Clapton

The Ultimate Illustrated History

UPDATED EDITION

Chris Welch

Voyageur
Press

Quarto is the authority on a wide range of topics.

Quarto educates, entertains and enriches the lives of our readers—enthusiasts and lovers of hands-on living.

www.quartoknows.com

First published in 2011 by Voyageur Press, an imprint of Quarto Publishing Group USA Inc.,
400 First Avenue North, Suite 400, Minneapolis, MN 55401 USA.
Hardcover edition published 2011. Softcover edition published 2014. This edition published 2016.
Telephone: (612) 344-8100 Fax: (612) 344-8692

quartoknows.com
Visit our blogs at quartoknows.com

10 9 8 7 6 5 4 3 2 1

ISBN: 978-0-7603-5019-5

The Library of Congress has cataloged the hardcover edition as follows:

Welch, Chris, 1941-
  Clapton : the ultimate illustrated history / Chris Welch.
    p. cm.
  Includes index.
  ISBN 978-0-7603-4046-2
1. Clapton, Eric—Pictorial works. 2. Rock musicians—England—Biography—Pictorial works. I. Title.
ML419.C58W45 2011
787.87166092—dc22
[B]
                        2011006957

Editor: Michael Dregni
Design Manager: Katie Sonmor
Designed by: John Barnett/4 Eyes Design

Printed in China

On the front cover: Eric Clapton portrait, early 1990s. *Terry O'Neill/Getty Images*
On the frontispiece: Slowhand's hands, 1989. *Luciano Viti/Getty Images*
On the title page, top left: Eric Clapton plays with Cream at the band's first live appearance, at the Windsor Festival on July 31, 1966. *David Redfern/Redferns/Getty Images*
  Top right: Clapton performs with Delaney and Bonnie in Copenhagen in 1970. *Jan Persson/Redferns/Getty Images* Bottom left: Clapton at the Meadowlands Arena, East Rutherford, New Jersey, on August 7, 1990. *Time Life Pictures* Bottom right: Clapton performs during his Seventieth Birthday Concert Celebration at Madison Square Garden on May 1, 2015. *Kevin Mazur/Getty Images*
On the back cover: Clapton's hybrid Fender Stratocaster "Blackie." *Robert Knight Archive/Redferns/Getty Images*

Author's Note

Riding with Mr. Clapton

IT WAS MY FIRST WEEK AT *MELODY MAKER* IN **1964** when I met a young Mod named Eric Clapton who played guitar with the "latest pop group," the Yardbirds. The weekly British newspaper where I'd managed to secure a job as features writer was known as the bible of the music biz. Established in 1926, it had been covering the world of jazz, blues, and rock for forty years. During that time, its journalists had interviewed every star from Louis Armstrong to Bob Dylan and the Beatles. I was on exalted ground when I entered the Fleet Street office for the first time in October 1964.

News editor Ray Coleman had deadlines in his soul and specialized in exclusive interviews with John Lennon. When he "asked" me to interview the Yardbirds, it was a direct order—get the story or else! So it was with some trepidation that I tracked down the group at a coffee bar in London's Fleet Street. The idea was to get an "angle." Were they breaking up? Were their fans revolting? Was the guitarist going to quit?

As it turned out, the noisy bunch of R&B musicians were funny, charming, and easy to interview. They even had an angle. Singer Keith Relf told me in all seriousness they

"it's all denied."
—Eric Clapton, 1968

hoped their latest single, "Good Morning Little Schoolgirl," *wouldn't* be a hit. They risked losing all their fans if they "went commercial," they feared. Hooray, I had my headline. The news editor would be pleased, and I'd keep my job.

However, the band's cool dude in the smart Ivy League jacket and fashionable haircut smiled. I suspected he could see right through me. He clearly thought the rest of the band was being silly. Eric Clapton was a dark horse, someone special, a man with a different agenda. He was deadly serious about the blues, and I soon realized he was seriously good at playing the guitar.

It was a joy in the 1960s to be given a mandate to spend all my time digging groups and discovering bright new talents from Steve Winwood to Jimi Hendrix. But the man who held constant appeal and always made wonderful music was Eric Clapton. There he was with the Yardbirds at the Marquee Club, then with John Mayall's Blues Breakers, and onwards to super group Cream. I was fortunate enough to witness Cream's first rehearsal and went to all their small club gigs. Watching Clapton wail the blues in those early days was a treat.

We talked, too, at his Chelsea flat about his ambitions and influences, wreathed in smoke and getting pleasantly stoned. He'd tell me how Cream was breaking up but that nobody should know. "It's all denied," he'd grin.

When the band Blind Faith was proposed, I found myself jamming on drums with Clapton at his country home. We were supposed to be doing an interview, but he soon grabbed a guitar instead: Playing a Buddy Holly tune was more his idea of fun. I didn't get the Blind Faith gig but was in seventh heaven for half an hour. And so I saw Blind Faith in Hyde Park and his shows with Derek and the Dominos when "Layla" was unveiled, and I went on tour with the Eric Clapton Band to experience the wilder side of rock 'n' roll.

It was the greatest thrill to see Cream reunited at the Royal Albert Hall and Madison Square Garden in 2005. Clapton was much the same as when we met for our first interview in years. Older, wiser, but that friendly knowing grin was just as disarming.

It is a privilege to be able to tell his story and look back on his achievements in this book, drawing largely from my own encounters and past conversations. Mr. Clapton always thanks audiences at his shows with a particular salutation. It's one I'd like to offer him now as autumn leaves fall. "God bless you, Eric."

A tribute to one of the most famous guitars in the world—Eric Clapton's Fender Stratocaster nicknamed "Blackie."
Fender Musical Instruments Corporation

preface

The Crossroads

"NOW IT IS TIME FOR THE MOST BLUESWAILING YARDBIRDS!" The compere can barely contain his excitement as he introduces the band one by one. Wild applause greets our heroes as they gird up their guitars. "Here they are—on the lead guitar, Eric 'Slowhand' Clapton!"

If you wanted a wild night with the hottest R&B bands in England, then London's Marquee was *the* place to hang out. The Animals, Spencer Davis Group, and the Who were just some of the attractions playing nightly during the 1960s at the club on Soho's Wardour Street.

One of the best loved was the Yardbirds. Fronted by blond-haired singer Keith Relf and starring Eric Clapton, they whipped up fans with furiously fast versions of R&B classics. As the band tore into their hottest number, "Too Much Monkey Business," the dark and cavernous Marquee became a sticky sauna, with sweat pouring from the walls and chewing gum stuck to the floor.

The smartly dressed Mods and their girlfriends who patronized the London blues clubs knew their stuff. They may never have seen Chuck Berry or Muddy Waters live, but

Eric Clapton stands in a field in his native Surrey, England, in 1993. *Terry O'Neill/Getty Images*

they recognized R&B when they heard it played with such passion. Most of all they admired the smartly dressed guitarist with the cool haircut who seemed to be a man with a mission. He played the blues with a skill and authenticity so much better than anybody else toting a guitar around town in March 1964. That's the night when Eric Clapton and the Yardbirds were captured "live," recording their debut album at the Marquee.

Keith Relf, blowing his harmonica and straining his vocal cords to be heard above the 30-watt guitar amps, may have been the leader. But to discerning ears the main attraction was Clapton. He exuded an air of authority. Here was a musician who knew he was damn good, patiently waiting for his chance to take care of business.

Yet Clapton never hogged the show. The proof of his brilliance came when he was finally given space to cut loose. Then he'd launch into a stream of sublime improvisations. This calm, adult attitude entranced his followers and suggested he had semimystical powers.

Londoners in those days were divided between those who had seen the guitarist in action and those who had only heard the rumors. "Have you heard Eric Clapton?" Those who confessed they hadn't felt the irritation and jealousy of the excluded.

What was so special about him? Guitarists abounded in pop music and had so for decades. Whether you called the music they played rock 'n' roll or R&B, an electric guitar lay at the heart of the matter. America's pioneers had set the standards, all the way from jazz giants Charlie Christian, Barney Kessel, and Les Paul to blues legends B. B. King, Freddie King, T-Bone Walker, and Chuck Berry.

There were hordes of brilliant session musicians tucked away in recording studios on both sides of the Atlantic, diligently playing all those spine-tingling but anonymous guitar licks on countless hit records. The pop groups of the 1960s also had their own capable lead guitarists, such as Hank B. Marvin with the Shadows, George Harrison with the Beatles, and Keith Richards with the Rolling Stones.

What drew faithful fans to Clapton was the feeling of being summoned to hear the truth. When Clapton played, it seemed like the real thing and not some clumsy, overwrought pastiche. Even so, with the Yardbirds, his style had yet to mature. At the Marquee, he betrayed the nervous, restless energy of youth. But it was in this hothouse environment of small clubs that the guitarist learned his craft. Soon his fame would spread way beyond London to the rest of the world.

Eric Clapton's remarkable journey took him from impoverished "underground" cult figure to rock icon and international celebrity. Along the way he'd devote himself to hardcore blues with John Mayall's Blues Breakers and then devise the world's first super groups with Cream and Blind Faith. He would evolve into a singer with a warm, unpretentious vocal style and develop as a composer whose songs, from "Layla" to "Wonderful Tonight" and "Tears in Heaven," would reach out and touch millions of record buyers.

After the Cream years, when he was thrust into the role of a guitar hero alongside the flashier Jimi Hendrix, Jeff Beck, and Jimmy Page, he would seek to work in a more low-key fashion. He even went so far as to disguise his name, billing himself as Derek and the Dominos. Whether he courted celebrity or not, celebrities tripped over themselves to engage his services. Bob Dylan, John Lennon, George Harrison, Duane Allman, Roger Waters, Elton John, and Phil Collins all wanted Clapton to share a stage or studio with them.

The mystery for many was how a mild-mannered youth growing up in Surrey, England, came to be hailed as the world's greatest white blues artist. As Huddie Ledbetter, better known as Leadbelly, once said, "The white man cannot sing the blues because he's got nothing on his mind." But just as American blues artists such as Muddy Waters had been influenced by Robert Johnson, so the sheer power of the blues—its lyrics, themes, and underlying feelings—could speak to anybody, black or white. And especially to a lonely lad who thought of himself as an outsider.

Whatever the circumstances, Clapton had somehow unlocked the door to blues power—a fact easily communicated to anyone who heard him play from his earliest days. He was certainly in the right place at the right time. His life story parallels the unexpected development of the blues in lands far from the Deep South. It was a phenomenon that had enormous social effects and one that ultimately fired up the rock music that came to dominate twentieth-century pop culture.

Just as Clapton was influenced by his heroes, he, too, became an enormous inspiration to dozens more would-be guitarists trailing in his wake. Many would go on to develop their own careers, notably Peter Green of Fleetwood Mac and Mick Taylor with the Rolling Stones, who both avidly listened to Clapton whenever he played a gig. Even Hendrix said he'd only come to London to launch his career in 1966 if he could meet Eric Clapton. It was a condition his manager, Chas Chandler of the Animals, was only too happy to fulfill.

Clapton has always been a good-humored, polite, friendly, usually modest, and generally happy man with a boyish sense of humor. Fond of practical jokes, unworldly in a disarming way, he charms everyone he meets. The darker side of Clapton could only be explained by the pressures placed on him by a sometimes alarming, stressful outside world.

Clapton had to cope with a confused childhood background even before he came into contact with the wildly disorganized characters that populate the music business. It was only his detachment and inner strength that enabled

Rare early recordings by Clapton, at times joined by Jimmy Page, appeared on the compilation *Guitar Boogie* 1971.

Early cuts by Clapton were released on the three-volume compilation *Blues Anytime* 1968.

Three tracks by Clapton and the Powerhouse appeared on the 1966 compilation *What's Shakin'*.

him to deal with the crazier aspects of being in a band, endlessly on the road. Nevertheless, he would become prone to bouts of suspicion, often unable to trust those around him.

He would retreat into his own world and became cold and detached. Whereas just playing the guitar was once enough to soothe away problems and troubles, in the aftermath of several crises he gradually became drawn into a web of drug and alcohol addiction. Already bruised by his years with Cream, he was shocked by the death of his friend Hendrix in 1970. At the same time he was involved in a complicated love affair with his best friend George Harrison's wife, Pattie Boyd, who he eventually married.

The commercial flop of his cherished song "Layla" (dedicated to Pattie) and attendant problems promoting his new band Derek and the Dominos all added to his general unhappiness. In October 1971, another musician friend, Duane Allman, was killed in a motorcycle accident. It all seemed like an omen to Clapton, attached as he was to the legend of Robert Johnson, who had also died young under tragic circumstances.

For a while he persevered by fulfilling his duties. Clapton performed alongside George Harrison and Bob Dylan at the Concert for Bangladesh in New York in August 1971. But this would prove to be one of his last public appearances as he retreated to his Surrey mansion. Refusing to answer calls, locked away from prying eyes, he rapidly descended into heroin addiction.

It blighted his life during the early 1970s and caused many of his oldest fans to give up on him as a lost cause. But showing enormous resolution and strength of character—and with the help of friends, loved ones, and his manager, Roger Forrester—Clapton returned a stronger, more successful artist than even his more ardent admirers in the 1960s could have imagined.

Recovering from his heroin habit, he made a historic appearance at London's Rainbow Theatre in January 1973 for an all-star concert organized by well-wisher Pete Townshend, who helped reintroduce him to a waiting and loyal army of fans. Accepting medical help, Clapton gradually weaned himself off drugs and drink and at the same time rebuilt his reputation and career with such hits as "I Shot the Sheriff" and his comeback album, *461 Ocean Boulevard*. Clapton may have been singing more than playing guitar—and he seemed to be veering away from the blues—but he was back and, most importantly, alive and kicking.

In subsequent decades, an Armani-suited, sober, and reliable Clapton evolved, singing, composing, enjoying hit records, and once again playing great guitar. Here was the Eric Clapton who could sell out twenty-four nights at the Royal Albert Hall in 1990. He was also the gossip columnist's delight, reported to be dating any number of superstar models and rock chicks.

He was so well liked that even the Queen of England decided to give him a couple of awards, first the OBE (Order of the British Empire) and then the CBE (Commander of the British Empire). Of course she may have been advised about his charity work that included setting up the drug and alcohol dependency treatment facility, Crossroads Centre, in Antigua.

Clapton jams with one of his blues heroes, Buddy Guy, in 1969. *David Redfern/Redferns/Getty Images*

Clapton with Muddy Waters and Johnny Winter
in Chicago, Illinois, on June 12, 1979.
Paul Natkin/WireImage/Getty Images

During the 1990s, Clapton suffered two more severe personal blows. In August 1990, his close friend, guitarist Stevie Ray Vaughan, was killed in a helicopter crash in Wisconsin shortly after playing as a guest on Eric's own tour in 1990. The following year, in March 1991, Clapton's four-year-old son, Conor, plunged seven hundred feet to his death from an open fifty-third-floor window in his mother's Manhattan apartment.

These were emotional shocks that could have left Clapton unwilling to perform again. But it would have been no use to anyone to give up. He decided to carry on, and the loss of his son was mourned in the best possible way with the moving song "Tears in Heaven."

Into the new millennium, Clapton was ready to confront his past and pay tribute to all those musicians who had been part of his remarkable journey. He agreed to play one more time with his former boss John Mayall. He even reformed Cream in 2005 and in a surprise gesture returned to the spotlight with Jack Bruce and Ginger Baker in sellout shows in London and New York. The Cream reunion signaled to the world that it was cool to bury any hatchets

still sticking into the shoulders of rock. Afterward, the Police and Led Zeppelin both decided to get back together.

Eric himself didn't really need reviving. He had been working virtually nonstop during a recording career spanning forty-six years. During that time he unleashed a legacy of critically acclaimed bestselling albums, among them *Layla and Other Assorted Love Songs* (1970), *461 Ocean Boulevard* (1974), *Behind the Sun* (1985), *Pilgrim* (1998), and *Journeyman* (1989).

More recent albums—such as *Riding with the King* (2000), *Reptile* (2001), *Me and Mr. Johnson* (2003), and *Back Home* (2005)—have continued to ensure him an important place in a constantly changing music scene. In 2010 came his nineteenth studio album, *Clapton*—the same title as his first solo effort back in 1970.

The grizzled and happily married sixty-five-year-old was perhaps showing his age as he sang a sad and reflective version of the old standard "Autumn Leaves." A far cry from "Too Much Monkey Business" and "Steppin' Out." But it showed that Eric Clapton had finally arrived at his personal crossroads and chosen which way to go.

B. B. King, Buddy Guy, and Clapton perform at the 20th Annual Rock and Roll Hall of Fame Induction Ceremony at the Waldorf-Astoria Hotel in New York City on March 14, 2005. *Scott Gries/Getty Images*

1. when the Rooster crowed

Childhood and the Blues, the Roosters, and Casey Jones and the Engineers, 1945–1963

ERIC PATRICK CLAPTON IS A PURPOSEFUL NAME that suggests strength and confidence. Yet his real name is the rather more humble Eric Clapp. He was born in Ripley, Surrey, England, on March 30, 1945. Ripley is a pleasant country village, about thirty miles from London. He was brought up by his grandparents, Rose and John Clapp, whom he was led to believe were his parents.

Clapton was fond of his grandmother Rose, who always took a keen interest in his career. She was known to telephone music magazines to correct any stories about Eric, especially those concerning his date of birth, much to his amusement. Although he rarely mentioned it in interviews, he learned at a young age that his "sister" Patricia was really his mother. She'd had an affair with a Canadian Air Force pilot stationed in England during World War II. He had returned to Canada before the birth of his child. Clapton's mother was just sixteen years old. After the baby's birth she moved away and Clapton's grandparents assumed parental duties at their home on The Green, Ripley.

The Roosters rock, circa 1963. From left, Clapton with his Kay guitar, drummer Robin Mason, singer Terry Brennan, Clapton's friend Tom McGuinness on guitar, and pianist Robin "Ben" Palmer.

Such affairs were considered scandalous at the time and led to the decision to create an illusory family background. Clapton discovered the truth about his real father at the age of twelve when his mother reappeared on the scene. He explained later: "When I was young I made a conscious decision that I didn't want to know anything about him, because it would be too painful, disappointing, and disruptive."

Despite these complications, Clapton led a happy childhood and was well looked after by his grandparents, who, he confessed, "spoilt him." He went to Ripley Primary School and St. Bede's Secondary Modern before enrolling at Kingston School of Art with the intention of studying stained-glass design. His grandfather worked as a plasterer and bricklayer and expressed little interest in art or music. Clapton, however, had been listening to pop music on the radio from an early age.

Among Clapton's formative experiences was hearing records by Chuck Berry occasionally played by the BBC on a Saturday morning children's show. Clapton was only ten years old when he heard his first blues record, by Sonny Terry and Brownie McGhee, featuring Terry's howling harmonica.

Then Clapton spotted his first guitar, being played on a TV show in 1958. It was actually a Fender bass guitar used to back U.S. rock 'n' roll star Jerry Lee Lewis on his greatest hit, "Great Balls of Fire." Clapton thought the bass was a regular guitar, but it didn't matter. He was smitten with the idea of becoming a guitarist. If only he could get one, it could be a means of escape from humdrum village life.

Like many British teenagers in the late 1950s who couldn't afford the real thing with guitars in short supply, Clapton decided to make his own. He tried carving a Stratocaster body shape out of a block of wood, but gave up when it came to crafting a neck and fretboard. His grandparents took pity and bought him a plastic Elvis Presley–branded toy guitar. Now he could mime to Gene Vincent records while posing with his guitar in front of a mirror.

At the age of fifteen he was given a real Hofner acoustic guitar that proved equally hard to play with its warped neck. He discovered a few chords but gradually lost interest. In his late teens he took an increasing interest in art and yearned to lead a bohemian lifestyle. From the age of fifteen he began visiting London by train on weekends to mix with fellow "ravers" and beatniks.

In 1961, traditional jazz was the music of choice for the bohemian crowd. "Trad," as it

"I was the one that used to get stones thrown at me because I was so thin and couldn't do physical training very well! One of those types. I was always the seven-stone [98-pound] weakling. I used to hang out with three or four other kids who were all in that same kind of predicament. The outcasts. They used to call us the loonies."

—Eric Clapton on his childhood, *Rolling Stone*, 1974

Jerry Lee Lewis in his "killer" pose at the piano.

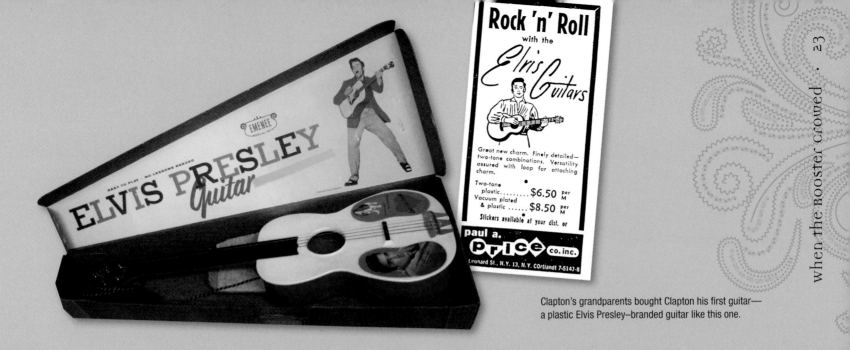

Clapton's grandparents bought Clapton his first guitar—
a plastic Elvis Presley–branded guitar like this one.

was known, would soon be supplemented by R&B and folk music. As Clapton hung out in Soho coffee bars and skiffle cellars, he met and heard twelve-string guitarist Long John Baldry performing what seemed like an authentic blend of folk and blues. Baldry was part of a growing revivalist movement that despised the commercial pop scene. They wanted to re-create the authentic African-American blues they heard on imported records.

On Friday nights the faithful gathered to play the latest records from the States, including the Chess album *The Best of Muddy Waters*. Clapton began to discover a host of bluesmen, such as Howlin' Wolf, Blind Willie Johnson, Otis Rush, Buddy Guy, and his particular favorite, Robert Johnson.

He was blown away by an album of Johnson recordings called *King of the Delta Blues Singers*. On first listen he found the anguish expressed in the lyrics too much to handle. He was also greatly impressed by Big Bill Broonzy; as he said years later: "I'd never heard anyone like him."

Despite all these early influences, Clapton had virtually given up trying to play the guitar, but he was taking the music he was discovering seriously and began to identify with the some of the more rebellious bluesmen. Somehow the angry voices and music from the past seemed to assuage his own teenage confusion caused by his unconventional family relationships.

Clapton went to Kingston-on-Thames Art College in September 1961 and while supposedly studying spent a lot of time drinking in the local pub at lunchtime and playing records. There he heard his fellow students digging LPs by Muddy Waters, Chuck Berry, and B. B. King. He also learned about the coolest of the rock 'n' roll stars, the late Buddy Holly. By now Clapton began to feel the urge to play again and not just listen to records. He got out his old guitar and started practicing. He tried to play the licks and riffs he'd heard on his favorite blues records. It wasn't long before he was assiduously adding his own ideas to develop a truly personal style.

"I can see that that's probably what it was. It was some kind of . . . it was me identifying with some, some kind of cry of suffering, yes—pain, because I had a very confused, tumultuous childhood. I mean no one has a perfect childhood but mine. . . ."

—Eric Clapton on his early love of the blues as a "cry of pain in the music," David Frost television interview, 1994

Gene Vincent's first LP, *Bluejean Bop!*, from 1956.

The Best of Muddy Waters on Chess Records, straight from Chicago.

The next step was to join a band. His art studies were neglected as he spent a lot of time playing in local folk clubs. He was expelled from college in July 1962 as his tutors felt he wasn't taking the course seriously. He enjoyed his new-found freedom, visiting more London clubs and sitting in. In September 1962, he got his first electric guitar, a Kay model advertised in the music press. For a while he played in a duo with guitarist Dave Brock. Then he met fellow guitarist Tom McGuinness at the Station Hotel in Richmond.

McGuinness was born December 2, 1941, in Wimbledon, London. He had been looking for a guitarist to form an R&B group, having quit his rock 'n' roll covers band. His girlfriend, Jennifer Dolan, had told him about a Kingston student she knew who could play blues guitar. It was thanks to Jenny that in January 1963 the eighteen-year-old Clapton and twenty-two-year-old McGuinness formed their pioneering R&B group the Roosters, named in honor of "Little Red Rooster," the Willie Dixon–penned, Howlin' Wolf blues.

McGuinness and Clapton became good friends. In 1963, the pair, together with Jenny, went to see one of their rock 'n' roll heroes. "Jenny was at art school with Eric and we all went to a concert in Croydon to see Jerry Lee Lewis," McGuinness recalls. "Bearing in mind Eric and I weren't working and she was an art student, somehow we managed to afford tickets for a box at the Fairfield Hall."

Jerry Lee was on the same bill with Gene Vincent and Heinz, the blond-haired singer who came to fame with the Tornados and had a 1963 solo U.K. hit with "Just Like Eddie." "Heinz had a really feeble voice and sounded as wimpy as you could imagine," McGuinness continues. "Right in the middle of his set a row of Teddy Boys stood up and each had a printed card with a letter on it. They held up the cards to the audience and it spelled out 'Jerry Lee Is King.'"

McGuinness and Clapton were highly amused. They couldn't wait to see Jerry Lee either. The pair clearly shared the same sense of humor and a love of R&B. "Jenny had been at Kingston Art College with Eric and she just mentioned that he was one of the people there who was interested in the blues," McGuinness says. "We're talking 1962–63, and it was a bit like being a member of a secret society. Just meeting someone who had actually heard of Howlin' Wolf or John Lee Hooker was great."

Before the birth of the Roosters, McGuinness had gone for an audition with the Dave Hunt Band at the Station Hotel in Richmond. "It turned out it wasn't really a blues band," he says. "It was Dave Hunt's Confederate Jazz Band. But they wanted to make the transition to R&B and Dave was auditioning for someone to play guitar. I had phoned him to get an audition and at the end of the call I asked what instrument he played. He said, 'Trombone,' and put the phone down. I then knew it doesn't sound right, but I was desperate. So I went with Jennifer to the Station Hotel and immediately knew I was in the wrong place because there were three trombonists, string bass, piano, and drums. They were doing Joe Turner Kansas City–style blues. Lovely stuff but not what I wanted to play."

McGuinness was spotted trying to sneak away and was asked to plug in his amp and play along to their version of "Kansas City." McGuinness expected to play with a honky-tonk, Jimmy Reed groove, but had to play in E flat with a big band swing feel. "There was no cohesion at all," he remembers. "I told them it wasn't the band for me and left. But I heard later that the person who got the job was Ray Davies. I got off stage and Jenny said, 'How was it?' And I said, 'It was horrible.' And she said, 'Oh well, this is Eric and he *loves* the blues.'"

McGuinness continues: "When I was introduced to Eric Clapton, we just hit it off. We reeled off names to each other like Sonny Boy Williamson, Elmore James. I literally came off stage and there was Eric. I guess Jennifer had asked him to come down. We talked a bit and decided we'd try to get a band together, which became the Roosters."

The new group included Clapton and McGuinness on lead guitars backed by Robin "Ben" Palmer on piano, singer Terry Brennan, and Robin Mason on drums. Their drummer owned a car, which proved very useful. But there was one member missing: The Roosters couldn't find a bass player willing to play with an R&B group. Nevertheless, they began rehearsing at a pub in New Malden, and among the tunes they attempted were John Lee Hooker's "Boom Boom," Muddy Waters' "Hoochie Coochie Man," and Larry Williams' rocker "Slow Down."

Clapton's new Kay guitar was fitted with light-gauge strings that made it easier to bend the notes but were prone to breaking, causing delays while he had to restring. Once underway, his playing greatly impressed Palmer, who had made a previous attempt to form a group with McGuinness. The semiprofessional Roosters began playing parties and clubs and made lots of friends.

"It was pretty unstructured," McGuinness says. "None of us had any idea about how to get gigs. I got Ben Palmer in on piano because the year before, Paul Jones [later of Manfred Mann], Ben, and I had tried to get a band together. And we could not find a single other musician who wanted to play R&B. We usually got disgruntled jazzers playing drums or no-hopers playing bass."

Settling some myths about their origins, McGuinness adds, "Brian Jones was never in the Roosters, but confusingly Eric now insists that Paul Jones *was* in the Roosters. Paul wasn't."

McGuinness continues: "Eric was laboring, having been thrown out of art school. When the Roosters began rehearsing at a pub, I remember Eric turning up after spending the day plastering or helping his grandfather lay floors. We didn't have much equipment and we never found a bass player. But we never worried about it because we were very young and enthusiastic."

Howlin' Wolf concert poster, 1950s.

The classic album, *King of the Delta Blues Singers*, that opened the eyes of many blues fans to Robert Johnson's legacy. It was first released in 1961.

Chuck Berry's genre-busting hit "Maybellene" from 1955.

They were all still discovering the source of their favorite music as they began playing tunes by T-Bone Walker, Jimmy Reed, and Fats Domino. One day McGuinness played Clapton a single by Freddie King called "Hide Away" with "Have You Ever Loved a Woman" on the B-side. The single was actually owned by singer Brennan. "Terry was really into black music and not just the blues," McGuinness says. "I'm pretty sure we played 'Have You Ever Loved a Woman' with Terry singing, but not 'Hide Away.' Terry would sing and play harmonica and we'd all take long solos. We only had one amplifier. It was a Selmer Truvoice and through that we put two guitars and Terry's vocals. I don't remember us being very loud, but Ben Palmer had to hammer his piano to be heard as he didn't have a microphone."

"We weren't really professional and we didn't have any money," Clapton remembers. "The drummer did have a car, although it was actually his mum's car, you know? I remember how everybody went through one amplifier. Even the vocalist Terry Brennan had a microphone that plugged into the amp. It was doomed really! But it was fun and it was a proper blues band. . . . I guess I was learning about the kind of music I wanted to play."

"Hide Away" was the first time Clapton heard Freddie King's note-bending electric guitar style, also used by T-Bone Walker and B. B. King. It was a great influence on Clapton and would transform his playing.

McGuinness: "Eric and I would swap solos. We were both at the same stage in our playing, which was not very far along. We had the absurd confidence of youth."

The Roosters lasted from January to August 1963, during which time they played at such venues as the Wooden Bridge Hotel in Guildford, the Scene and Marquee clubs in Soho, and at the Jazz Cellar in Kingston—a venue that was actually up two flights of stairs. Palmer remembers that Clapton was the best musician in the band and that his playing "seemed like a miracle." "He would solo effortlessly and at length. He really got people excited and was pretty deafening, too, with his thirty-watt amplifier."

The Roosters played twice at the Marquee in Oxford Street, opening for hit-making group Manfred Mann in 1963. Tom: "We made a pound each. The Marquee was packed out, but that's all they paid the support band. We probably got the gig through Paul Jones. After the second gig I went to see Manfred, who was handling the money. He said, 'Are you all right for next week?' And I said, 'No, no, we want more money.' Ben, our pianist, had to come all the way from Oxford. Manfred was shocked and said, 'You don't understand. There are bands that would kill to play this support spot.'"

The Roosters didn't survive mainly because the members with proper day jobs couldn't see themselves ever becoming full-time players. The Roosters' last crow was at Uncle Bonnie's Chinese Jazz Club at the Aquarium in Brighton, Sussex. It was high summer and the seaside resort was full of foreign students attending language schools.

"There were all these smart French students in college-boy haircuts," McGuinness recalls. "We were the interval band supporting a trad jazz outfit.

We started setting up the amp and electric guitars and could hear lots of grumbles. We started playing and they started booing! They were shouting 'Le jazz hot! Le jazz hot!' Terry got very annoyed with them, jumped off the stage, and started a fight with a couple meek-looking students. Terry wore very smart Italian-cut suits but he was quite a tough geezer. I don't think we got paid for the gig!"

The afternoon had begun so peacefully with McGuinness and Clapton enjoying the town's funfair attractions. "Before the gig Eric and I went down to the pier and found a donut-making machine," McGuinness continues. "It spewed out hot-ring donuts coated in sugar. We had a donut-eating competition to see who could eat the most. I think we had a pack of six donuts each for two shillings. But I can't remember who won!"

It was a stunt typical of Clapton's boyish sense of humor that McGuinness grew to love. "A lot of things you read about Eric are quite heavy and doomy and there was a lot of sadness in his later life. But I remember us arranging to meet in an arts cinema in Shaftesbury Avenue, London. They were showing a complete series of *Batman* films, like fifteen episodes one after the other."

McGuinness got there for the afternoon screening, but Clapton wasn't there. Not wanting to miss the start of the show, McGuiness bought a ticket and sat down. "About ten minutes into the film I heard this laugh somewhere in the cinema. So I thought 'Eric's in.' Every time I heard this laugh I navigated my way through the darkness to where he was sitting.

"We got on really well in the brief period we were together. He was two or three years younger than me, but he'd led a relatively unstructured life. He'd gone to an art school when he was twelve years old. Not the Kingston College he went to later, but a specialist school for young art students. I'd had a sheltered upbringing and, although we were both completely immature, he seemed worldlier than me. One night we were walking back from a rehearsal after missing the last bus. We got our guitars out. They were held up with string as we didn't have any proper straps."

McGuinness and Clapton had confessions to make. "We told each other that we . . . really liked the Beatles! We started trying to play 'Misery.' We were just having fun and Eric never ever showed that he had any thought that one day he might become a professional musician. We got on really well and then it was over."

After the Roosters, Clapton jammed with Alexis Korner's Blues Incorporated at the Ealing Blues Club in West London, where the R&B revival was gaining strength. In a sweaty cellar where water dripped from the ceiling onto the drummers, Clapton mingled with future Stones Mick Jagger and Charlie Watts.

Then he heard about a new group being put together at the Scene in Ham Yard. It wasn't long before Clapton and McGuinness were reunited in an outfit fronted by Brian Casser from Liverpool. Casser had previously sung as Cass and the Cassanovas. He'd come to London to seek his fortune and recorded "One Way Ticket," a single released in 1963 under the name of Casey Jones and the Engineers.

Buddy Holly and the Cricket's first album, *The 'Chirping' Crickets*, 1958.

Howlin' Wolf recorded the blues classic "The Red Rooster" in 1961. It was subsequently covered by numerous blues and R&B bands under the title "Little Red Rooster."

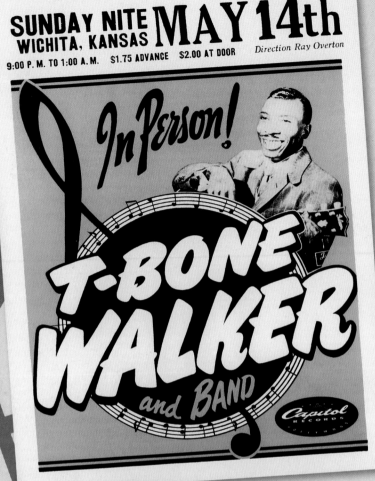

T-Bone Walker concert poster, 1950s.

Big Joe Turner's Kansas City blues were an early influence on the Roosters.

As Casey didn't have a regular band, he needed to recruit some "Engineers." His drummer, Ray Stock, bumped into Clapton at the Scene. Clapton said he'd join the Engineers—but only if he could bring along his pal McGuinness. Casey Jones and the Engineers got together in October 1963 with vocalist Casser, Clapton on lead guitar, McGuinness on bass, and drummer Stock.

At their first gig, the band was expected to back female cabaret artist Polly Perkins in a nightclub in Macclesfield, Cheshire. They had driven miles from London under the impression they'd be playing the blues. Nobody knew the chords to her chosen song, "Who's Sorry Now," and the whole evening was a terrible embarrassment.

McGuinness: "We turned up and there's Eric and me, who could just about play a Chuck Berry tune, being expected to back Polly Perkins. We didn't even know she was going to be there. She came in and said, 'Oh, you are my backing group, are you?'

"And she handed us the sheet music for 'Who's Sorry Now.' She carried on like a trouper and ignored the complete shambles we were making of her song behind her. She only did three songs before leaving the band to get back to its Chuck Berry covers."

They had several more engagements lined up all over the country. At first McGuinness and Clapton enjoyed the novelty of being on the road away from home. "For the first time it felt like being in a professional band," McGuinness remembers. "Casey had a record out on Columbia and it got some radio play. As a result he got some gigs. He also had a manager and a van we all traveled in and Ray Stock was a good drummer. So it was quite a good band. But Casey couldn't sing. He was a great frontman with a lot of 'bottle' who could chat to the audience. He had a Liverpudlian sense of humour. Everybody from Liverpool is a comedian! But he wasn't a great singer."

The music also started to get them down. "We'd play at the Scene and then all these records come on in the interval and we would think what we were playing wasn't very good in comparison."

Clapton decided to quit and skipped the next Casey Jones gig without telling McGuinness. It was an early example of the way Clapton would deal with untenable situations—by simply walking away. McGuinness discovered Clapton had left only after hearing the news from Clapton's friend, Guy Stevens, a DJ at the Scene. (Stevens later worked for Island Records and ran the influential Sue label. He also produced *London Calling* by the Clash.)

McGuinness was annoyed that Clapton had simply decided not to show up. McGuinness soon quit as well. Their erstwhile bandleader didn't seem too upset. Casser formed Casey Jones and the Governors and relocated to Hamburg, where he enjoyed a couple of hit records and gained a sizeable following.

Neither the Roosters nor the Engineers recorded anything with Clapton on guitar, but McGuiness thinks there may have been one extremely rare recorded example of their time together: "I have a dim recollection that Eric and I went into a Record-A-Disc booth at Waterloo Station and recorded together. I guess it was probably us imitating *Goon Show*–style voices. I doubt it was music."

Freddie King's instrumental single "Hide Away," 1960.

Clapton later described Casey Jones and the Engineers as "a heavy pop show and I couldn't stand that for long. I was such a purist and they were playing Top Twenty stuff which was disastrous."

McGuiness went on to join the highly successful Manfred Mann group and switched to bass guitar.

More R&B groups were enjoying national pop success in the wake of the Rolling Stones and soon an opportunity would open that seemed tailor-made for Clapton's talents.

The Rolling Stones had moved on from the Crawdaddy Club in Richmond and were rivaling the Beatles' with hits such as "Come On" and "I Wanna Be Your Man." The Stones were swiftly replaced at their Crawdaddy residency by the Yardbirds, an upcoming R&B outfit from Kingston whose lead guitarist, Anthony "Top" Topham, was about to leave. Once again the call went out for "the guy from Kingston Art College who used to play guitar."

One thing was certain. The Yardbirds would be playing strictly the blues. Clapton wouldn't have to back any lady cabaret singers.

"The funny thing about trying to hold a band together in those days was that neither Eric nor I had a telephone," McGuinness says. "In order organize a gig we'd have to write to each other. I've still got Eric's letters to me. We kept in touch and I sat in with him in the Yardbirds a couple of times in December 1963."

Clapton recalls that after playing with his first two groups he was beginning to feel like an experienced performer. "By the time I was in the Yardbirds, I was already a kind of a veteran," he remembers. "I had done the Roosters and Casey Jones, but I didn't really know how to go about things properly. However, I was clear in my mind about what I *wanted* to do. And I was finding other people with the same sort of musical taste.

"I was always playing in pubs and coffee bars in the Kingston and Richmond area. I'd go to the Eel Pie Island club on the Thames on a Saturday night and see Ken Colyer and Kenny Ball, who were really good jazz players. They would play music that I'd never heard before. They had an incredible record collection and the DJ would play bluegrass, jazz, and blues. There were also great record shops in Charing Cross Road and New Oxford Street in London where you'd could find Folkways albums and blues records. My eyes were being opened all the time to the spectrum of music. That whole period was a very exciting time for me."

Freddie King, the Texas Cannonball, was an early proponent of the blues played on a Gibson Les Paul.

"'Hide-Away' was the first time Clapton heard Freddie King's note-bending electric guitar style, also used by T-Bone Walker and B. B. King. It was a great influence on Clapton and would transform his playing."

—Tom McGuinness

2. A Band of Brothers

The Yardbirds, 1963–1964

When Eric Clapton joined the Yardbirds, he enlisted with a band of brothers, eager to fight their battles for fame and success together. As teenagers they were caught up in the excitement of an era when youth were enjoying a degree of freedom undreamt of by previous generations. No more boring office jobs. Instead there would be lucrative record contracts, celebrity status, and screaming fans.

It didn't always work out like that. There were plenty of contracts, but not necessarily lucrative. The "fans" weren't always screaming praise but quite often abuse, at least at their first few gigs. That was because the Yardbirds had the unenviable task of following the hugely popular Rolling Stones into a residency that Jagger & Co. had vacated at the Crawdaddy Club in Richmond. It was a tough job to win over the Stones fans. But the Yardbirds eventually acquired a secret weapon—an excellent new lead guitarist.

Many British pop groups were hardened working men from "Up North" who had endured playing sleazy night clubs in Hamburg and Liverpool. The Yardbirds were nice,

The Yardbirds embark. For an early publicity image, the band of brothers was photographed in a rowboat on the Serpentine Lake in Hyde Park on April 23, 1964. Clockwise from bottom left: Keith Relf, Paul Samwell-Smith, Jim McCarty, Chris Dreja, and a not-too-pleased-looking Eric Clapton. *Tony Gale/Pictorial Press Ltd/Alamy*

polite, middle-class art students from the leafy suburbs of Richmond and Kingston. The original group consisted of lead guitarist Anthony "Top" Topham, Keith Relf on vocals and harmonica, guitarist Chris Dreja, bassist Paul Samwell-Smith, and drummer Jim McCarty.

McCarty was actually born in Liverpool but his father was from London, and the family eventually moved south to Teddington. McCarty went to Hampton Grammar with Paul Samwell-Smith, where they formed a school group playing tunes by Buddy Holly and the Crickets.

"I used to be in the Boys Brigade and played marching drums. When we got a band together we played at the school dances doing all the old rock stuff," McCarty recalled. "We were called Sean and the Country Gentlemen, named after the Gretsch guitar." The Gentlemen were McCarty, Samwell-Smith, and Brian Smith on guitar with singer Sean Newcombe, who modeled himself on Elvis Presley.

"[Newcombe] had swept back hair," McCarty said. "Paul played lead guitar and it wasn't until later that he switched to bass. He was mad on Cyril Davies and he modeled himself on his bass player, Rick Brown, who came from the Screaming Lord Sutch band."

Upon leaving school, the Country Gentlemen disbanded. Some weeks later McCarty bumped into Samwell-Smith, who explained he was getting into R&B. Said Samwell-Smith: "Come round to my house and I'll play you a record by Jimmy Reed at Carnegie Hall." McCarty thought it sounded like rock 'n' roll with a blues feeling.

By then Samwell-Smith had started performing country blues with Keith Relf in the Metropolis Blues Quartet. They played Leadbelly songs on the beatnik scene around Kingston. "Paul said that after listening to Jimmy Reed they wanted to go electric and do Chuck Berry and Howlin' Wolf tunes," McCarty explained. "We went out and bought a few of the 'in' records, like Slim Harpo's 'Rainin' in My Heart.' R&B was the new thing and we thought it was really exciting, so different from the usual pop stuff. We used to go and see the Rolling Stones, and that's when we got the Yardbirds together."

Samwell-Smith and Relf abandoned the Metropolis Blues Quartet, while McCarty brought in Chris Dreja and Anthony Topham, who were both at Kingston Art College. "Paul and Keith wanted to form a blues band, so we started rehearsing," McCarty said. "There were actually two bands until both conglomerated into the Yardbirds."

McCarty's group had included Topham, Dreja, and a harmonica player called Jamie. They had played alongside the Metropolis Quartet at a pub in Norbiton. McCarty: "Then Keith and Paul wanted to form this electric band instead of playing acoustic blues, so in the end we got together and it was Paul, Keith, Chris, and myself and Tony Topham."

The new, unnamed outfit began playing gigs at Ken Colyer's club at Studio 51 in Soho and at the Ricky Tick Club, Windsor. McCarty says their first appearance was in 1963 at Eel Pie Island where they supported Cyril Davies' All-Stars. The tiny island on the Thames at Twickenham was reached by a footbridge. A narrow path led to a rundown hotel that had been used as a jazz and blues club since 1956. Jeff Beck and the Tridents were among the many groups who played in the spooky old hotel ballroom, which has long since been demolished.

Concert poster, the Cavern, Liverpool, England, January 22, 1964.

THE BIG R & B NIGHT

FOR ALL BELIEVERS IN GENUINE RHYTHM & BLUES MUSIC

AT THE CAVERN

THIS COMING WEDNESDAY

22nd JANUARY, 1964   7.15 p.m. TO 11.15 p.m.

PRESENTING THE RENOWNED AMERICAN RHYTHM & BLUES ARTISTE IN PERSON

1 SONNY BOY WILLIAMSON

OF PYE-INTERNATIONAL RECORDS "HELP ME" FAME

PLUS

A TRULY EXCITING NEW R & B COMBO DIRECT FROM LONDON

2 THE YARDBIRDS

PLUS

MERSEYSIDE'S OUTSTANDING R & B BAND

3 THE MASTER SOUNDS

FEATURING EX "MOJO" ADRIAN LORD

PLUS

LIVERPOOL'S PROMISING THREESOME

4 THE PAWNS

AND INTRODUCING THE ALL-COLOURED COMBO

5 THE CHAMPIONS

THIS SHOW YOU MUST NOT MISS!

PLEASE BE EARLY — 7.15 p.m. START.   MEMBERS: **3/6**

VISITORS ARE ESPECIALLY WELCOME!   Admission for Visitors: **4/6**

AT THE CAVERN

10 MATHEW STREET (off North John Street)

LIVERPOOL 2.   Telephone: CENtral 1591

The Yardbirds perform on the British television show *Ready Steady Go!* at Television House, Kingsway, London, on May 22, 1964. From left, Paul Samwell-Smith, Chris Dreja, Keith Relf, Jim McCarty, and Clapton playing a Gretsch Chet Atkins Model 6120. *Val Wilmer/Redferns/ Getty Images*

"We played a few songs and then Cyril Davies asked Keith the name of the band," McCarty continued. "Keith checked a short list of names he'd prepared and chose the Yardbirds. It wasn't named after Charlie 'Yardbird' Parker. It was from one of the beat poets like Jack Kerouac. A yardbird was a hobo who bummed lifts on trains across the States from the old railyards. When Cyril announced, 'That was the Yardbirds,' it was the first time I'd heard the name. We were quite influenced by the Cyril Davies All-Stars who used to double up tempos on the bass. That became Paul's big thing, doubling the tempo—and, of course, playing the songs for a long time."

When they heard the Rolling Stones were leaving their residency at the Crawdaddy after being poached by their new manager Andrew Loog Oldham, Samwell-Smith and Relf approached the Stones' promoter, Giorgio Gomelsky. They explained that if he needed a band he should come and check them out. His assistant, Hamish Grimes, went to see them play at Studio 51 and reported back favorably to Gomelsky.

Gomelsky signed the Yardbirds, becoming their manager and working hard to control the unruly teenagers and turn them into a group as big as the Rolling Stones. Gomelsky was a wild character full of bustling energy and enthusiasm. A multilinguist, he was a Russian émigré with a Swiss passport, who spoke with a heavy accent. With his black beard and wild eyes, he reportedly was often mistaken for Fidel Castro in America.

To the youngsters now in his care, Gomelsky seemed a worldly, parental figure. His family background was fascinating. He was born on an Italian boat en route from the Persian Gulf to Italy in 1934. His father was a Russian doctor who had fled a purge in the Soviet Union. In 1943, the family moved to Switzerland, and Gomelsky came to England in 1955 with the intention of making jazz films. But it was difficult to overcome trade-union obstruction, and he became involved with the National Jazz Federation that ran the Marquee. He wound up being a pop promoter and manager instead of a film director.

"I was going around London trying to turn people onto the new rhythm and blues bands," Gomelsky recalled. "It took months to get a journalist down to see the Rolling Stones at the Station Hotel, Richmond. I only started a club because nobody else would do it and in the end it was so successful we were thrown out. There was a whole page in the *Daily Mirror* about the Crawdaddy Club. The director of the brewery asked his secretary, 'Is that our Station Hotel, Richmond? Close it down immediately.' We had to find another place, and so we went to the Richmond Athletic Association club. We soon had fifteen thousand members."

Gomelsky struck lucky promoting the Stones, but when his new protégés took over it wasn't so easy to convince the regular club-goers. By some accounts, a few stopped going to the Crawdaddy, complaining that Relf, who had a blond fringe and played the maracas, looked too much like Brian Jones or Mick Jagger. But McCarty insists, "There was a terrific reaction to us and we thought right away that we'd make it. We never really died the death."

Still, the Yardbirds had a problem with their guitarist. Topham's worried parents were pressuring the sixteen-year-old to leave the group. Although the Yardbirds had begun to win over fans and get more work, Topham quit in October 1963, resulting in an urgent search for a replacement.

"Top was the youngest guy in the band," McCarty said. "He was at art school and his parents were quite keen that he should finish his studies. Keith and Chris knew there was a guy at art school called Eric Clapton who was supposed to be a good blues player and a bit of a character. So we auditioned him. I'd never met him before, but he used to come to some of the gigs. He fit in well. Was he shy? No,

A portrait of the guitarist as a young Mod: Looking thoroughly disgusted with the whole pop world, Clapton poses for a Yardbirds promotional photo in Hyde Park on April 23, 1964. *Tony Gale/Pictorial Press Ltd/Alamy*

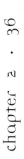

quite cocky, really! He already had a bit of an image and was quite famous on a small scale. He didn't quite have his own style together then. He used to copy blues guitar solos.

"He soon became quite popular. Keith had his fans and Eric had his fans. Then it got into that thing where the guitarist became bigger than the lead singer, which was unknown in those times. Usually the lead singer was the frontman. Keith was a nervous type and a little insecure."

"I knew Keith Relf and a guy called Roger Pearce from the pubs and parties we all used to go to," Clapton later recalled. "Those two would play Django Reinhardt stuff like the Hot Club de France with acoustic guitars, playing 'Sweet Georgia Brown.' I just hung out with them for a while. They told me about this band they had, and I also knew their guitar player, Tony Topham.

"When he had to leave they asked me to join. I thought, 'Well why not?' although I was quite happy doing what I was doing actually, which was learning Big Bill Broonzy stuff and playing in pubs on acoustic guitar for beer money.

"I later went down to see the Yardbirds at the Crawdaddy and was fairly critical of them, especially the guitarist. I was watching them one week and playing with them the next."

The Yardbirds respected Clapton's growing reputation. They also felt that he was much better looking than their previous guitarist and would attract more girl fans. They had just one rehearsal with Clapton at the Great Western Pub in Richmond and he was unanimously voted in. Clapton celebrated by buying himself a new Fender Telecaster.

He was by far the best musician in the band and also had deep knowledge about the blues. He thus cherished firm ideas about what the band should play, which caused some friction between McCarty and him. And Clapton, who came from a working-class background, didn't always get on with the rather posh Samwell-Smith, whose father owned an electrical business.

Nevertheless, they were now committed to making the band a success—and managed to have some fun along the way. Clapton, Dreja, and Relf shared a flat and even Clapton's relationship with Samwell-Smith warmed when it came to sharing band jokes. Jim McCarty remembers Clapton loved custard-pie jokes in particular and would even stick a pie in his own face to get a laugh.

Even so, there remained fundamental disagreements between Clapton and the band. "The thing that saved me in all of those situations was I had an extreme lack of ambition in terms of commerciality and conventional ideas about success," Clapton later explained. "I did not want to go anywhere special. I was quite happy to stay put.

"I was a bohemian or what we used to call 'beats' or 'traddies.' We had all kinds of names! I wore a duffle coat and a combat jacket and skin-tight jeans and army boots. I liked the crowd that I hung out with and was more interested in entertaining the people in the pub than playing for audiences. That didn't do a lot for me. And of course the Yardbirds was all about crossing that line and getting into pop magazines and being on TV and becoming famous, and that was absolutely repugnant to me."

Ticket, Sonny Boy Williamson and the Yardbirds, R&B Festival, Town Hall, Birmingham England, February 28, 1964.

Guitarist at work: Clapton wails on his Fender Telecaster with the Yardbirds. *Jeremy Fletcher/Redferns/Getty Images*

"That was a joke on my surname: slow hand clap-ton. The thing with my technique is that I have to re-learn it over and over again in the presence of other musicians. That's why I always make sure that the band and I have got a good long stretch of rehearsals. Because I'm a lazy bastard and I think it's very important for me with my personality that I walk into a rehearsal room with the least amount to offer. I have to work twice as hard. The other guys will come in hot from doing a session the day before and I'll be all over the place. It's a challenge for me to climb back up again."

—Eric Clapton on his nickname "Slowhand," *Q*, 1990

The group couldn't fail to be impressed by Clapton's tendency to be a bit of a style freak. He was always smartly dressed in the latest fashions and way ahead of the rest of the group. He shopped for clothes in the West End with Dreja, who was an old school pal. Clapton knew all the shops to get the best gear and would turn up at a gig or photo shoot with a close-cropped hairstyle despite the fact the rest of the group was sticking to their Stones-style long hair and getting thrown out of clubs and hotels as result.

"He was a style guru," said Dreja. "One minute it would be plastic raincoats and bouffant hair and the next minute it would be crew cuts and Ivy League clothes. Eric was always very style-conscious because of his art school background."

Clapton may have seemed a tad arrogant at times, but this was due to his inherent shyness. When performing with the group he was a driving force, but could still appear reticent. Audiences noticed not just his playing but the cool attitude that set him apart. "Although it's hard for people to believe now, I have to say Eric wasn't a guitar virtuoso at that point," said Dreja. "He was still learning licks and sometimes he wouldn't play lead guitar, he'd go and stand behind his amp. He had an amazingly charismatic image though."

Fans poured back to the Crawdaddy to see the revitalized Yardbirds, and the group began drawing huge crowds all over England. Management went into overdrive. Gomelsky's assistant Grimes ran their publicity campaign, dreaming up slogans such as "The most blueswailing Yardbirds." He also dubbed Clapton "Slowhand," a pun on the slow handclapping that ensued when the show had to stop while he replaced a broken string.

Gomelsky secured a contract with EMI's Columbia label, having turned down a bid from rival Decca. Meanwhile, the Yardbirds were invited to support visiting American bluesman Sonny Boy Williamson, who came to Britain as part of the American Blues Festival, a package tour that included Muddy Waters, Memphis Slim, and Willie Dixon.

The Americans arrived in October 1963, and a concert at Croydon's Fairfield Hall went so well that Williamson decided to stay on in Britain for another six months. He was supported by such groups as the Animals, Gary Farr and the T-Bones, and the Yardbirds. It was the first time Clapton had the chance to play with a real American blues artist, and he was as impressed by Williamson's capacity for drinking whiskey as he was by his harmonica playing. Clapton recalled one night when Williamson came on stage with the band, fell through the curtains, dropped all his harmonicas, and ended up in a heap on the floor.

Gomelsky arranged for the Yardbirds to be recorded live backing Williamson at the Crawdaddy on December 8, 1963. Clapton's guitar solos worked well with the harmonica, even if he was nervous and in awe of the irascible, unpredictable bluesman.

"We never had any rehearsals with Sonny Boy before we played a gig. We just had to pick up the number," McCarty recalled. "We were all trying to find the beat and the key. When you listen to the recordings you can hear us petrified, wondering when to come in and when to end. For some reason he'd finish and I'd do a drum roll."

The album wasn't released in the United States until 1966 as *Sonny Boy Williamson and the Yardbirds* on Mercury. Despite his unconventional approach to life and performing, Williamson loved his young band and was in tears when he had to leave the country. He died in Helena, Arkansas, on May 2, 1965.

In addition to the live session with the blues legend, the Yardbirds recorded demo studio tracks in February 1964, including John Lee Hooker's "Boom Boom" and Billy Boy Arnold's "Honey Hips." Gomelsky knew that the band would always go down well live, but there was something lacking in their recordings. "We did [the demos] in a studio and just couldn't get that live sound," McCarty said. "There was no excitement and we thought they sounded dead. Techniques were behind in those days and it was still the days of men in white coats running the studios as if it was a scientific procedure. Doing a live recording seemed the answer to our problems. It was Giorgio Gomelsky's idea to record our first album during a club gig."

Gomelsky had secured the group a weekly residency at the Marquee. On March 20, 1964, the Yardbirds cut a live session there that included an exciting version of Howlin' Wolf's "Smokestack Lightning," a number that gave Clapton plenty of space to freak out. The result was *Five Live Yardbirds.* Despite the cold March weather, the club was so packed that the heat became unbearable and the group played in puddles of sweat. "We wanted to re-create the scene we had going at the Crawdaddy at the Marquee," Gomelsky explained. "[The recorded Marquee show] consisted of two sets climaxing with wild rave ups. Everybody started dancing at the Crawdaddy like lunatics and were hanging from the ceiling. It was almost like a ritual. I realized, 'We can't capture this on a single.' I began to think, 'Why not present the Yardbirds' forty-minute set on an album?'"

Gomelsky recalled much panic as they set up primitive recording equipment in cramped conditions at the back of at the club. They used an engineer named Phillip Wood, who owned an Ampex recorder he'd used to record the Animals with Sonny Boy Williamson in Newcastle. "Phillip was a sweet man but he walked with a limp and it took him ages to change the microphone positions on the stage," Gomelsky continued. "However, we recorded two sets, enough for an album. During the first set we sorted out any problems. Then we took a forty-five-minute break when everybody went to the pub."

"I don't remember who was in the crowd that night," McCarty said, "but I've since heard David Bowie and Phil Collins were there. When you listen to the recordings now, it all sounds incredibly fast. I don't know if the machine sped up the sound, but the whole idea was to whip the crowd up. So it was all a bit manic."

Here Come The Yardbirds, Epic's New English Act

NEW YORK—Epic Records has dealt with England's EMI for yet another English rock act, a vocal-instrumental quintet called the Yardbirds, according to Bob Morgan, A&R exec producer at Epic.

First U.S. release by the group is "I Wish You Would," already reported as making the grade in England.

The crew is currently the regular quintet at the Crawdaddy Club, the nitery that launched the Rolling Stones, currently a top British act here. Group is headed by Keith Relf, harmonica player and featured soloist.

Epic is riding high with singles and LP dates by the Dave Clark Five, another acquisition from EMI. Others include Cliff Richard, Rolf Harris and Scottish singer Andy Stewart.

Announcement of the Yardbirds' first single, "I Wish You Would," in the U.S. music-industry magazine *Cash Box* from August 15, 1964.

The Yardbirds' first single, a cover of Billy Boy Arnold's "I Wish You Would," released in the U.K. on Columbia in 1964.

After Lord Ted Willis made disparaging remarks about Mod music in the English House of Lords in 1964, the Yardbirds and fans invaded his home at Shepherds Green, Chislehurst, Kent, England, in an effort to convert him. Although taken by surprise, His Lordship invited the Mods into his home to discuss matters. Afterwards, the Yardbirds performed while His Lordship relaxed in his lawn chair. *Jeremy Fletcher/Redferns/Getty Images*

Clapton talks to an early admirer, Lady Willis, during the band's demonstration at Lord Willis' home. *Trinity Mirror/ Mirrorpix/Alamy*

"We played twice as loud and fast as normal," Dreja confirmed. "After all, it was a high-energy era. Speeded up or not, everything was played with incredible verve. But we approached it as just another gig at the Marquee. Apart from doing a sound balance in the afternoon, we thought it a huge laugh. None of us took it seriously except for Keith Relf's father, Bill, who stood on the stage with a contraption like a fishing rod with a mike on the end to capture the audience noise. The audience loved it. It was a great night."

Gomelsky insisted it was an honest recording. "There were no overdubs. And we didn't speed up the tapes. We didn't have the equipment to do that kind of stuff. There was no desire to cheat in any way. Possibly the machine wasn't calibrated properly, but what you hear is what the band played."

The Yardbirds' cover of the blues standard "Good Morning Little Schoolgirl" as learned from Sonny Boy Williamson and released in the U.K. on Columbia in 1964. © Colin Underhill / Alamy

Dreja remembered the thrill of being on stage: "It was a great audience and of course we were all very young. And Eric was just making his way as a guitarist. We decided to record the gig because although we were exciting on stage, we had failed to make our mark as a recording band.

"I remember another night at the Marquee when in walked a very tired-looking bunch of guys who were the Moody Blues. They had just spent twenty-four hours recording their big hit 'Go Now.' We thought it amazing they'd been so long recording one song. We didn't realize the importance of spending so much time in a studio. We thought that was all a bit of a joke."

"I don't know if they took the recording seriously or not," Gomelsky later pondered. "Maybe the band wasn't totally involved because no one knew how it would come out. We were just having a go. Certainly the group took the playing seriously. I remember Eric kept on breaking strings, but he did that anyway because he played with such ferocity."

Although the Marquee show went well, there was a near disaster later. Paul Samwell-Smith, who nursed ambitions to become a producer, ran a section of tape and accidentally erased one of their best numbers, "I Wish You Would."

"Paul was just getting into production and thought he was a bit of a clever clogs," McCarty said. "He pressed one of the buttons and erased a whole chunk of tape. That's why 'I Wish You Would' was never on the original album. We all shouted 'What are you *doing*?' Then we just fell about laughing."

Dreja remembers Samwell-Smith saying, "What does this button do?" "He hit 'erase' and wiped the track. We thought it was funny but that was our attitude, I'm afraid. I remember Eric and myself filling in Performing Rights forms with fake names like E. Ville. We didn't realize we were cutting ourselves off from a source of income."

The Yardbirds' show with American bluesman Sonny Boy Williamson at London's Crawdaddy Club was recorded and released as an LP in later years.

Despite Samwell-Smith's slip, he later became a successful producer, working with artists such as Cat Stevens. Most of the Marquee session was salvaged, and *Five Live Yardbirds* proved a moderately successful album on its U.K. release in January 1965. The group had already released their debut single, a studio recording of "I Wish You Would" coupled with "A Certain Girl."

"It got into the charts for one week in July 1964," said McCarty. "We got a phone call from Giorgio at seven a.m. saying, 'Come on, we're going to do

Following the release of their first recordings, the Yardbirds made many publicity appearances, including signing records and autographs in music shops. Clapton looks none too happy to comply. *Jeremy Fletcher/ Redferns/Getty Images*

Ready Steady Go! on TV today because somebody has dropped out.' So we took taxis to the studio and we did 'I Wish You Would' and because of that it went straight into the charts. It was all very spontaneous."

In October 1964, the band released a version of the blues standard "Good Morning Little Schoolgirl." BBC radio refused to play it, but the record scraped into the charts at No. 44. It was clear the Yardbirds needed more than R&B covers to make an impact. Their songwriting ability hadn't developed, but they could try experimenting with somebody else's material. They would have loved a Beatles song, but in the end they chose an unusual number called "For Your Love" written by Graham Gouldman, who would later create 1970s hitmakers 10cc.

The record was a big hit, but it spelled the end of the Yardbirds' relationship with their string-breaking fashion guru. Eric Clapton was about to quit the band of brothers.

THE CLASSIC ALBUMS

Five Live Yardbirds

The band's first LP, *Five Live Yardbirds*, released on Columbia in 1964.

"On the lead guitar, Eric 'Slowhand' Clapton!"

Amidst a flurry of cheers as the breathless compere makes his announcement, the young Yardbirds guitarist launches into Chuck Berry's "Too Much Monkey Business." Rarely has any artist been caught in the act of launching his career with such an exhilarating introduction and fanfare.

We can forgive the flubbed note at the end of Clapton's fretboard fury. And we can't forget that most of the attention at the Marquee Club on the cold wintery night when the Yardbirds recorded this legendary live album was supposedly on singer Keith Relf. Yet even back in March 1964 all eyes were on the brilliant young guitarist bobbing about on stage and smiling at the madness of it all.

The idea was to capture the excitement the band had been generating at club gigs ever since they took over from the Rolling Stones. The venue in London's Soho had become the Yardbirds' home, where they regaled fans with their manic "rave up" style. The band can be heard having huge amounts of fun as they storm into "I Got Love if You Want It" and "Smokestack Lightning." But amidst the wailing harmonica and thrashing drums is also discernible the sound of Clapton developing his early guitar style.

It's all about nervous energy and frantic speed and is far removed from his more mature playing with John Mayall's Blues Breakers several years later. But there's no doubting his energy and commanding presence. He can even be heard summoning the courage to sing alongside bass player Paul Samwell-Smith on their school boyish "Good Morning Little Schoolgirl." It had been Clapton's idea to choose the number for a single, and although Relf sang it on the record, it was Clapton who sang it at gigs.

There aren't many lengthy solos from Clapton but when he does get a chance to shine you can hear his burgeoning confidence. When the album was released, many thought that the tapes had been speeded up, as Clapton & Co. seemed to be playing so fast.

On "Five Long Years," they play at a more manageable tempo and we sit on tenterhooks waiting to hear Clapton cut loose. He only gets one chorus, but this track provides some of his best work on the album. "Here 'Tis" is another Bo Diddley classic that the boys take at a furious tempo, interspersed with hoarse cries of "Whoa ho ho!" It all sounds like a runaway freight train. The best bit comes when Clapton trades phrases with Samwell-Smith. "Here it comes!" yells Relf, launching into a battle cry that sounds like "Isle of Wight!" until you realize he's singing "I'm all right!"

If this recording sounds panic stricken, that's because guitar strings were being broken, people were tripping over wires, and recording equipment was being blasted by needle-busting volume. And amidst the chaos the tape of Clapton's feature number "I Wish You Would" was accidentally erased. No wonder his days with the Yardbirds were numbered.

3. where's eric?

The Yardbirds and the Blues Breakers, 1965

ERIC CLAPTON LOOKED MISERABLE. The Yardbirds were playing "Smokestack Lightning" to a handful of people at a South London venue called the Bromel Club, and the guitar player was itching to get off stage. "You look fed up," said one of his fans. "You noticed," said Clapton with a wry smile. Just a few weeks later, he was gone, and the group was desperately seeking a replacement.

The guitarist had enjoyed his first brush with fame and now he was throwing it all away. Just after he left, the Yardbirds' latest single, "For Your Love," shot to No. 2 on the U.K. chart in March 1965, fulfilling the group's dreams of stardom. Along with the rest of the group, Clapton had experienced the kind of pop mania that all 1960s pop stars were accorded, including the attentions of frantically screaming girls. Clapton admits he was pleased and amused at first to be the object of idolization. But he began to have doubts about the validity of his role as a pop idol.

"To be honest I thought it was a little bit disproportionate," he says. "I could only use my own standards of behavior as a term of reference. If I went to see a great performer playing,

Five live Yardbirds: The band rocks through their show at Woolwich, England, on January 21, 1965.
From left, Chris Dreja, Paul Samwell-Smith, Jim McCarty, Keith Relf, and Clapton. *Pace/Getty Images*

One of the last happy publicity shots of the former band of brothers. *GAB Archive/Redferns/Getty Images*

The Yardbirds' pop single "For Your Love" was the last straw for Clapton.

I would stand and listen and maybe at the end, if I had any kind of nerve, I'd go up and tell him I was a fan and mention that I'd bought his album. Because I was a bit of a mod myself, I ended up with lots of mod girls all yelling at me! I thought, 'This is not the real thing, this is something else.' It was interesting but I was wary of it."

So in the midst of all the excitement, the guitarist decided to walk out. What had gone wrong? In a great huff he proclaimed that he was leaving because the band had "gone commercial." He really disliked "For Your Love" and couldn't relate to the doomy theme or its bongos and harpsichord backing. It was produced and arranged by Paul Samwell-Smith. Clapton wasn't pleased when their manager, Giorgio Gomelsky, suggested that henceforth Samwell-Smith should be the group's musical director.

Even though the B-side, "Got to Hurry," featured one of Clapton's best recorded guitar solos with the Yardbirds, he was unhappy with the move from blues to pop. His discontent had shown itself even before the release of the disputed single when he failed to turn up to a show at an Odeon theater and the group had to perform as a four-piece with Chris Dreja on lead. Clapton suspected the group had already been checking out his replacement and realized that his own behavior had worried them. Increasingly withdrawn and dogmatic, he was no longer the cheerful joker who once enjoyed spraying his mates with beer in the van after a gig.

"I was kind of elbowed out," Clapton later said. "The decision was made by Giorgio Gomelsky and the other guys. They thought I was going to be the difficult one and it was not worth their while keeping me on. There was clearly a big market for what they had to offer and they made the most of it, as far as I could see.

"Years later I bumped into Jimmy Page and Jeff Beck at a reception with the Queen at Buckingham Palace, and they told me they didn't have the greatest time in the Yardbirds, either. By the time they got to America and were touring with those two playing guitar, apparently it was getting pretty ugly in the band. The time I was in the band was probably their best period, when we were playing at the Ricky Tick and the Crawdaddy at the Station Hotel. That was the peak of the Yardbirds, and I thought 'I Wish You Would' was a great record.

"I was happy to go but at the same time I was very confused. It seemed like a repeat pattern of where I'd been before because Casey Jones wasn't a very satisfying experience. There was always this thing about someone *else* having an idea about how you should be presented. What I now realize is that the burden of being 'in a group' where you have to toe a party line. It's a fairly poisonous existence because there is always a dictator in there somewhere who is going to tell you what you're supposed to look like and how to behave and even the kind of music you're supposed to be producing. I remember when the Yardbirds appeared on the Beatles' Christmas show, our manager Giorgio thought we should wear a uniform. So we went to a Soho tailor and had some suits made. It was great meeting the Beatles, but after that I steered clear of becoming part of a cooperative group, until Cream came along."

Jim McCarty explained further: "Eric Clapton just didn't like 'For Your Love.' Instead he suggested various Motown-type things for us to do like 'Putty in Your Hands' and 'Hang on Sloopy.' But we all liked 'For Your Love,' which we thought was very commercial. Graham Gouldman wrote for the Hollies, but 'For Your Love' was his first big hit."

The production featured extra session musicians, and Samwell-Smith stayed in the control room rather than playing bass in the studio. Jazz organist Brian Auger played harpsichord, Denny Peircy was on bongos, and Ron Prentice added the bowed bass. There wasn't much space for the guitar player.

"I thought it was a bit silly really," Clapton recalled. "I thought it would be good for a group like Hedgehoppers Anonymous. It didn't make any sense in terms of what we supposed to be playing. I thought 'this is the thin end of the wedge.'"

The news of Clapton's departure hit the headlines in the music press. In March 1965, *Melody Maker* reported, "Clapton quits Yardbirds—'too commercial.'" It was announced he'd be replaced by Jeff Beck. Keith Relf told the newspaper, "It's very sad because we are all friends. There was no bad feeling at all but Eric did not get on well with the business. He does not like commercialisation. He loves the blues so much I suppose he did not like it being played badly by a white shower like us! Eric did not like our new record 'For Your Love.' He should have been featured but he did not want to sing or anything and he only did a boogie bit in the middle. His leaving is bound to be a blow to the group's image at first because Eric was very popular. Jeff Beck, who is very very good was recommended to us by session man Jimmy Page, who is the guv'nor."

Once again Eric Clapton was a loner, out a group and out of the limelight. As he explained to anyone who would listen, "The Yardbirds put me in a very strange frame of mind. I was all screwed up about my playing and didn't like anything I did. I had lost my values. I was ready to go off and paint or do something else. I just didn't know what. My attitude within the group got really sour and it was kind of hinted that it would be better for me to leave. I was starting to feel very lost and alone. The Yardbirds were tying me down. I wanted to get a step further on and they wanted more and more discipline."

"I wanted to be in Freddie King's band or Buddy Guy's band, that's the band I wanted to be in—the real thing. I didn't want to be in a white rock band, I didn't want to be in a black rock band, I wanted to be in a black blues band. . . ."

—Eric Clapton on leaving the Yardbirds, 1994

"If I hadn't left the Yardbirds I wouldn't have been able to play real blues much longer because I was destroying myself."

—Eric Clapton, *Rave* magazine, 1965

Concert poster, March 10, 1965.

The flipside of "For Your Love" was the blues-powered "Got to Hurry," featuring one of Clapton's best recorded guitar solos with the Yardbirds.

It seemed his career might be over before it had really begun. But the blues were just around the corner, waiting to bring him back to life and back to the guitar. Recalling his time with the Yardbirds, Clapton said, "I was fooled into joining the group. I fooled myself, attracted by the pop thing, the big money, traveling, and chicks. It wasn't until I'd been doing it for eighteen months that I started to take my music seriously. I realized that I wanted to do it for the rest of my life, so I had better start doing it right."

His old group watched cautiously to see how things would pan out for the renegade. His first step was to join John Mayall's Blues Breakers. The all-important telephone call from the bandleader came just two weeks after becoming unemployed.

"It was 'Got to Hurry,' the B-side of 'For Your Love' that got Eric the job with John Mayall," said Dreja. "I often wonder what thoughts went through Eric's head when he left the group at the point when 'For Your Love' did so well. But it wasn't a mistake from his point of view, as it kept him in the blues idiom a lot longer.

"None of us had a crystal ball in those days to predict what would happen. The main thing was this explosion of energy. We could all do what we liked. The thing about Eric is that he is one of those people who have incredibly close relationships with others for very short periods of time. He's very intense. Then something triggers inside him and a wall comes up. We'd all had intense relationships with Eric and then prior to us playing on a Beatles' Christmas show, he started to disappear. He spent a lot more time on his own. From being your brother he became quite distant. He was no longer really part of the band. There are intense relationships within bands and if you don't support each other and you don't have that integral family thing, they tend not to work."

In the aftermath of Clapton's departure, the Yardbirds continued to record and toured the States with Jeff Beck and later Jimmy Page, who joined on bass before switching to lead guitar. The pair forged the kind of aggressive heavy rock that led to the creation of Jimmy Page's New Yardbirds, which ultimately became Led Zeppelin in 1968.

The old Yardbirds broke up that year but remain revered as pioneers, with groups such as Aerosmith proclaiming them an early influence. (In a tragic sequel, founding member Keith Relf died in May 1976 at age 33, electrocuted by his guitar while practicing at home.)

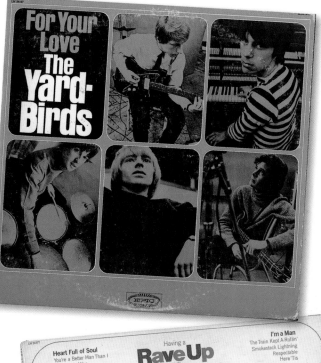

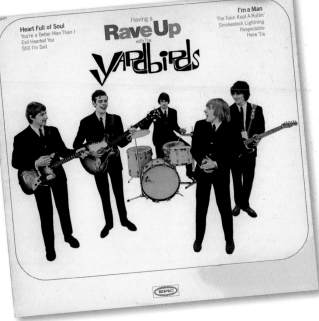

Even with Clapton gone from the Yardbirds and ably replaced by Jeff Beck, the band continued to release older recordings that featured Clapton—although with Beck on the album covers of *For Your Love* and *Having a Rave Up with the Yardbirds*.

John Mayall was a former art student who led a truly bohemian life and played a pivotal role in the development of blues appreciation in Britain alongside contemporaries Alexis Korner and jazz trombonist Chris Barber. Mayall was born in Macclesfield, Cheshire, England, on November 29, 1933. As a child, he studied the George Formby ukulele and banjo tutor book and learned how to play stringed instruments. But at the age of thirteen he became fascinated by piano boogie-woogie. Says Mayall, "From that point on I was addicted!"

After three years in National Service, including time in Korea, Mayall returned to England in 1954 and studied at Manchester College of Art, where he met his future wife, Pamela. He planned to become a commercial artist, but also formed his own band called the Power House Four. Mayall played boogie and blues on the art school piano during the lunch breaks. Soon music and bandleading would take over his life.

When Mayall's parents divorced, he had to move into his grandfather's house. Rather than share a room, he decided to construct his own treehouse in the garden. "I spent a lot of time up there and it became quite sophisticated," he recalled. "I had a water tank attached to the outside and a power line running from the main house."

The local press reported on the strange structure appearing in suburban Manchester and explained how the eccentric tree-dweller, then known as Johnny Mayall, climbed up into his treehouse via a rope ladder. When he married Pamela, Mayall carried his bride up the ladder in front of cameramen and reporters. The house was later ordered demolished by the town council due to nonpayment of taxes.

Conversely, for the sheet music of the Yardbirds' next single, "Heart Full of Soul," which featured Jeff Beck's guitar, a dour-looking Clapton was pictured on the cover.

Proficient on piano, organ, harmonica, and guitar, as well as singing, Mayall sought solace in the blues and formed the first of a succession of groups that evolved into the Blues Breakers. Encouraged by Alexis Korner, Mayall moved to London in 1962, and during the 1960s his touring band would be considered a musical college for dozens of musicians, many of whom went on to more famous groups. In fact, the role of lead guitarist with John Mayall became a much sought-after post, although the hard life on the road and relatively low pay did not encourage them to stay. Ex-Mayall musicians included Peter Green, John McVie, and Mick Fleetwood, who later formed Fleetwood Mac; Jack Bruce, who helped form Cream with Clapton; Mick Taylor, who later joined the Rolling Stones; and drummer Aynsley Dunbar, who went on to play with Frank Zappa.

Eric Clapton became a Blues Breaker in May 1965 and stayed until June 1966—with a crazed break in the middle that would become the stuff of legends. Whenever he disappeared, the cry would go up "Where's Eric?!"

"Joining John Mayall suited me fine because he had a blues band and I was a purist then," Clapton says. "For me, in those days, blues was the only kind of music and I didn't like anything else."

Clapton had seen the Blues Breakers at the Flamingo Club in Soho and wasn't that keen on John Mayall's rather shrill voice. "He seemed to know what he wanted to do but not exactly how to do it. There were few people around then who could do anything properly. It was all very rough. But when I joined the band he chose me for the way I played and he didn't tell me *how* to play."

Clapton took over from Mayall's previous guitarist, Roger Dean. "I don't know if John had wanted to replace him but I was intrigued by the offer," Clapton continued. "It was a very powerful band and it wasn't just John Mayall, God bless him. He was the focal point and the custodian, and it all came from his choice of musicians. He always had great people passing through."

Clapton went to stay at Mayall's house in Lee, South London, living in a small room and getting to know more about his employer's lifestyle. Mayall had a strict anti-drink rule within the band, and on one occasion bassist John McVie was chucked out of their van on the road between London and Birmingham, accused of being seriously drunk.

"John got turfed out of the van in the middle of some awful place, up north at the top of the M1," Clapton recalls. "He was swearing and cursing, but the next day everything would be as right as rain, as if nothing had happened."

The van became legendary among Mayall's musicians. It had a bunk bed, but only for the use of the bandleader. The rest of the group had to sit at the front while Mayall slumbered in the back; his sidemen could sleep in the van

A pleased-looking Clapton was pictured with John Mayall's Blues Breakers. From left, Mayall, Hughie Flint, Clapton, and John McVie. *Michael Ochs Archives/Getty Images*

only when they drove to Manchester, where Mayall could stay the night at his mother's house. "He was an amazing man," says Clapton. "He'd didn't get you a hotel to stay in. So there were disadvantages being in that band."

Despite the privations of touring, there was no doubt Clapton's presence boosted the Blues Breakers' popularity and drew increasing numbers to their gigs. But Clapton was restless. For him it was just another job and not particularly well paid, either.

It might have seemed that joining John Mayall's Blues Breakers was like jumping from the frying pan back into the fire in terms of dictatorship. But Clapton was always loyal to the Mayall regime. "The only bit that was anything like the Yardbirds was the band uniform, which one I quite liked because it was Ivy League," he says. "It was a sort of pale-blue Dacron blazer with black shirts and I thought, 'This is good' because it was sorta jazzy. We looked like a jazz band. John Mayall was always a canny guy in terms of the arts. When I first met him, I was quite impressed by how many things he had going on."

Clapton continues: "He was an intellectual and very well read. He had an incredible knowledge of the kind of music I was most interested in, which was Chicago blues. I stayed with John for most of the time I was in his band. John and I were the real blues fanatics in the Blues Breakers. I would encourage him to do much more hard-core stuff. He was doing the crowd-pleasing things, like taking his shirt off while doing 'Parchman Farm.' That was the Mose Allison part of the set. But I was trying to get him to play songs by Otis Rush and Howlin' Wolf and contemporary Chicago blues, which was flourishing at the time."

"With John Mayall I can play how I like. I'm a very passive person but I can make chords on a guitar sound vicious and violent. When I do, it is all the bad things I've seen coming out. Sometimes I don't play for days, but when I pick up the guitar a stream of feelings pour through it."

—Eric Clapton, *Rave* magazine, 1965

Yet despite these serious musical intentions, Clapton didn't want to spend all his days stuck in a van on the M1 driving north in the rain. An alternative was driving south—in search of sunshine.

And so Clapton abruptly quit the Blues Breakers in August 1965 and went to stay with former Roosters pianist Ben Palmer in Oxford. He wanted to hang out with friends who preferred drinking wine and listening to jazz records rather than working. One drunken night while staying in a flat in London's Covent Garden, Clapton's mates planned a wild adventure. They would form a group called the Glands and set off around the world, stopping off to play and earn their keep.

The original plan was to re-create Cliff Richard's movie, *Summer Holiday*. When they couldn't find a London Transport bus to convert into a mobile home, they bought an American Ford station wagon to be driven by Bernie Greenwood, who had played saxophone with Chris Farlowe and the Thunderbirds. The Glands also included singer John Bailey and bassist/trumpeter Bob Rae. Palmer would play piano, and Clapton would pack his trusty Gibson Les Paul. Bailey went ahead to Greece, where he thought he could get them some nightclub dates.

But when the merry party arrived in Athens, no dates had been booked. They scrounged up work at a club called the Igloo, but the management expected them to play the latest pop hits. It wasn't exactly what Clapton had in mind. "We didn't get a chance to play any blues at all," Palmer said. "Instead we covered numbers by the Who, Stones, and Kinks."

"The job with Mayall had become—just a job," Clapton later explained. "So I wanted to go and have some fun as well. We ended up in Greece playing Rolling Stones songs, anything to get by. We met this club proprietor who hired us to open for a Greek band that played Beatles songs."

The house band was called the Juniors, but sadly they were involved in a car crash a few weeks later that killed some of the members. As a result, Clapton was expected to take over. "I found myself obliged to play with both bands," he recalled. "I was a quick learner and picked up all the Beatles and Kinks songs they were doing. But I began to realize I was trapped and the proprietor wouldn't let me go. Then he fired the rest of our band, and I was stuck there with this Greek band."

After a couple of weeks the British lads discovered their hotel bill wasn't being paid and they weren't receiving any money for playing at the club. They wanted to return home, but the club owner advised them that as they had no work permits they'd all be arrested. Clapton was ordered to stay at the boss' house, and the others weren't allowed to remove their instruments from the club. The Glands were also forced to play two concerts at a local cinema one Sunday morning.

"We were prisoners surrounded by heavies and in a state of kidnap" recalled Palmer. Their final show ended in a riot when the Glands played the Stones' "Satisfaction" nonstop throughout the show in protest.

In the confusion that followed, Palmer managed to sneak their instruments and gear away with the help of Greek fans. Clapton, however, was locked into the venue's office by the management, who clearly regarded him as the ringleader.

In desperation, Palmer sold their amplifiers and raised enough money to buy train tickets home. Clapton escaped by claiming he needed to buy some new guitar strings for that evening's gig. Instead, he headed for the station where he met Palmer. The pair hid in the toilets until a trans-European train arrived.

Once safely back at London's Victoria Station, as Clapton got off the train he told Palmer to "Hang on a minute" and dashed to the nearest telephone. He phoned John Mayall and asked for his old job back. Mayall said yes and Clapton jumped into a taxi and went straight to his house. He was back in the Blues Breakers once more. This time they'd do more than drive to Manchester in the rain for yet more club gigs—they'd go into Decca studios and make an album. The results would prove a turning point in Eric Clapton's career and establish him as a serious force in music.

TONIGHT at
BLUESVILLE CLUB
THE BATHS HALL
7.30-11 p.m.

Nanda and Ron Lesley Present
The Big R and B Beat Show
of 1965

THE BOSS ORGAN GRINDER
John Mayhall
and his
Bluesbreakers

Featuring the Superb Blues Guitar of
ERIC CLAPTON

MEMBERS 5/-   GUESTS 6/-
Free Sweets! Ciggies! Discs!

THE CIVIC HALL, GRAYS
TUESDAY, FEBRUARY 1: THE ORIGINAL SOUND OF
JOHN MAYALL'S
BLUESBREAKERS
WITH WONDERFUL ERIC CLAPTON
TUESDAY, FEBRUARY 8 THE
RAM JAM BAND
WITH GENO WASHINGTON
8 P.M. ONWARDS   COME EARLY!

Concert advertisements, 1965–1966.

4. steppin' out

The Blues Breakers and Cream, 1966

WHEN ERIC CLAPTON RETURNED to John Mayall's Blues Breakers, he found a new man in the ranks. Jack Bruce had joined on bass guitar, having replaced John McVie, who Mayall had sacked for alleged excessive drinking. Bruce was a dynamic bass guitarist, harmonica player, and singer. Yet the fiery Scot had also been sacked, in his case from the Graham Bond Organisation. His dismissal had been the result of a violent altercation with raucous drummer Peter "Ginger" Baker.

Jack Bruce would stay only a short while with the Blues Breakers. He left to take a better-paid gig with the Manfred Mann group. But his tenure was long enough to impress Clapton. He had already seen Bruce with the Bond Organisation and was well aware of his abilities. As fellow Blues Breakers, they improvised in a way that Clapton found challenging and inspiring. Swapping ideas and blending solos, the guitarist felt he was being pushed by a musician of equal stature.

"When I got back with John Mayall, Jack was on bass and we hit it off really well," Clapton recalls. "Then he left to go with Manfred Mann, and John got John McVie back.

John Mayall and Eric Clapton from the cover of the *Blues Breakers* LP, with Clapton reading the new issue of *The Beano* comic book that gave the record the nickname, "The Beano album."

I decided that playing with Jack was more exciting and he was more creative. Most of what we were doing with Mayall was imitating the original records, but Jack was something else. He had no reverence for what we were doing and began composing new parts as he went along. I had never heard that before and it took me someplace else."

Clapton's return to the Blues Breakers after his Greek expedition with the Glands was a source of joy for crowds turning up at Mayall gigs. Clapton was hailed as the prodigal son and became a conquering hero in the eyes of his army of fans, who'd shout "Give God a solo!" It was alleged that graffiti proclaiming "Clapton is God" began appearing on walls all over London.

Clapton remains unconvinced of these scrawled messages. "Did I ever see them on walls?" he begins. "No. Never. It was probably some agency putting them up. It got all blown out of proportion. I could never understand what all the fuss was about and I didn't really take it to heart."

Clapton was still an "underground" cult hero, but the record industry was waking up to his presence. A single featuring him and the Blues Breakers playing "I'm Your Witchdoctor" and "Telephone Blues" was produced by Jimmy Page and released on Andrew Loog Oldham's Immediate label in October 1965. The tracks came from sessions recorded during Clapton's first tenure with Mayall earlier in the year.

Both appeared on the 1968 anthology *Blues Anytime Vol. 1*. In his sleeve notes, blues enthusiast and producer Mike Vernon wrote about "the spine-chilling guitar work of Eric Clapton," and enthused, "Eric has emerged from the depths of the rock 'n' roll clique to become the finest British guitarist working in the modern blues idiom."

"I'm Your Witchdoctor," a fast, jazzy number, had spooky effects and heavy echo on the guitar. By contrast, "Telephone Blues" was slow and dragging with stop-time breaks. *Blues Anytime Vol. 1* also had some ramshackle tape-recorded snippets featuring Clapton with Page on second guitar. On the slow, dragging "Snake Drive," Clapton was backed by Bill Wyman on bass and Rolling Stones' tour manager Ian Stewart on piano. "Tribute to Elmore," another Clapton–Page collaboration, proved most disappointing, while a turgid "West Coast Idea" showed Clapton still in throes of shaping his style.

In November, Vernon invited Clapton and Mayall to record some Chicago-style blues numbers. "Lonely Years" and "Bernard Jenkins" were given limited single release on the Purdah label in August 1966. Both tracks later appeared on the Ace of Clubs compilation *Raw Blues* issued in January 1967, together with tracks by Otis Spann and Champion Jack Dupree.

"Lonely Years" was a brave attempt at re-creating 1930s American blues in a 1960s British recording studio. One microphone was used to capture the vocals, harmonica, and guitar. The same technique was used for "Bernard Jenkins," a lively instrumental featuring Mayall's boogie piano overlapping Clapton's guitar.

John Mayall's Blues Breakers' first single, "I'm Your Witchdoctor," Immediate Records, 1965.

Much more important was the creation of the first album that properly showcased that "spine-tingling guitar." Decca released *Blues Breakers*, produced by Mike Vernon, in July 1966 to universal acclaim. At last fans could hear Clapton given free rein to express himself in a professional studio alongside like-minded souls. The LP with its iconic cover design became known as "The Beano Album" because the cover shot showed an amused Eric casually reading the popular British children's comic alongside his more po-faced colleagues.

Much of the credit for getting the album off the ground lay with Vernon, who badgered Decca Records into taking on the Blues Breakers. He told them that unless they signed the group they'd miss out on Clapton, a star in the making.

Clapton's sound and style was firmly established during the sessions that took place without fuss or ceremony at Decca's Number 2 studios in West Hampstead, London, in April 1966. Clapton arrived armed with a Gibson Les Paul Standard and a 60-watt Marshall combo amplifier. Using vibrato and smooth phrasing, Clapton delivered his own version of the American blues that had been pioneered by his idols Freddie and Albert King.

Although now regarded as a milestone in his career, Clapton remains bewildered by the album's perceived significance: "When we did the *Blues Breakers* album we had been on the road so long we could just go into the studio and play our set," he later explained. "My recollection of that day at Decca was of unloading the gear, taking it in, playing, packing up the gear, and leaving."

The engineer on the session, Gus Dudgeon, was alarmed at the volume levels that Clapton was generating through his amplifier, fearing serious distortion. Vernon and Dudgeon had to find a way to deal with the problem without discouraging the musicians in the throes of creativity.

In the end, Clapton just played as loud as he liked, and the result was a collection of powerful performances, with "All Your Love" and "Hideaway" graced with particularly sparkling solos. These were matched by the confident instrumental "Steppin' Out," while Clapton's solo on Mayall's "Have You Heard" was also a sublime piece of carefully constructed improvisation. Eric even sang a bit on Robert Johnson's "Ramblin' on My Mind."

Critics and fans alike were delighted with the bestselling album, as was the bandleader. "The album did really well in the charts," Mayall later recalled. "And it really helped me to get known in America."

Despite this success, the guitar player was getting itchy feet again.

On the road in the Mayall bandwagon was less fun than ever, and Clapton still felt restricted in his playing opportunities. The seed of an attractive idea was germinating, growing, and taking root. Eric had started to think seriously about forming his own group. He was partly inspired by seeing a visiting American blues guitarist at work.

The British children's comic book, *The Beano*, issue 1242 from May 5, 1966: Clapton's choice of reading material during the cover shoot for the *Blues Breakers* album.

the Beano guitar

In 1965, Clapton purchased a used, five-year-old 1960 Gibson Les Paul Standard at Lew Davis' guitar shop on Charing Cross Road, London. That Les Paul would soon become legendary—in part for the glorious bluesy tone Clapton coaxed from the guitar on the *Blues Breakers* album, but also because it was soon lost or stolen during Clapton's summer in Greece, never to be found.

One of the few known photographs of Clapton with the famous 1960 Gibson Les Paul Standard guitar that became known as the "Beano guitar." The image appeared on the back of the *Blues Breakers* LP. Playing through his Marshall JTM45 combo amp, Clapton created a deep, overdriven tone that would be imitated forever after.

"That was the best Les Paul I ever had . . . just a regular sunburst Les Paul that I bought in one of the shops in London right after I'd seen Freddie King's album cover of *Let's Hide Away and Dance Away*, where he's playing a gold-top. It had humbuckers and was almost brand new—original case with that lovely purple velvet lining. Just magnificent. I never really found one as good as that. I do miss that one."

—Eric Clapton in *Guitar Player* magazine

In December 2010, Gibson launched a reissue of Clapton's iconic 1960 Gibson Les Paul Beano guitar, with PAF humbucker pickups and aged sunburst finish. *Gibson Guitar Corporation*

"Eric was the first to evolve the sound with the Gibson and the Marshall amps; he should have total credit for that. I remember when we did 'I'm Your Witchdoctor,' he had all that sound down, and the engineer, who was cooperating up to that point, but was used to doing orchestras and big bands, suddenly turned off the machine and said: 'This guitarist is unrecordable!' I told him to just record and I'd take full responsibility; the guy just couldn't believe someone was getting that kind of sound on purpose."

—Jimmy Page

"I went to see Buddy Guy at the Marquee, and he had a pickup band of bass and drums," Clapton explains. "They were irrelevant really because he played the whole thing on his own. What it said to me was 'This is possible.' If you were a good enough guitar player, you could just do it as a trio. It was what Jimi Hendrix did when his turn came around. It seemed to me so free. You could go anywhere, change direction, and do whatever you liked. Being in a fairly rigid structure like John Mayall's Blues Breakers, we had a set we played every night and I was kind of thinking about that as a problem. A trio was a way of breaking free."

As early as March that year, Clapton had confided to journalist Nick Jones that he been thinking about his future plans but was finding it very difficult. "Forming a blues band in England is like banging your head against a brick wall," he told Jones. "Nobody wants to record it."

He also revealed that he was well aware of his abilities. "I have a power and my guitar is a medium for expressing that power," he explained. "I've worked it out by myself. It's nothing to do with technique and rehearsing. It is to do with the person behind the guitar who is trying to find an outlet. My guitar is a medium through which I can make contact with myself. It's very lonely."

Chicago bluesman Buddy Guy wails on his Fender Stratocaster. Inspired by seeing Guy at London's Marquee Club, Clapton dreamed of creating a pure blues band. The result, instead, was Cream.
Elliot Landy/Redferns/Getty Images

So Clapton was already in a receptive mood when Ginger Baker turned up at a Blues Breakers' gig in Oxford one night in May 1966. Baker asked to sit in, and his passionate, dynamic drumming transformed the sound of the band. Clapton was excited and impressed. When they chatted afterward, Baker looked him in the eye and asked, "How about getting a group together?"

Clapton was keen and suggested another possible member. He knew a good bassist who would be ideal:

"By then I had seen Ginger and Jack Bruce play with Alexis Korner and with Graham Bond and, of course, Jack had joined John's band for a while. When he played with [the Blues Breakers] it really took off and it was like 'Wow!' With the greatest respect to John McVie, Jack is a driving bass player. He can move around like a guitarist and he really shook that band up. I started making mental notes about how this would affect my future. I was thinking I could have a Buddy Guy–style trio with a composing bass player.

"When Ginger Baker showed up at the Blues Breakers gig, I think he'd probably already been to see Robert Stigwood with the idea of forming a band. He'd got the bit between his teeth. I don't know what he would have done if I had been easier about Jack. Because he didn't want Jack in the band and I did. That was my condition, although at that point I didn't know there was any enmity between them.

"After Ginger came to see me play he gave me a lift home and asked if I was interested in doing something. Then I said, 'Yeah. How about Jack? Wouldn't that be great?' Then he said, 'No, I don't think so.' I don't remember him saying who else he would have got on bass. I can't imagine who we could have got for that kind of format. Unless, of course Ginger's scheme had involved a bigger band. My feeling was he'd got fed up with everything he'd done and wanted to start something really fresh."

In the end Baker agreed to the idea of Jack Bruce being incorporated into the band, realizing he couldn't get Clapton without him. And he also knew that Bruce, despite their frequent rows, would be an important asset.

"We went to Ginger's house and set up in his front room," Clapton continued. "But it might have been more of a talk than a rehearsal. We just wanted to see if we could get in tune with each other. I think they had a row even then! I was only an onlooker. I couldn't understand what all the fuss was about. With the greatest respect to both of them, and I love them dearly . . . I've got three daughters and the youngest reminds me of Ginger and Jack. They just scrap over everything. It happened all the time and didn't seem to have any rhyme or reason."

There was a pressing reason for the first row, however. Baker had informed *Melody Maker* of the supposedly secret group. The result was an announcement that appeared in the July 11, 1966, issue under the headline:

Eric, Jack & Ginger Team Up

A sensational new Group's Group starring Eric Clapton, Jack Bruce and Ginger Baker is being formed. Top groups will be losing star instrumentalists as a result. Manfred Mann will lose bassist, harmonica player, pianist and singer Jack Bruce; John Mayall will lose brilliant blues guitarist Eric Clapton and Graham Bond's Organisation will lose incredible drummer Ginger Baker. The group say they hope to start playing at clubs, ballrooms and theatres in a month's time. It is expected they will remain as a trio with Jack as featured vocalist.

The news item caused a storm among the managers of the three established bands. The star players protested that it was untrue and demanded a retraction. Baker got into trouble with Bruce for leaking the story before Bruce had a chance to inform Manfred Mann, but two weeks later there came an official announcement in *Melody Maker*:

Bruce-Clapton-Baker Group Debut

All star group's group consisting of Eric Clapton, Jack Bruce and Ginger Baker, announced exclusively in the MM *two weeks ago, has been signed by Robert Stigwood.*

"They will be called Cream," Stigwood told the MM. *"And they will be represented by me for agency and management. They will record for my Reaction label and go into the studios next week to cut tracks for their first single. Their debut will be at the National Jazz and Blues Festival at Windsor in July."*

The phrase "group's group" referred to an earlier *Melody Maker* article in which members of different groups were asked to vote for their favorite musicians for inclusion in a mythical all-star band. Among those who received the highest votes were Eric Clapton, Jack Bruce, Steve Winwood, and Ginger Baker. As it turned out, all

four would eventually work together either in Cream or their successor, Blind Faith. By then, the phrase "group's group" would be supplanted by the more assertive "super group."

Cream certainly had enormous potential and provided the ultimate showcase for three of the most exciting musicians on the British scene. The man who had engineered its creation was undoubtedly Baker, their uncompromising, temperamental, and highly individual drummer. Known as Ginger because of his flaming red hair, he was born in Lewisham, London, on August 19, 1939. He grew up in the South London surburb of New Eltham during World War II and remembers the sound of antiaircraft guns blazing away near his mother's home.

As a teenager he was a keen racing cyclist, which helped develop his leg muscles, competitive spirit, and stamina—useful attributes when he eventually took up drumming. His first instrument was the trumpet, which he played in an Air Training Corps band. He switched to drums, having entertained his schoolmates by playing with a ruler on his desk between lessons and banging knives and forks on the kitchen table at home. Leaving school, he joined various bands from the age of sixteen, including Bob Wallis and His Storyville Jazz Men. Among his musical influences were early jazz drummers such as Baby Dodds and Zutty Singleton, but he later began listening to Max Roach and Baker's favorite British drummer, Phil Seamen.

When he couldn't afford a new drum kit, Baker made one himself out of Perspex and spare parts. Always a forceful personality, Baker was often fired from groups, either for being too loud or for clashing with his bandleaders. However, he established a name for himself on the London modern jazz scene and was encouraged by Seamen, who saw him playing at the Flamingo Club.

Baker began to play with musicians migrating from jazz to R&B, where they could play with more freedom. He joined Alexis Korner's Blues Incorporated in August 1962, taking over from Charlie Watts. The bass player with Korner was Jack Bruce, and the two soon formed a powerful rhythm section.

Jack Bruce was born John Simon Asher Bruce on May 14, 1943, in Bishopbriggs, Glasgow, Scotland. His parents traveled to Canada and the United States when he was a child, disrupting his education. But at seventeen he received a scholarship to study cello and composition at the Royal Scottish Academy of Music in Glasgow. He found the academy too strait-laced, however, and was disappointed to discover that none of his tutors shared his enthusiasm for the Modern Jazz Quartet.

Bruce left the academy and Scotland to find work in England. There, he joined the Murray Campbell Big Band in Coventry and went on a disastrous tour of Italy. When the promoter absconded with all the money, Bruce was stranded in Milan for six weeks.

Back in Britain, he joined Jim McHarg's Scotsville Jazz Band. At a gig in Cambridge he spotted Baker jamming with Dick Heckstall-Smith. Bruce sat in and so impressed the others that Heckstall-Smith recommended him for a regular gig with Alexis Korner. Baker was also installed in Korner's Blues Incorporated, alongside Graham Bond. This heavy version of Alexis' group played at the Marquee until February 1963. Baker and Bruce quit Blues Incorporated along with the band's alto sax player, Graham Bond, and formed the Graham Bond Trio. Guitarist John McLaughlin joined, Bond began playing Hammond organ, and the group became known as the Graham Bond Organisation. Dick Heckstall-Smith and his tenor sax replaced McLaughlin, Bruce switched from upright to electric bass, and the group recorded two albums for EMI Columbia, *The Sound of '65* (1965) and *There's a Bond Between Us* (1966).

Their manager, Robert Stigwood, promoted the band by putting them on a package tour with Chuck Berry. Although a popular live band, the rather ferocious-looking musicians found difficulty gaining acceptance as a pop group. Lyricist and poet Pete Brown was a great fan of the Bond Organisation and saw them as a blend of Muddy Waters and Charles Mingus. The group tried hard but couldn't get a hit single to help them move up the ladder. Bond began to crack under the strain, and Baker took over the finances and running of the band. This change didn't go down well with Bruce, and eventually the pair had a row onstage at a club in Golders Green, North London. When Baker started playing loudly through one of Bruce's bass solos, the two began pulling faces at each other. The situation escalated to the point where Baker bounced a drum stick off Bruce's head and Bruce threw his bass at Baker, demolishing his drum kit (Bruce happened to be using an upright bass at the time). The pair then began fighting and rolling over the floor. The audience was stunned and the rest of the band had to pull them apart. Bruce was promptly sacked but insisted he "was leaving the band anyway."

Baker later protested that it was Bruce playing through *his* solo and that it was a band decision to fire their bassist. Whatever the causes of the dispute, it wasn't the sort of behavior the Modern Jazz Quartet would have tolerated.

Amid this history of rows, torments, and frustrations, the band Cream was born. Eric Clapton hoped at last to find freedom, success, and personal happiness with his newfound friends.

Except, of course, the blues trio didn't quite work out as expected.

Blues Breakers drummer Hughie Flint remembers the shock when Mayall discovered his guitarist was planning to leave the group, yet again. It turned out Mayall had read a story in the *Melody Maker* revealing that Clapton was rehearsing with a band in a school hall in North London. Flint thought that Mayall fired Clapton over the Cream affair, but Clapton claimed they actually fell out over a mutual girlfriend.

"I was an absolute sex manic in those days," Clapton says. "At the end of our collaboration we were fighting over one woman and we fell out big time." Mayall agreed they were both "into the ladies" but can't remember which girl they were supposedly fighting over. At least they weren't fighting over the guitar solos.

Even as Cream were getting together for their first rehearsals, Clapton began to wonder if he'd made the right decision.

"When I went to Cream I thought it was going to be a higher platform of the same thing I'd done before," he said, looking back. "But it wasn't. I loved Cream and what it did. But I knew there were some things going on. So it was 'How long do I put up with this?'"

Cream was famous even before the band formed, as rumors and news accounts reported on the possible debut of the "super group." From left, Jack Bruce, Ginger Baker, and Clapton pose for an early studio publicity photo.
© Pictorial Press Ltd / Alamy

John Mayall's *Blues Breakers with Eric Clapton*,
London Records, July 1966.

Few dreamed that an album recorded at a few casual sessions at London's Decca studios one afternoon in 1966 would have such a lasting impact and become an important milestone in Eric Clapton's career. After the enthusiasm of his early recordings with the Yardbirds, the serious atmosphere engendered by British blues pioneer John Mayall gave Clapton the platform to perform in a more productive and sympathetic setting.

The results were magical. Clapton's guitar flies away with almost mystical inspiration, and his lyrical tone and deep feeling for the blues were unheard of in the context of the times. The introductory bars of Otis Rush's "All Your Love" set the scene for Clapton's domination of both the band and the entire album. His chiming chords eventually give way to a faster tempo where harsh, angry stabs bring the piece to a determined climax. But this only serves a curtain raiser for the remarkable tour de force that is "Hideaway," Clapton's interpretation of the Freddie King theme.

On this instrumental showcase the playing gets better chorus by chorus. Clapton's improvisation is inspired, and he executes a faultless, snaking solo full of surprises and delights. He would later claim he just showed up at the studio, played, packed up, and went. But he must have known he was on a roll and creating something special. "Hideaway" is just one of a series of brilliant performances boosted by the first flush of youth and searing ambition.

The rest of the band, comprising leader John Mayall on vocals, keyboards, and harmonica, bassist John McVie, and drummer Hughie Flint, all do their level best to keep up. There was no doubting their individual talents. Mayall would go on to spend a lifetime leading bands, McVie later helped found Fleetwood Mac, and Flint would enjoy hit records with McGuiness Flint.

But as the public flocked to buy *Blues Breakers* and put it in the charts, there was no doubt the guitar player sporting the whiskery sideburns and reading *The Beano* comic book on the LP cover deserved most of the attention. Such was the rapid maturity of his playing that it was hard to believe it was the same Clapton who once broke strings with the Yardbirds.

Yet more brilliance occurs in the slow blues "Double Crossing Time," where Clapton holds onto notes with spine-tingling tenacity. It seems there is nothing that he can't play. "Have You Heard" is another source of delight, and here he plays so passionately it's enough to make strong men cry.

"Steppin' Out" is another unfettered instrumental and one that became a regular showstopper both at Blues Breakers gigs and later on with Cream. We also hear his debut as a lead singer on a stirring version of Robert Johnson's "Ramblin' On My Mind."

This was the record that took Decca by surprise and kickstarted the British blues boom. But in a sense it was also the first Eric Clapton solo album and one of which he can remain justly proud. If nobody had picked up another guitar and played the blues after Clapton recorded "Ramblin' on My Mind," it might not have mattered.

ODEON THEATRE
BIRMINGHAM
THE CREAM
EVENING at 7-30 p.m.
SATURDAY
DECEMBER **23**
REAR STALLS
£1·00
B5
No ticket exchanged nor money refunded
THIS PORTION TO BE RETAINED   [P.T.O.

5. fresh cream

Cream, 1966–1967

The press release that officially announced the creation of Cream was positively biblical in tone:

AND THEY WILL BE CALLED CREAM . . .

After all the denials and controversy surrounding news of their birth, the world's first super group was ready for action. One of Cream's earliest rehearsals took place at Ginger Baker's home in Braemar Avenue, Neasden, North London. "As soon as we played it was total magic," recalled Baker.

Clapton remembers it somewhat differently. "We were going to be a blues trio that would play small clubs," he explains. "But the guys were pretty strong, forceful personalities and I hadn't taken that into consideration." Clapton soon found that his ambitions to be group leader "went out of the window." He realized Baker was the driving force and Bruce was also vying for leadership.

Cream perform on the British television show *Ready Steady Go!* in early 1966. © *Pictorial Press Ltd / Alamy*

"I just let them get on with it and backed off," Clapton continued. "After the fights had died down at rehearsal I'd start playing a riff and one of them would say, 'What's that? Maybe we could do that.'" Clapton also recalled that their first attempts at finding material were hesitant and uncertain, but gradually a cooperative system of writing evolved and a working set list emerged. "We didn't have any songs but we played a lot of blues, tunes like 'Cat's Squirrel' and 'Lawdy Mama,'" Bruce recalled.

It was in a school hall in Kensal Rise, North West London, that Cream put on its first performance, a showcase for *Melody Maker* in July 1966. The audience comprised a troop of junior Girl Guides known as Brownies, a grumpy caretaker sweeping the floor and raising clouds of dust, and manager Robert Stigwood. The group had minimal equipment. Baker tapped on a snare and bass drum, while Clapton and Bruce relied on a couple of Marshall amps.

Clad in white bell-bottom jeans, Clapton looked cool with his guitar slung low at the hip. He also seemed distracted by some young girls who had been lured by the sound of a "pop group" and were giggling and peering through the door from the street. Asked how he felt about the band's impending debut at the National Jazz and Blues Festival, he replied, "Nervous."

The trio set up on the corner of the darkened hall amidst a sea of cigarette butts. Baker was wearing a red beard and looked like a demon from the underworld as he crouched over his drums. Bruce was ready for action, wearing a harmonica harness and clutching his six-string bass.

Despite Clapton's inner misgivings about a leadership role in the band, there was no doubt that the rhythm section was waiting on his instructions. He promptly took charge, counting in the first tune to assail the ears of their tiny audience. It was an old jug band number called "Take Your Finger Off It." It started well but ground to an abrupt halt. "You mucked up the end," the guitarist said pointedly to the bass player. "Yes, I did, didn't I?" grinned Bruce.

Stigwood looked concerned. When his protégés resumed playing, he whispered, "Are they any good?" It was an honest inquiry, and the reply from *Melody Maker* was reassuring. "Yes, they're brilliant."

After blasting the school hall with their premiere performance, Cream adjourned to a nearby café. Bruce drove the Ford Transit van with Clapton and Baker sharing a bench seat. The whole party was nearly wiped out when the driver jumped a red light at a busy intersection. Nothing was said beyond a sharp intake of breath and the only comment was an intense glare from Baker. It was nearly "Goodbye Cream" before the first tour had been booked.

Safely ensconced in the café and eating eggs and chips, the band discussed their ambitions and presentation plans for their debut show. Clapton proposed having a live turkey and a stuffed bear with them on stage, adding, "I'm going to have a hat with a cage on top and a live frog inside. It would be nice to have stuffed bears on stage too. We'd ignore them and not acknowledge their presence at all." He seemed influenced by the Dada school of surrealist art that inspired one of his favorite comedy outfits, the Bonzo Dog Doo Dah Band.

Cream's first live appearance was at the Windsor Festival on July 31, 1966. Seeking a replacement for his famed Beano guitar, Clapton played another Gibson Les Paul, here fitted with a Bigsby vibrato tailpiece. Note the wear and tear on Ginger Baker's crash cymbal. *David Redfern/Redferns/Getty Images*

Asked to define Cream's musical policy Clapton described it as "Blues Ancient and Modern." Bruce came up with "Sweet and Sour Rock 'n' Roll." Clapton was impressed and thought it was an even better name than Cream. Asked if there would be any jazz influences, Clapton was adamant: "I'd say jazz is definitely out and sweet and sour rock 'n' roll is in."

After just a few days of rehearsals Cream were ready to play to a larger audience than a bunch of Brownies. The band members had been playing in different bands for years and didn't need much practice to make perfect. "Most people have formed the impression of us as three solo musicians," Clapton said at the time, "clashing with each other. We want to cancel that idea and be a group that plays together."

Clapton was still keen on his idea of a blues trio in the Buddy Guy tradition, respectfully playing numbers by Robert Johnson and Son House. But it was clear they'd need more original material if they were going to be a successful recording act and not just another R&B revival outfit.

Bruce wrote one of their first songs, "N.S.U.," whose initials stood for Non-Specific Urethritis. Explained the composer, "It was about a member of the band who had a venereal disease. I can't say which one . . . except he played guitar."

To assist with the writing process, London beat poet Pete Brown was called in to help provide some lyrics. At first he teamed with Baker, but eventually formed a writing partnership with Bruce, resulting in a slew of successful hit singles that would transform Cream's fortunes, although they got off to a shaky start.

Pete Brown was born in London on Christmas Day 1940. He had been writing poetry since the age of fourteen, inspired by the American beat poets of the early 1960s. Brown became involved in the jazz and R&B movement and promoted a jazz and poetry concert at London's St. Pancras Hall in 1961. The event featured many upcoming musicians, including Ginger Baker, Dick Heckstall-Smith, and Graham Bond. When Cream formed, Baker remembered Brown from his poetry readings and invited him to help write some lyrics.

Meanwhile, on July 29, 1966, Cream performed a secret warm-up gig at the Twisted Wheel Club in Manchester. Ben Palmer, Clapton's old friend and former pianist with the Roosters and the Glands, drove them there. It was a learning process for all of them, not least for Palmer, who discovered he was expected to be their roadie and was required to set up the stage as well as be the driver. He confessed he'd never even plugged in an amplifier before. Baker had to help him out. Cream, like so many bands at the time, was still in the throes of inventing the rock industry.

The National Jazz and Blues Festival held in Windsor was the band's official debut, and Cream were billed on Sunday July 31, 1966, alongside Georgie Fame and the Harry South Orchestra. A ten-thousand-strong crowd turned out to greet the new group, but the skies opened up just as they came on stage. It was hard for spectators to see the trio through the downpour, let alone any stuffed bears. But there was no doubting the power of the music. They

Concert advertisement, August 1966.

Cream's first single, "Wrapping Paper," was released in the United Kingdom on Reaction Records on October 7, 1966.

Advertisement from *New Musical Express* on October 7, 1966, announcing the release of "Wrapping Paper."

played three numbers that would become permanent features of Cream shows: a take on Willie Dixon's "Spoonful," "Traintime," and "Steppin' Out." The roar of the crowd was music to their ears.

Melody Maker reported, "Then came the moment thousands had been waiting for—the debut of Cream. They kicked of with 'Spoonful,' 'Sleepy Time' and Jack Bruce's harmonica and vocal feature, 'Train Time' [*sic*]. Eric Clapton's incredible guitar induced the audience to shout and scream for more, even while he was playing more! And Ginger's solo using bass drums called 'Toad' sent the crowd potty."

After the show, Stigwood hosted a party for Cream at his apartment in Regents Park. Bruce and Baker seemed happy to be celebrating their victory at Windsor, but Clapton was spotted sitting on the floor in a corner of the room looking glum. Stigwood wanted to find out why he appeared so upset. It seemed that he wasn't at all happy with what the group was doing and it hadn't been right from the start. And frequent backstage conflicts didn't help his frame of mind.

"There was a constant battle between Ginger and Jack," Clapton later recounted. "Although they loved one another's playing. I was the mediator and I was getting tired of that."

But they were committed now and there was work to be done. Cream were still expected to play a succession of club bookings earning them just £45 a night. These were mostly leftover gigs from Baker's days with the Graham Bond Organisation. As a result, fans able to squeeze into small venues such as the Cooks Ferry Inn in North London or Klooks Kleek at the Railway Hotel, West Hampstead, saw Cream close up and personal. When they played at the Marquee Club on August 16, they broke the house attendance record, and queues formed hours before the doors opened.

The band's success took promoters by surprise, and it was a while before the group realized they should ask for more money. By now they had recruited another roadie, Mick Turner, who drove a second car to gigs to help split up the convoy.

Just three months after their formation, Baker refused to complete a gig after a row with a promoter. Baker had demanded they get paid extra money for extra time on stage. Clapton and Bruce carried on playing without a drummer and later agreed that Baker should be fired. He was swiftly reinstated, but in the aftermath the group was deemed to be more of a cooperative venture.

Fresh Cream was released on December 9, 1966, in the United Kingdom and in March 1967 in the United States. It reached No. 7 in the U.K., No. 39 in the United States.

Cream perform in 1966. © Pictorial Press Ltd / Alamy

Cream, during happy times. From left, Clapton, Jack Bruce, and Ginger Baker. *Jan Olofsson/ Redferns/Getty Images*

Clapton gamely tried to laugh off these rows and ignore the feuding, but it was becoming more of a strain.

During September and October 1966, Cream played a string of U.K. dates. One of the most intriguing was on October 1 at the Polytechnic in central London. Jimi Hendrix had arrived in town and showed up with his manager, Chas Chandler of the Animals. Hendrix wanted to sit in, but the band was dubious about his abilities. When he finally joined them on stage, Cream were in a state of shock. He was brilliant. It was the first time another guitarist had been allowed to sit in with Cream. It was also the last. Clapton later confessed he was surprised by the newcomer. "I don't think I'd ever heard of him before, although he had been hanging out in Greenwich Village for quite a while from what I could gather," Clapton said, adding, "Funnily enough Roger Waters and Nick Mason of Pink Floyd had hired Cream [to play the show] when Nick was a college entertainments secretary at the London Polytechnic. They were both in the audience as students to see us play.

A stylish Clapton in prime 1967 style. © *Pictorial Press Ltd / Alamy*

"Then this guy shows up and asks to play. He looked like he might know what he was on about. He got up and did a Howlin' Wolf song, 'Killing Floor,' which is a very difficult thing to play. It's got a tricky bass line and you need to know what you're doing. I thought 'This guy is a player.'

"I had seen Buddy Guy, Memphis Slim, and Muddy Waters, but here was a young guy doing what they'd do but had somehow brought it into the decade of the 1960s. He was certainly doing something new."

The next important step for the group was to cut a single. Stigwood was determined to have a commercial record that would raise the group's profile. The result was "Wrapping Paper" (released on Stigwood's Reaction label on October 7, 1966), written by Pete Brown and Jack Bruce.

It may have seemed like cleverly obtuse marketing to come up with something quirky. Rather than blast away with guitar solos, they'd attempt a production number aimed at the charts. But fans were deeply disappointed when they heard a Lovin' Spoonful–style ditty backed by an old-fashioned

piano and Bruce humming the melody. And where was the sound of Clapton's guitar? This was worse than the "For Your Love" affair with the Yardbirds. (However, those loyal Cream fans who bought the 45-rpm single were mollified by a resounding "Cat's Squirrel" on the B-side.)

Reviews were less than enthusiastic, and one critic described the record as "Too weird for us." It struggled to get to No. 34 in the *Melody Maker* chart in November. As a film buff, Brown had combined various movie images to create lyrics he hoped would match the music that became "Wrapping Paper." He later confessed his first attempt at writing for Cream was not his best efforts. Even so, he was excited to see it get into the Top 40. The record company explained the single's poor showing by claiming that thousands of copies were "withdrawn due to a pressing fault."

Still, Cream were sufficiently impressed by Brown's talents to persevere with him. Initially, Brown was supposed to write material with Baker, but after several demo tracks Bruce and Brown found they could write more successfully together. The fact that Bruce and Brown came up with the bulk of the new material and were credited on the record labels as joint composers began to rankle Baker, who thought the split unfair and realized he would miss out on royalties. Clapton understood how Baker felt, but he thought it too difficult to come up with a three-way split when he wasn't writing much himself and Bruce and Brown were so prolific.

The real sound of Clapton with Cream was finally revealed on their album *Fresh Cream*, released on Reaction in December. The iconic cover depicted the band members clad in flying jackets and goggles, and the album shot to No. 6 on the U.K. charts. Any confusion caused by "Wrapping Paper" was cleared up by the inclusion of their take on such blues classics as "Spoonful," Muddy Waters' "Rollin' and Tumblin'," and Skip James' "I'm So Glad." There were also Jack Bruce originals "N.S.U.," "Sleepy Time," and "Dreaming," while Baker's songwriting was showcased on "Toad."

The band released a much better new single, "I Feel Free," written by Bruce and Brown, which, coupled with "N.S.U." as the B-side reached No. 11 in January 1967. It was on the A-side that Eric unveiled his famous overdriven yet articulate "woman tone" guitar sound. He wasn't pleased with his performance, however, and wanted to re-record his track. This proved impossible and was another cause for frustration.

But it wasn't all doom and gloom for Clapton. Beyond the confusion caused by "Wrapping Paper" and occasional tantrums at gigs, Cream were undoubtedly a success. The most exciting news was that *Fresh Cream* would be released in the United States. Ahmet Ertegun, the legendary head of Atlantic Records, had agreed to a deal with Stigwood to release their records on his Atco label.

The way ahead was clear for Eric Clapton to make his first trip to America with a band he felt sure could knock 'em dead. Clapton was heading for the land where his beloved blues were born. He was starting to feel important—and free.

"Guitar-slinging heroes with sideburns, wild and woolly clothes, blazing away on all strings, are a phenomenon peculiar to the rootin' tootin' British pop scene. They set trends, make or break groups and draw an almost fanatical fan worship."

—*Melody Maker*, 1967

Just before leaving England for the first U.S. tour, Cream perform on the British television show *Top of the Pops* in January 1967. © Pictorial Press Ltd / Alamy

TOFT'S
35 to 39 GRACE HILL, FOLKESTONE   TEL. 38173
Established 10 years
ONE OF THE COUNTRY'S LEADING AND MOST FAMOUS CLUBS
Fridays & Sundays 8 - 11   Saturdays 8 - 11.45

Cream

plus

support

Saturday, February 18th

6. strange brew

Cream, 1967–1968

AMERICA WELCOMED CREAM and made Eric Clapton a star. Lionized by fellow musicians, admired by his fans, Clapton himself claimed he'd never played better in his life. Whatever pressures were involved in working with Jack Bruce and Ginger Baker, they ensured Clapton was pushed to his limits—and the results were often astounding.

Cream set off for their first U.S. tour at the end of March 1967. On arrival in New York, they guested on concerts set up by radio DJ Murray "the K" Kaufman. Murray the K had helped the Beatles and Rolling Stones by playing their records in the early days of the British Invasion. Now he was presenting an ambitious package of British and American stars under the banner of *Music in the Fifth Dimension* at the RKO Theater on 58th Street in Manhattan.

On the bill were R&B artists Mitch Ryder, Wilson Pickett, and Smokey Robinson, who were pitched again with invading rockers the Who and Cream. The latter pair formed an alliance, as they rebelled against the strict format of the disaster-prone package show.

Poster, Ricky Tick Club, Guild Hall, Southhampton, England, March 13, 1967.

There were five shows daily: after each one, the theater was cleared and a new audience ushered in. Every act was allocated fifteen minutes and expected to fit in three songs. But Cream's improvised solos were so long they had to cut their set down.

Even so, the shows ran over. Only three concerts could be held on the first day. While it was hoped children on holiday would pack out the midday shows, the theater was often half empty. Smokey Robinson and the Miracles and Simon and Garfunkel never even showed up.

Even though they were advertised as "Direct From England," Cream were low on the bill and the Who created a greater impact with their explosive stage act. Murray kept a strict eye on all the musicians and ensured they didn't leave the venue during the day. Nevertheless, Clapton enjoyed his first taste of the Big Apple as he told *Melody Maker* back in London:

"The Murray The K Show was great—too much! We played there for a week and audience was mostly thirteen to fourteen year old teeny boppers. Everybody went down well and as we only had two numbers each, we pulled the stops out. The Who stole the show. They only had to smash everything up and everybody was on their feet. We did 'I'm So Glad' and 'I Feel Free' but the show had nothing to do with music. Nothing whatsoever. We took the whole show as a joke.

"Wilson Pickett and Mitch Ryder were topping the bill. Smokey Robinson dropped out and refused to do it because it wasn't his scene. But New York is incredible. Everybody is so hip to the music scene. Taxi drivers talking about James Brown—can you imagine that in London? The best musical times we had were in Greenwich Village. It became like an English Musical Appreciation Society.

"I sat in with a couple of the Mothers of Invention and Mitch Ryder at the Café Au Go Go where Jimi Hendrix used to play. The Mothers are musically one of the best bands in America. They are really sending up the psychedelic scene. When they are on stage they exaggerate everything and you can't keep a straight face."

Eric made lots of friends during trips to the Village, including Al Kooper, musician and A&R man who famously played organ on Bob Dylan's "Like a Rolling Stone." Clapton also met his lifelong idol, B. B. King.

"I'd first heard of B. B. King during my 'musical student' period when I was looking for albums in music stores," Clapton says. "I didn't realize he was a guitar player and thought maybe he was fronting a big band doing Jimmy Witherspoon type stuff. It wasn't until I was in Cream and playing at the RKO Theater that I saw him live. I went down to the Café Au Go Go with Al Kooper. He was going to start Blood, Sweat and Tears that night. B. B. King was playing in this café and at the end of the night I got up and we jammed together. I had no idea how great he was until then. We became fast friends and he became a huge influence on me in the way I played the guitar. Did anybody record our jam? Well, somebody had a reel-to-reel tape machine but somebody said they'd lost the tape, so I don't know whatever happened to that."

As the Murray the K Shows drew to a climax, Cream planned a riotous finale. Clapton explains: "We had all these fourteen-pound bags of flour and eggs we were going to use on stage on the last night. But Murray got to hear about it and said we wouldn't get paid if we did. So we spread them all around the dressing rooms. The whole cast joined in and Pete Townshend ended up swimming around in his dressing room fully clothed in a foot of water when his shower overflowed.

"It was said that Murray spent thirty thousand dollars on the show and lost twenty-seven thousand dollars and it was rumored we wouldn't get paid. He was very distraught, throwing his hands up in the air. He hadn't bargained for the casual English approach and expected us to be leaping around doing a James Brown thing. It just wasn't our kind of show."

continued on page 92

"We are the first group to do what we are doing in America—to go on stage and just improvise. . . . It works for us because all three of us have got something to say."

—Jack Bruce, 1968

Cream perform at the Falkoner Centret, Copenhagen, Denmark, on March 6, 1967, part of a tour that took them around the United Kingdom and Scandinavia, then back through England. *Jan Persson/Redferns/Getty Images*

Clapton leans against his wall of Marshall stacks during soundcheck in Copenhagen. *Jan Persson/Redferns/Getty Images*

Opposite: Handbill, Fillmore Auditorium, San Francisco, California, August 22–27, 1967. *Artist: Bonnie MacLean*

strange

Clapton relaxes backstage at the Murray the K *Music in the Fifth Dimension* show at the RKO Theater in New York City on March 31, 1967. *Michael Ochs Archives/Getty Images*

Throughout much of 1967, Clapton played his 1964–1965 Gibson SG Standard, nicknamed "The Fool" after the Dutch artists collective The Fool that painted the guitar. It was acquired in 1974 by Todd Rundgren. *Courtesy Nigel Osborne/Jawbone Press*

"The Fool were . . . two Dutch artists, Simon and Marijke, who had come over to London from Amsterdam in 1966 and set up a studio designing clothes, posters, and album covers. They painted mystical themes in fantastic, vibrant colors and had been taken up by the Beatles, for whom they had created a vast three-story mural on the wall of their Apple Boutique on Baker Street. They had also painted John Lennon's Rolls-Royce in lurid psychedelic colors. I asked them to decorate one of my guitars, a Gibson Les Paul, which they turned into a psychedelic fantasy, painting not just the front and back of the body, but the neck and fretboard, too."

—Eric Clapton, *Clapton: The Autobiography*, 2007

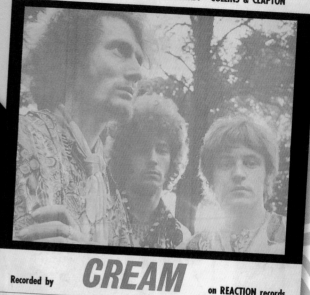

"Strange Brew" and "Tales of Brave Ulysses" were released in the United Kingdom on May 26, 1967, and in July 1967 in the United States.

Cream perform onstage at Los Angeles' Whisky A Go Go on September 4, 1967. *Michael Ochs Archives/Getty Images*

Clapton jams with his hero, B. B. King, at New York's Café
Au Go Go in September 1967 with Elvin Bishop at right.
Michael Ochs Archives/Getty Images

Cream were back touring Great Britain and Scandinavia in autumn 1967. They performed on Danish television's *Toppop* on November 11, 1967. *Jan Persson/Redferns/Getty Images*

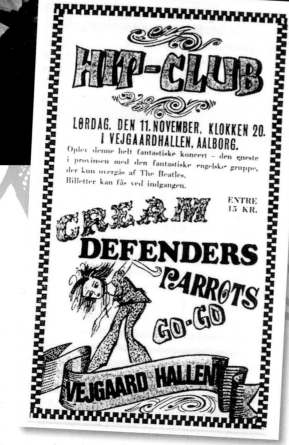

HIT-CLUB

LØRDAG, DEN 11. NOVEMBER, KLOKKEN 20.
I VEJGAARDHALLEN, AALBORG.

Oplev denne helt fantastiske koncert - den eneste i provinsen med den fantastiske engelske gruppe, der kun overgås af The Beatles.
Billetter kan fås ved indgangen.

ENTRE
15 KR.

CREAM
DEFENDERS
PARROTS
GO-GO

VEJGAARD HALLEN

Concert advertisement, November 1967.

behind the scenes with cream

Donal Gallagher, brother of Irish guitarist Rory Gallagher, served as a roadie with Cream touring Europe and North America. He took these snapshots from backstage, offering a rare look at life on the road with the group.

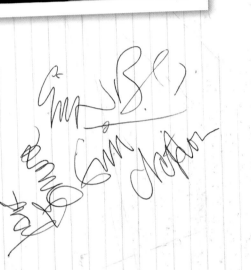

Cream meet the Bee Gees. Both groups were managed by Robert Stigwood and both were on top of the charts in 1967–1968, Cream as a hard-rock super group, the Bee Gees as the next Beatles. Meeting in a Copenhagen hotel lobby in February 1968, from left: Robin Gibb, Jack Bruce, Colin Peterson, Vince Melouney, and Ginger Baker. Seated: Barry Gibb, Maurice Gibb, and Clapton. *Jan Persson/ Redferns/Getty Images*

continued from page 81

Cream's next step was to record their second album, *Disraeli Gears*, at Atlantic's Manhattan studios. It marked a step forward for Clapton both as a songwriter and singer. Ahmet Ertegun, the head of Atlantic who had first seen Clapton performing during a visit to London, encouraged him in this expanded role.

"Ahmet Ertegun first heard me play when I got up and jammed with someone at the Scotch of St. James Club in London one night," Clapton remembers. "He heard me the way nobody else would have done, because he was coming from the blues and jazz and he knew what I was up to. Ahmet became an important part of my life from then on."

They soon formed a strong friendship. Ertegun, the astute American record boss, also formed an unlikely partnership with Robert Stigwood, Cream's risk-taking manager. Their double act greatly amused Clapton.

"Robert Stigwood was really good to me and we loved him, you know?" Clapton says. "He had his foibles and he was a very eccentric character. But I became friends with Robert and we remained so for many years afterwards. I think he made some very wise decisions. Getting us onto Atlantic was very important. And the relationship between Ahmet Ertegun and Robert is one of the most precious things in my memory.

"The way they would carry on was so funny. They were really vicious to one another in a loving way. It was an incredible relationship. Sometimes it was physical, but it was mainly just a lot of humor—roasting each other all the time. The repartee was vicious. Very cruel, but very funny. It was the kind of thing you only get from really close friends.

"I really wanted Ahmet to be a part of my life from the moment we met. It was just such an honor to work with him, and also Tommy Dowd and all of those Atlantic guys. I never really got to know Jerry Wexler that well because he was in another part of the company. But I spent a lot of time with Ahmet, who was very supportive.

"Robert didn't really know what we were trying to do. He kind of humored us and thought that maybe Cream could be viable financially. I'm sure he would rather have seen us go onto a more commercial route. But Ahmet was the one who knew how to keep us broadly in the right direction by being true to the right music. I knew he really understood and that made me feel really secure. . . .

"Somebody said to me that Ahmet saw me as the leader of Cream. But I didn't know that at the time. At some point he may have thought about getting me out of there. But I didn't ever get that feeling. As far as I could see, he was supportive of the whole group. He just wanted to make sure I was happy to be there. He never tried to drive a wedge between me and the others and didn't manipulate anything."

Still, when Clapton came under pressure, he invariably turned to his manager in London for advice.

"After a fairly bad night on tour, Robert was the one I'd call up. The bad nights got to be very regular. I remember one tour of the States we were playing almost every night for six months. I'd call him after a show and it was in the middle of the night for Robert. I'd say 'You've gotta get me home.' He would listen and be very kind to me. He was a father figure to all of us in a way."

Cream only had a few days left on their visas to spend in Atlantic's eight-track studio while recording *Disraeli Gears*. The album was produced by American arranger and musician Felix Pappalardi and engineered by Tom Dowd. Pappalardi was born in the Bronx in 1939. A former singer and guitarist, he turned producer working with the Youngbloods in 1966. Then he heard *Fresh Cream* and was determined to meet the band. Ertegun set the wheels in motion for Pappalardi to become Cream's producer, and the result was a much more professional sounding record.

"*Disraeli Gears* was a great album," Clapton says. "We worked very hard on it, but we didn't think it was that important, you know? We were always looking to the future. Making records was odd for us because we didn't see

"Sunshine of Your Love" was released in February 1968 in the United States and on September 6, 1968, in the United Kingdom.

Cream fan club flyer. *Collection Donal Gallagher*

ourselves as naturals in that environment. We were stage players and we liked the freedom of going off and doing really crazy things and taking risks. That doesn't really work in the studio."

The *Disraeli Gears* sessions were spread over several days in April 1967 and another week in May. The material ranged from the sublime "Strange Brew," "Sunshine of Your Love," and "Tales of Brave Ulysses" to the ridiculous "Mother's Lament," which was a Cockney music hall song.

Eric's guitar work was more experimental and prone to freak-out effects. He also took the plunge and sang lead on "Strange Brew," co-written with Pappalardi. "Tales of Brave Ulysses" was another Clapton theme with lyrics by his pal Martin Sharp.

Recalls Clapton: "It took me a long time to get started as a writer. I still don't really rank myself very highly in any of the fields I work in, whether writing, playing, or singing. I think of myself as a journeyman. These days I like to think more about 'How can I satisfy myself?' And how, 'How hard do I have to work before I'm content?'"

Clapton the bluesman was at his best on "Outside Woman Blues," a 1920s classic. Meanwhile, "Strange Brew"/"Tales of Brave Ulysses" was issued as Cream's third single in the U.K. in May 1967 and in July in the United States. Their next single from the album, "Sunshine of Your Love"/"SWLABR," was released in the United States in February 1968 and September in the U.K. "Sunshine" soared to No. 5 on the U.S. Billboard charts. While Clapton, Bruce, and Brown took the composer credits, the drummer was miffed that he wasn't included. However, the song became Cream's signature tune.

Disraeli Gears was released in November 1967 in a striking LP sleeve illustrated with red and yellow fluorescent colors. It was designed by Martin

Cream returned for their second American tour, opening in Santa Monica, California, on February 23, 1968. From left, Clapton, Ginger Baker, and Jack Bruce. *Roz Kelly/Michael Ochs Archives/Getty Images*

Poster, Earl Warren Showgrounds, Santa Barbara, California, February 24, 1968.

Clapton picks his large Guild acoustic guitar while performing with Cream on the back of a truck in Copenhagen on February 5–6, 1968, during the shooting of the film *It was a Saturday Night*. *Jan Persson/Redferns/Getty Images*

Program, U.S. tour 1968.

Handbill, Fillmore Auditorium, San Francisco, California,
March 3, 1968. *Artist: Lee Conklin*

Handbill, Shrine Auditorium, Los Angeles, California,
March 15–16, 1968. *Artist: John Van Hamersveld*

Poster, Fillmore Auditorium and Winterland, San Francisco, California,
March 7 and March 8–10, 1968. *Artist: Stanley Mouse*

COLISEUM
Wabash at 15th Street
KK 11 13   SATURDAY 8:30 p.m
MEZZANINE   TRIANGLE PRODUCTIONS present
APL.   THE CREAM
27   THE MOTHERS OF INVENTION
1968   ADMISSION $4.50
            No Refunds or Exchange!

SILVA PRODUCTIONS PRESENTS

CREAM

Cream perform onstage in 1968. *Michael Ochs Archives/
Getty Images*

Poster, Memorial Auditorium, Sacramento, California,
March 11, 1968.

Sharp, Clapton's Australian artist friend who worked for *Oz* magazine in London. The album's original title was simply *Cream*. Then came an idle conversation between Baker and Cream roadie Mick Turner about racing bicycles. Turner mentioned such bikes were fitted with "Disraeli gears" when he meant "derailleur gears." The group instantly seized on the mistake.

Cream's reputation in America was strengthened by eleven shows at Bill Graham's Fillmore Auditorium in San Francisco during summer 1967. Later, they played Los Angeles, Boston, New York, and Detroit. But it was at the Fillmore and larger Winterland venues where Cream began to stretch out and solo ad lib during sets lasting well over an hour to standing ovations

Back in the U.K., they were welcomed as heroes at London's prestigious Saville Theatre, owned by Beatles' manager Brian Epstein. In November 1967, *Disraeli Gears* peaked at No. 4 in the U.S. album chart and reached No. 5 in the U.K.

Despite such success, shocking rumors began to circulate that Cream were about to split up. These were hastily denied. Behind the scenes, the group was still busy recording material for their blockbuster double LP, *Wheels of Fire*, being produced by Felix Pappalardi. This would include the seminal Bruce–Brown compositions "White Room" and "Politician" featured on the "studio" sides.

Eric Clapton plays Guild F-50 . Complete specs in Guild Catalog 704B. Write to Guild Musical Instruments, Hoboken, New Jersey.

Advertisement for Clapton's endorsement of Guild guitars.

Poster for cancelled show, Electric Factory, Philadelphia, Pennsylvania, April 12–14, 1968.

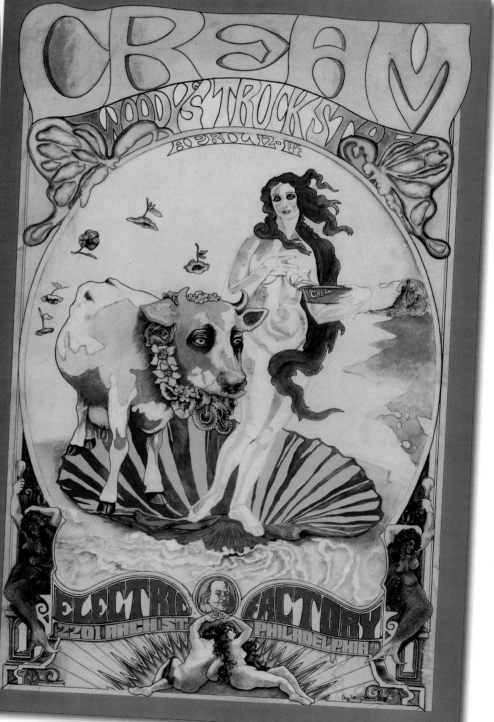

Cream's "Anyone for Tennis" was released in May 1968 and was the theme song to the biker flick *The Savage 7*.

Poster, Robertson Gym, University of Santa Barbara,
Santa Barbara, California, May 24, 1968. *Artist: Chuck Miller*

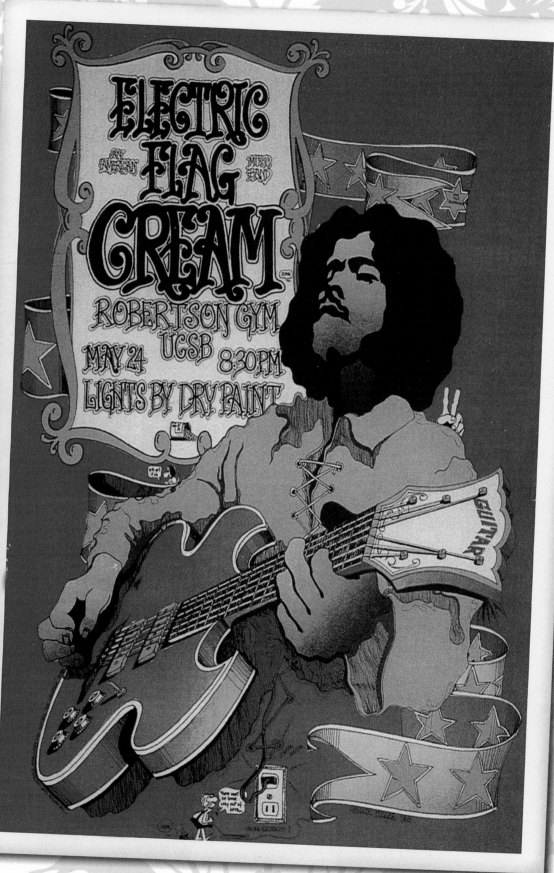

In February 1968, Cream commenced their second major U.S. tour. Performances from their Fillmore and Winterland shows in March were captured for the "live" section of *Wheels of Fire*, including "Crossroads," "Spoonful," "Traintime," and "Toad." The LP in its distinctive silver cover was released in August 1968 and immediately topped the U.S. charts.

As rock music grew ever more powerful, it was ironic that Cream began to complain about the volume unleashed by their array of Marshall amplifiers and speakers. Clapton, Bruce, and Baker all began to suffer from ringing ears after shows—and blamed each other for playing too loudly. Said Baker: "I couldn't hear myself play, it was so loud. The last year of the band the volume got so awfully loud that it just ruined it for me. It hurt my ears."

There were other problems too—notably the continuing rows between the bassist and drummer that so upset their guitarist; the sheer exhaustion of touring; and even worse, an unexpected critical backlash.

Clapton had been used to good reviews in the British music press. Then, out of the blue came an attack from *Rolling Stone* magazine that knocked him sideways. It demoralized Clapton and hastened the demise of Cream.

Clapton himself came up with ideas that might have kept them going longer: "I thought the group needed help and talked about bringing in another player. I wanted Stevie Winwood to come in. I had been exposed to some more current music which was achieving something where I felt we were falling short. It was a lot to do with making records, believe it or not. Specifically it was about 'The Big Pink' album [*Music from Big Pink*] by the Band that was a really well crafted record.

"Our *Wheels of Fire* was half live, and I didn't know if that was right. To me it didn't seem to work. Our live stuff wasn't making it for me on record. So I thought if I'm going to make good records I needed more players. I liked the fact the Band were swapping instruments and liked that fluidity. I liked the structure in their writing.

"Cream was trapped in some kind of spin. We'd got onto the bandwagon of whistle-stop touring across America for months on end. The only recompense was to come up with some new thing in the middle of a song. That was the light at the end of the tunnel. We'd hit some improvising moment that was coming good. Mainly we were trapped in other people's expectations.

"*Disraeli Gears* was written mostly by Jack and Pete Brown and produced by Felix Pappalardi and in a way that was a bit too poppy for me. With all this going on, I felt I needed a break to reevaluate. But I hadn't got anywhere to go. I just wanted to stop and think. But I didn't think 'Sunshine of Your Love' was too poppy. We kind of nailed it with that one. I was very proud of the heavier stuff we did, like 'White Room.' They have lasted in my own repertoire, and I have played them a lot. Stevie Winwood would have been a good addition to Cream, but whether it would have worked is another thing. There might have been a lot of conflict between him and the other two guys."

Clapton shared the opinions of Baker and Bruce that Cream's volume was getting far too loud on stage: "Oh, yes: My hearing was ruined as a result. I've

Poster, Community Concourse, Exhibit Hall, San Diego, California, May 19, 1968.

still got whistling in my ears all the time, which is a mild form of tinnitus. It doesn't bother me, but that's where it comes from. I was standing right in front of two 100-watt Marshall stacks. I would turn one on just for solos and I had no ear protectors. It was madness.

"I remember one night, me and Ginger stopped playing and Jack just carried on. I don't think he cared. At that point we were pretty ruthless about what we were doing. I was trying to kind of guilt trip him. 'What about me?' I fell very easily into a victim role in that band. It was an easy road to take. I wouldn't do it now but then I was like an old sulk, you know? I'd go off on my own. It was awful, really, but I was young. I was the youngest sibling and had no idea how to contest it. I disapproved of the way they were behaving and didn't want to get into childish arguments that went on and on. I just didn't want to go there and I would just withdraw.

"Personally the price was very high, especially being trapped in hotels. My experience of touring with Cream was I'd go off and make friends. It was normal for me to just hit the street and find the local underground scene and hang out."

Poster, Civic Auditorium, San Jose, California, May 25, 1968.

Then came the bad review that added fuel to the inner mounting flames of Cream's destruction. Clapton: "It might have been the second issue of *Rolling Stone* that ever came out. Jann Wenner came to interview me and I rambled on. It was at the height of my ego period and I probably made all sorts of claims about my position in the music world. It came out in the issue juxtaposed with a review of Cream that was really scathing. So you had me saying how great I thought I was—they called me the 'Master of the Blues Cliché' in the review.

"It was the first serious, critical review I'd ever seen specifically targeted at me and I fainted. I was in a restaurant with some friends in Boston. They said, 'Have you seen this magazine?' without knowing it had a bad review. I started to read it and began to feel really funny. I remember getting up and passing out. It was extraordinary how strong an affect it had on me.

"That not only confirmed what I thought about the group but what was happening to me in my role in the group. I still use that as a term of reference whenever I feel that I'm getting stale. I don't *want* to be the master of the cliché, you know?"

In July 1968, Cream's British fans were equally shocked when they read the front page news in *Melody Maker* headlined "Cream Split Up." A farewell tour was planned, and it seemed like the end of another Clapton era.

Said Clapton: "In a pop group, the first things you suffer from are jealousy and terrible insecurity. You keep wondering if what you are playing is out of date. You try to write pop songs and create a pop image. I went through that and it was a shame because I am and always will be a blues guitarist."

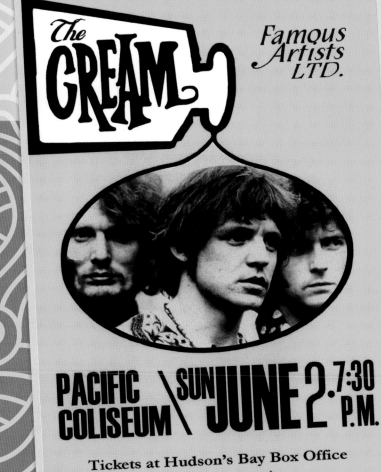

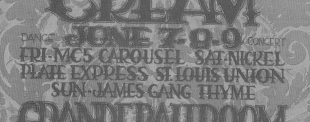

Poster, Pacific Coliseum, Vancouver, British Columbia,
June 2, 1968.

Poster, Grande Ballroom, Detroit, Michigan,
June 7–9, 1968. *Artist: Gary Grimshaw*

Wheels of Fire was released in July 1968 in the United
States and August 1968 in the United Kingdom. It hit
No. 1 in the United States, No. 3 in the U.K.

Disraeli gears

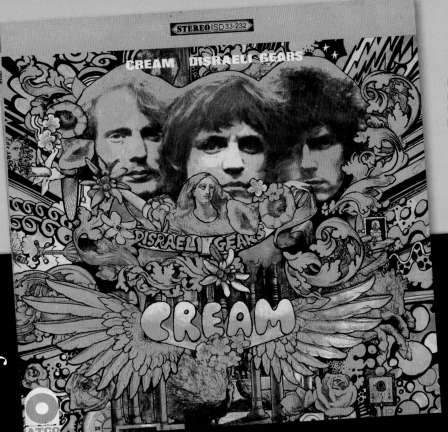

Following several delays, *Disraeli Gears* was finally released in the United Kingdom and United States in November 1967. It reached No. 4 in the U.S., No. 5 in the U.K.

In summer 1967, Cream found themselves competing with the Beatles, Jimi Hendrix, and Pink Floyd for hippie credibility. It was thanks to the combined forces of producer Felix Pappalardi, songwriters Jack Bruce, Eric Clapton, and lyricist Pete Brown that the trio, once thought of as a blues super group, achieved something suitably experimental for the psychedelic era.

Disraeli Gears shifted into drive after the Beatles' *Sgt. Pepper's Lonely Hearts Club Band* had already created a sensation. But Cream's offering was welcomed by underground fashion gurus, music critics, and even a general public who saw Cream's brave new sounds as the latest manifestation of long-haired pop. It was all thanks to the hit tracks "Strange Brew" and "Sunshine of Your Love," which emerged like pearls from a wild mix of styles, tunes, and themes.

While the album's material lacked thematic coherence, there was a strength in the overall performance and production that ensured ultimate success. A garish and colorful sleeve design and the peculiar album title all added to the mystique. It certainly made the LP a suitable accoutrement for those flocking to see the band at the Fillmore.

Given that Cream were usually identified as a combo devoted to lengthy solo work and blues improvisation,

it was a bold step for them to concentrate on song writing and lyrics. Clapton took his first steps as a composer with "Tales of Brave Ulysses" and while avoiding long solos, introduced new effects such as the Vox wah-wah pedal that gave his hand-painted Gibson SG Standard an edgy new sound.

But it was the riff on "Sunshine of Your Love" that caught the ear of guitar buffs. Its languid solo passage, with a quote from "Blue Moon," made Clapton seem even cooler in the ears of his fans. On "World of Pain," the guitar is double tracked, making use of the Atlantic studio's advanced facilities, and the E.C. wah-wah pedal goes into overdrive once more.

Those looking for more of Clapton's roots were rewarded with "Outside Woman Blues," where he accompanies his vocal with the famed "woman tone" guitar sound. Working overtime alongside Clapton of course was Ginger Baker, whose thunderous tom-tom rhythms help define "Sunshine of Your Love" as much as Jack Bruce's bass riffing and declaiming vocals. It is the chemistry between all three that spurs them on to such heights of creativity, whether in the studio or on the road.

The pity about *Disraeli Gears* is that it didn't lead on to ever-better-produced studio albums. If Cream had stayed together working under an even stronger producer, they might have achieved a true masterpiece, perhaps their own *Sgt. Pepper*. They needed someone to say that using tracks such as "Blue Condition" and the comic "Mother's Lament" was perhaps not the best idea.

Artistically Cream would show their true potential with the studio tracks featured on their *Wheels of Fire* (1968) double album and farewell set *Goodbye Cream* (1969). Nevertheless, *Disraeli Gears* was the best they could manage, given the time and circumstances. And it was of course a huge hit that has become a classic.

Cream went into Atlantic's Manhattan studio to work on their
second album from September 17 through 21, 1967. Atlantic
executive Ahmet Ertegun talks with Clapton and producer Felix
Pappalardi while taking a break from recording "Strange Brew."
Michael Ochs Archives/Getty Images

7. goodbye cream

Cream, 1968–1969

WHILE FANS WERE REELING FROM ERIC CLAPTON'S REVELATION that Cream were splitting up, *Wheels of Fire* was still rolling up the charts, making the decision seem all the more difficult to understand. The first double album to sell a million copies, it earned the band a platinum disc. Just as a wider audience was discovering the "underground" group, so the wheels were set in motion for them to bid farewell.

Soon after, Cream commenced their third and final American tour on October 4, 1968, at the Oakland Coliseum, California. They would earn some $60,000 a night as they played eighteen dates. The tour included three nights at the Los Angeles Forum— October 18, 19, and 20. The band also played Madison Square Garden in New York on November 2, where they appeared on a revolving stage. After the show, they were presented with platinum discs for *Wheels of Fire* by Ahmet Ertegun and Robert Stigwood.

Their final U.S. shows were held at Rhode Island Auditorium in Providence, Rhode Island, on November 4. Then it was back to England to play twice at London's Royal

Cream give their farewell performance at London's Royal Albert Hall on November 26, 1968.
Pictorial Press Ltd/Alamy

Albert Hall on November 26, 1968. Some 5,000 fans packed out each show, and Clapton expressed surprise when they received a warm and emotional ovation: "We hadn't played in England for over a year and had no idea we were so popular. I was amazed we played to such full houses. I didn't think anybody would remember us."

He was almost tempted to carry on with Cream when he realized the strength of feeling among their supporters. But the die was cast: He had to stand by his decision.

Cream's farewell at the Royal Albert Hall was filmed for BBC TV by director Tony Palmer, who had first met Clapton and Cream on the recommendation of Jimmy Page. His documentary on the group was screened as part of the BBC *Omnibus* arts show on January 5, 1969. The footage was later re-edited as a full-length film. An earlier Palmer documentary, *All My Loving*, had helped introduce the serious side of rock to a wider audience and paved the way for Cream to be so heavily featured on TV.

Palmer was music critic for the *Observer* Sunday newspaper and recalls that John Lennon had encouraged him to make *All My Loving*. "That film was essentially John Lennon's idea. I'd first met him while I was at University and met him again when I began working at the BBC. He told me the problem with rock music on BBC TV was it was restricted to shows like *Top of the Pops* and *Juke Box Jury*.

"These were highly successful pop shows but only reflected what was in the Top Twenty and not the more serious side. John said it was terrible because he knew a lot of musicians who wouldn't appear on either of those programs because they didn't want to play three-minute pop songs behind gyrating nubile dancers. Much as we liked gyrating nubiles, this was understandable. Lennon said, 'It's your duty to get these people onto television.'

"He gave me a list that included Jimi Hendrix, Frank Zappa, and Cream. At the time I said, 'I don't know these people. . . . .' John said, 'I'll make the introductions and you film them.' So we made this film, *All Your Loving*, which was then shelved by the BBC for eight months while they figured out what the hell to do with it."

While working on the project, Palmer went to see Cream play the Dome in Brighton, England, at one of their earliest gigs. "I just thought they were completely amazing. I had seen Eric playing in the Yardbirds, but at the Dome I was just swept away. These were all astonishing musicians. What always attracts me is musical skill and while I thought Cream's singles weren't too good, it was a revelation when I saw them playing in full flow. It made my blood tingle and hair stand on end. Jimmy Page introduced me to Eric when I went backstage. I was then determined to get Cream into the film."

Eventually *All My Loving* was broadcast and included a Cream sequence filmed in San Francisco. Palmer had also started a weekly arts show called *How It Is* for BBC TV with Michael Palin and Terry Jones doing comedy interludes. One show had Cream performing "We're Going Wrong" and "I'm So Glad" in a sequence filmed in San Francisco.

"White Room" was released in October 1968 in the United States and in January 1969 in the United Kingdom.

Palmer: "Gradually I got to know them quite well. Ginger Baker never ceased to be monosyllabic, but I could always talk to Jack. In fact, Eric got rather cross that I was always talking to Jack and not to him! Eric let it be known I should be talking to him and not the others. While filming *All My Loving*, we had Eric demonstrating playing guitar, Ginger on drums, and Jack . . . just grumbling. Those bits were not used in the *All My Loving* so we kept them and later used them in the *Cream* concert film. The interviews were done at the end of January 1968 at the Sausalito Inn in San Francisco, about nine months before Cream played their farewell shows at the Royal Albert Hall."

The plan to film the complete final shows was unveiled when manager Robert Stigwood phoned Palmer in August 1968 and asked if he'd come to his Mayfair office. "His very words were, 'Eric has asked if you'd like to film the

Cream returned one last time to the United States, playing their third and final U.S. tour beginning October 4, 1968, at the Coliseum in Oakland, California. Along the way, they posed for a group portrait in a rowboat in New York's Central Park in November 1968. From left, Clapton, Ginger Baker, and Jack Bruce. *Michael Ochs Archives/Getty Images*

farewell concert.' Palmer replied, 'What farewell concert?' Stigwood replied, 'We're not supposed to tell anybody but it's coming up.'"

A month before the concert was scheduled, Stigwood rang Palmer again and told him it was going to be at the Royal Albert Hall in November. There was a pause before Stigwood inquired, "How well do you know the people at the Royal Albert Hall?" Stigwood asked if he'd contact them. The brief was to mention classical music frequently and not mention Cream too often or discuss "the problems" in the band.

"This all seemed very bizarre," Palmer remembers. "But I went along to the Albert Hall and met the general manager to talk about the farewell concert. He said, 'There isn't going to be a Cream farewell concert.' That's when I realized there was a problem. 'We're not having that rock 'n' roll group here.' I realized why I'd been sent—to do a heavy pitch on behalf of Cream. I explained that speaking as the music critic of the *Observer*, I thought they were phenomenal musicians. 'Oh,' he said. He still had Bill Haley and the Comets in his mind, whose fans used to rip up the seats.

"At the end he reluctantly agreed they could appear. Then I lobbed in at the end, 'Oh and by the way, we need to film it.' 'You can't do that.' There was no discussion. I had won one battle and so I didn't want to get into another one."

Palmer reported back to Clapton and Stigwood and also asked the BBC to approve a film for *Omnibus*. "I'd got tentative permission from the BBC and when I went back to the Albert Hall management I could see why they objected. In the summer of 1968, the first color video machines had arrived. They used two-inch analog tape, and we had no idea how to edit the tape. The two upright spools had to be unlocked and placed on a bench. The video tape was then chopped and stuck together with sticky tape. Sometimes it worked and sometimes it didn't. I thought I'd never be able to edit what I could see."

"The second problem was that the color TV cameras were enormous. You couldn't move them. They weighed a ton. So I went back to the Albert Hall and asked, 'Is the problem the weight of the cameras?' It turned out they thought the cameras would go through the stage. So I said, 'How about if we reinforce the bit we're on and promise not to move them?' So luckily they agreed to that. All of this relates to Eric Clapton because on the first show I pointed out where the four cameras were situated when Cream arrived.

"Ginger was fine because he couldn't move anyway. I told Jack where he had to stand and said, 'For God's sake, don't move because I won't be able to see you.' We did the same to Eric, but at the first gig Eric turned his back on the camera the entire time. So I went back to see him and said, 'Eric, please, if you turn your back I can't see you!'

"'Sorry, I forgot.'"

Tony says that at the second concert Clapton was more cooperative—but not much.

Poster, Coliseum, Oakland, California, October 4, 1968.

Poster, Rhode Island Auditorium, Providence, Rhode Island,
November 4, 1968. *Artist: Mad Peck Studios*

Poster and advertisement, *The Cream Farewell Concert* film.

Ticket to the debut of *The Cream Farewell Concert* movie, Philharmonic Hall, New York City, February 21, 1969.

Meanwhile, Stigwood came up with another plan. He wanted separate films of Clapton, Bruce, and Baker. "If they were going to break up, he wanted to get the most out of them. In fact, only two films were made, one of Ginger driving across the Sahara Desert in North Africa and one with Jack in Scotland called *Rope Ladder to the Moon*. By the time we got around to making Eric's film he was so far gone it wasn't possible. Ginger was pretty far gone himself and that was one of the reasons he wanted to drive across the Sahara."

Cream were supported at the two sold-out shows at the Royal Albert Hall by two new groups, Yes and Taste, the latter featuring rising young guitarist Rory Gallagher. Cream were introduced by the late DJ John Peel, and Clapton appeared sporting a new short haircut and clutching a 1963 Gibson Firebird for use on the first show. At the second concert, he used a Gibson ES-335TDC.

Clapton received a standing ovation from fans at the Royal Albert Hall but was treated in a rather strange fashion once the show was over. Palmer: "I remember going backstage afterwards amidst the general euphoria and discovering that Ginger had disappeared. Jack was with his first wife, Janet, who had organized a party for him. But when I went in the dressing room, there was Eric sitting in a corner all on his own. It was weird that he had just played this amazing concert and nobody was taking any notice of him at all. So he and I went off quietly and had a drink. Stigwood the manager was nowhere to be seen."

Palmer felt that Clapton wasn't being given the support he deserved. "In the classical world, musicians are treated with great respect. For example, you call a conductor 'maestro.' That's a term of respect for his position. But nobody ever called Eric Clapton 'maestro'! He needed more help and respect, but his manager was more interested in chaining fans of the Bee Gees to the railings at Buckingham Palace because that would get a good picture."

Palmer felt that Clapton's quiet reticence backstage was born out his sense of being involved in a music business he didn't really understand. "He somehow found himself in a crazy world in which he wasn't totally at ease. His love of music was very pure. That's what gave him the most satisfaction and he was making music for the sake of it. That's what fired his imagination. But in terms of his personality I don't think he was particularly laid-back. I just think he was shy, self-effacing, kind, and gentle. A lovely chap who has wandered into a world full of maniacs!"

The *Cream* film was hailed as a popular success and watched avidly by the new generation of rock fans. There were some critics however who pointed out flaws in the production.

Palmer: "We filmed nonstop at both gigs at the Albert Hall so there was a lot of material. But it was all on two-inch tape we couldn't edit. The problem was what to do with all this material. Stigwood suggested we also do a theatrical feature. My version was taken and completed re-edited to make an eighty-five-minute version. We also had a film camera at the concert, just in case anything went wrong with the electronic monsters.

"But the material didn't quite sync up. I'm told that Eric threatened to kill me because there were non-sync shots of him playing. But it wasn't my fault. It's got my name on it, but that wasn't my work. The psychedelic bubbles, patterns, and slow motion—that was me. And yes, it was all rather primitive in those days, but we only had four cameras. Martin Scorsese used twenty-five cameras when he filmed the Rolling Stones."

Tony Palmer filmed Clapton again a few years later for his groundbreaking 1975 series *All You Need is Love*. "In the interview, Eric told me he thought that Cream at the end was just a waste and it wasn't honest music. But I always thought that all his subsequent groups were an attempt to get back to what they had in Cream. Just think. Without Cream, no Led Zeppelin.

"In the years following Cream there was a constant attempt to re-create that sense of pioneering spirit. I felt that Eric was trying to re-create those days with musicians who were nowhere near as good. He also did showcase gigs where everybody turns up and does a bit. There's George Harrison, Bob Dylan, and Eric Clapton. Fantastic. But it's just an event, not ongoing, creative music. Eric is a musician of formidable quality and he needs other people on stage with him of equal ability.

"He doesn't need people to warble along quietly in the background, thinking, 'Oh my God, I'm on stage with an icon.' He needs somebody to give him a run for his money. And he's an intelligent enough musician to respond, which is what happened with Cream. He needs to be challenged. We all need a quiet life at the end of the day, but if you've got any creative spark you need that challenge."

As the Cream chapter drew to a close, albums were unleashed that celebrated their reign, including their final official offering *Goodbye Cream* that depicted a smiling Clapton, Bruce, and Baker in vaudeville pose, clad in satin suits, and strutting their stuff. It was released in March 1969 with three studio tracks and three live pieces. One of the best studio tracks was "Badge," co-written by Clapton with his pal George Harrison, which was released as a single. Like "Sunshine of Your Love," it became a much-requested number in Clapton's future shows.

The other studio items were "Doing That Scrapyard Thing" and "What a Bringdown." The live tracks were "I'm So Glad," "Politician," and "Sitting on Top of the World," recorded at the Los Angeles Forum in October 1968. The album topped charts in both the United States and U.K.

More Cream albums followed over the next few years, including *Best of Cream* in July 1969. *Live Cream* was issued in April 1970, followed two years later in Mach 1972 by *Live Cream II*, produced by Felix Pappalardi from material remaining in Atlantic's vaults.

Goodbye was released in the United Kingdom and United States in February 1969. The album reached No. 1 in the U.K., No. 2 in the United States.

Farewell! Cream play their final show, at London's Royal Albert Hall on November 26, 1968. While Jack Bruce, Clapton, and Ginger Baker perform, DJ John Peel watches from the side, sitting on a chair in the shadows. *Estate of Keith Morris/Redferns/Getty Images*

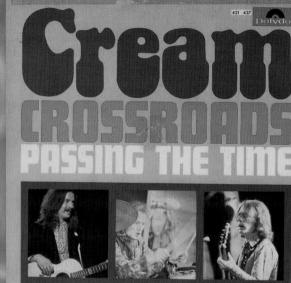

"Crossroads" was released in the United States in February 1969, but would not be released in Europe for several years.

In the aftermath of Cream, Clapton retreated to the mansion he had bought at Hurtwood Edge in Surrey and kept a low profile. His first appearance came in December 1968 when he guested on the Rolling Stones' *Rock 'n' Roll Circus* TV movie. He played on "Yer Blues" along-side John Lennon and Keith Richards. When reporters asked Clapton what he'd do next, he replied, "I'll probably join John Mayall's band."

He also took part in the filming of *Supersession*, a massive jam session with all-star guests and a variety of bands, including Led Zeppelin. Eric played alongside American multi-instrumentalist Roland Kirk, with Jack Bruce, Dick Heckstall-Smith, and Jon Hiseman. He later got to play with Buddy Guy, the man who had unwittingly inspired the creation of Cream.

The most significant development over the early months of 1969 was Clapton's increased involvement with Steve Winwood, the star of Traffic and former young genius with the Spencer Davis Group. Winwood had visited Clapton at Hurtwood Edge over the Christmas holidays, and they began playing together, revisiting much of the music they'd enjoyed in their youth, including the songs of Buddy Holly.

Somehow it seemed it might be a nice idea to form a group with Winwood. But who would play drums and bass and where would it all end? The music machine was already making up its mind about that. Another super group was in the making before Clapton could even pause to draw breath.

"Badge" was released in March 1969 in the United States and April 1969 in the United Kingdom.

Live Cream and Live Cream II were released in later years—1970 and 1972, respectively.

"One day, early in September, George drove me over to Abbey Road Studios, where he was recording. When we arrived, he told me they were going to record one of his songs and asked me to play guitar on it. I was quite taken aback by this and considered it a funny thing to ask, since he was the Beatles' guitar player and had always done great work on their records. I was also quite flattered, thinking that not many people get asked to play on a Beatles record. I hadn't even brought my guitar with me, so I had to borrow his. . . . The song was 'While My Guitar Gently Weeps.' We did just one take, and I thought it sounded fantastic. John and Paul were fairly noncommittal, but I knew George was happy because he listened to it over and over in the control room. . . . I felt like I had been brought into their inner sanctum."

—Eric Clapton, *Clapton: The Autobiography,* 2007

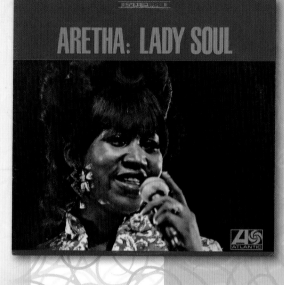

Clapton supplied the guitar obbligato to Aretha Franklin's "Good to Me as I Am to You" on *Aretha: Lady Soul*, 1968.

Clapton added his guitar on George Harrison's urging to the Beatles' "While My Guitar Gently Weeps," 1968.

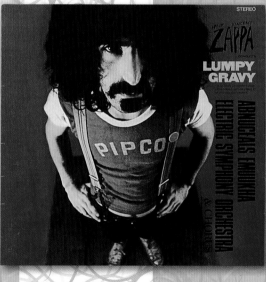

Clapton backed Frank Zappa on his *Lumpy Gravy*, 1968.

Clapton joins John Lennon and Keith Richards playing "Yer Blues" at the Rolling Stones' *Rock 'n' Roll Circus* at Wembley, London, in December 1968.
Mark and Colleen Hayward/Getty Images

8. can't find my way home

Blind Faith, 1969

THE LAUNCH OF BLIND FAITH WAS HEADLINE NEWS in the music press in February 1969. Hints had been dropped earlier when it was revealed Eric Clapton was hoping to team up with one of his best mates, Stevie Winwood. Not long after Cream's demise, *Melody Maker* announced on December 7, 1968, that Winwood's group, Traffic, had split. This breakup led to speculation about a "Winwood–Clapton tie-up."

Traffic was formed when Winwood left the Spencer Davis Group. Winwood, together with Dave Mason, Chris Wood, and Jim Capaldi, hit the charts with "Paper Sun" and "Hole in My Shoe" in 1967 and released the albums *Mr. Fantasy* and *Traffic*. Their innovative songs perfectly suited the hippie dreams of the psychedelic era.

But as the 1960s reached their climax, more changes were in the air. The Beatles played their last gig on the rooftop of Apple's London headquarters in January 1969. It seemed to trigger a response among all their disciples. It was cool to split and try something new.

Blind Faith launched their first U.S. tour on July 11, 1969, playing dates through August 24. The band performed here at Olympia Stadium in Detroit, Michigan, on August 1, 1969. *Robert Matheu*

Good times: Blind Faith ham it up for a band portrait in 1969. From left, Steve Winwood, Rick Grech, Ginger Baker, and Clapton. *Michael Ochs Archives/Getty Images*

When Clapton first indicated he wanted to work with Winwood, he thought the singer, guitarist, and organist was tied up with Traffic. Once Traffic split, *Melody Maker* buzzed with rumors. "Now both Eric and Steve are free with the break up of their groups, there is a strong possibility they may get a group together, or at least record."

In an age when musical ability was a hot selling point, *Melody Maker* had proposed the idea of a hypothetical "group's group," selecting the best musicians around to form an ideal band. The result of the magazine's 1966 poll was an imaginary lineup that included Eric Clapton, Ginger Baker, and Steve Winwood.

In fact, Winwood and Clapton had already duelled with their guitars at a Spencer Davis Group gig at London's Marquee Club one hectic night. Now, a new group would permanently marry their talents. As the pair began jamming on a regular basis, it was suggested they might record an album with Al Jackson and Duck Dunn, rhythmic lynchpins of Booker T and the MGs.

Still, much of the music press was suspicious about the formation of another much-vaunted super group intended to outgun Cream and create a new era for Clapton.

Poster, Hyde Park, London, June 7, 1969.

The last thing Clapton wanted was another Cream. He wanted to play in a more relaxed, laid-back style with less emphasis on the guitar hero role. He also wanted musicians with a less combative attitude.

What he got was Ginger Baker. Much to Clapton's dismay, the wild man of Cream was back on drums amid a wave of publicity and hype.

It seems that Clapton didn't have the heart to say no when Baker turned up at rehearsals. Baker himself recalls calling at Clapton's home in Surrey just as the guitarist was driving off in his Ferrari. Clapton was planning to visit Winwood at his cottage in Berkshire. Baker followed in his Jensen at high speed, and on arrival, all three began playing together on the concrete stage outside the cottage. The die was cast.

The band now called Blind Faith certainly had the potential to be a huge success. But compromises were being made from the start. They recruited bass player Rick Grech, who left his group, Family, to join them, and the new outfit was officially launched in April. When I interviewed Clapton at his home for *Melody Maker* that spring, I found him bereft of the group but playing host to various friends. As we adjourned upstairs to his music room, he picked up a guitar while I sat behind Baker's drum kit. We began playing "Well All Right," the Buddy Holly song that later appeared on the band's debut album.

continued on page 132

"For the first time, as far as I am aware, the dreaded word 'super group' reared its head. That's when I saw the red light, but I decided to go through with all of this and see where it was leading, because Steve was involved and because I had nothing else interesting going on. Subliminally, perhaps, my ambition was to re-create the Band in England, an idea that I knew was a huge gamble, which is probably why I named the new band Blind Faith."

—Eric Clapton, *Clapton: The Autobiography*, 2007

Blind Faith launched their first U.S. tour on July 11, 1969, playing dates through August 24. The band performed here at Olympia Stadium in Detroit, Michigan, on August 1, 1969. *Robert Matheu*

HANDLE WITH CARE
CREAM
DELICATE
AUCTION #21.
CHERRY RED 335

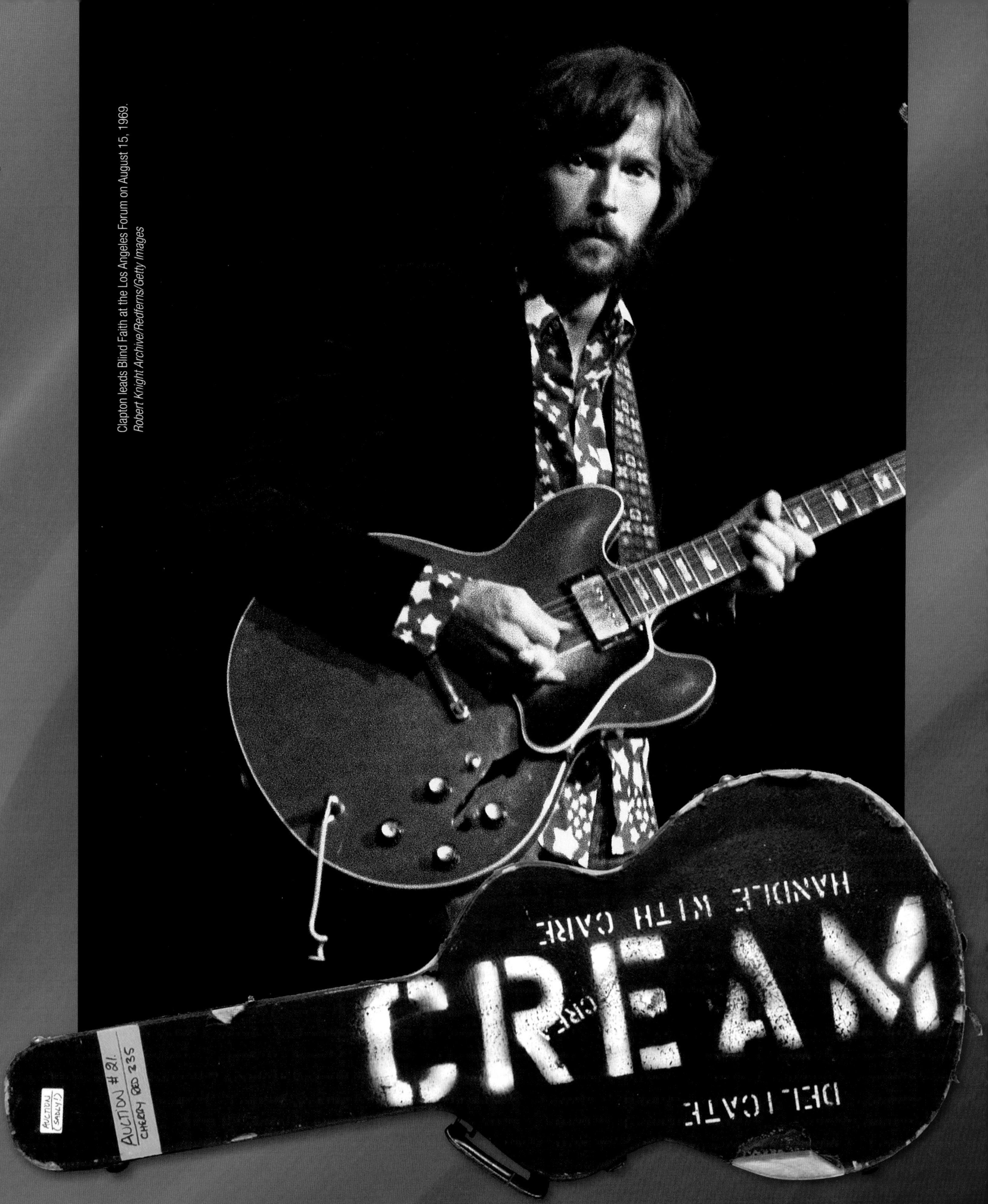

Clapton leads Blind Faith at the Los Angeles Forum on August 15, 1969.
Robert Knight Archive/Redferns/Getty Images

"Though the Yardbirds weren't yet in the big-money league, we were making enough for me to buy my first really serious guitar, a cherry red Gibson ES-335, the instrument of my dreams. . . . I had seen the Gibson in a shop on either Charing Cross Road or Denmark Street, where several music stores had electric guitars in the windows. To me they were just like sweet shops. I would stand outside staring at these things for hours on end. . . . When I finally bought the Gibson, I just couldn't believe how shiny and beautiful it was. At last, I felt like a real musician."

—Eric Clapton, *Clapton: The Autobiography*, 2007

Eric Clapton's 1964 Gibson ES-335, which he played with the Yardbirds, Cream, and Blind Faith. *Collection Guitar Center/Photo Robert Knight Archive/Redferns/Getty Images*

Hare Krishna!

Advertisement, Kennedy Center, Bridgeport, Connecticut, July 13, 1969.

Poster, Electric Circus, Toronto, Ontario, July 18, 1969.

continued from page 127

A group of hippies sat on the floor in a semicircle and listened respectfully while Clapton worked up a head of steam. I fearlessly delivered my best Buddy Holly and the Crickets–style tom-tom rhythms. In retrospect, this was the first duo version of Blind Faith, albeit to an audience of six. It felt like being in heaven, especially when Clapton smiled and nodded. At least he didn't stop playing, so something must have been working all right.

The band began recording an album at Olympic Studios in Barnes, with Jimmy Miller as producer under the watchful eyes of Robert Stigwood and Winwood's manager, Chris Blackwell. Rehearsals continued until the band was ready to make a live debut.

Free festivals were all the rage in London, so it was decided to showcase Blind Faith with a free concert in Hyde Park. On June 7, 1969, 100,000 fans ambled across the grass toward a makeshift stage. Most of the audience lay down in the sunshine and soaked up the vibes while others huddled under the trees. It was almost too peaceful as the heat and clouds of dope smoke had a pleasantly soporific effect. Nevertheless, expectations were high. The massed hordes clearly thought listening to Blind Faith was going to be an explosive experience.

When the band made their appearance, Clapton spent a lot of time casually leaning against his Marshall speaker stack. Baker later reported he was "puzzled" by his laid-back approach. Winwood, clad in red jeans and a purple shirt, sat at a Hammond organ and sang with passion, while a bemused Rick Grech did his best. Only Baker, red hair flying and bent over his silvery drum kit, made any attempt at rock showmanship.

The band played well enough, and there were many magical moments. When Winwood sang the beautiful "In the Presence of the Lord," the hushed thousands listened intently. Clapton, too, delivered an attractive solo on "Had to Cry Today." But it was Baker who won the loudest cheers, drumming away on "Do What You Like."

Said Winwood later, "Hyde Park was our first gig. Doing it in front of one hundred thousand people was not the best situation. Nerves were showing and it was very daunting. We couldn't relax like you can on tour."

During that sunny afternoon long ago, the set had included "Well All Right," "Sea of Joy," "I'd Rather See You Sleeping on the Ground," "Under My Thumb," "Can't Find My Way Home," "Do What You Like," "In the Presence of the Lord," "Means to an End," and "Had to Cry Today." Most of these songs would appear on the band's first album, which would not be released until September. The quartet clearly had great potential, yet a sense of anticlimax pervaded the park.

espite the altruistic nature of a free concert, the band was now expected to earn money on the road. They needed to tour, and America beckoned. Although nobody knew it at the time, British fans would never see the group perform again.

Clapton and Winwood wanted a group like the Band, but they soon found themselves under pressure to deliver more heavy rock. "And they loved it," Winwood said of the fans.

Blind Faith set off on a Scandinavian tour and played their first show at the Kulttuuritalo Hall in Helsinki, Finland, on June 12, 1969. The hall seated 1,300 and was only half full. The venue had hosted Hendrix and Led Zeppelin, but when Blind Faith arrived, most of the youth population was away on summer vacation.

The band had been billed as "New Cream," which didn't auger well, but this was changed to Blind Faith. The set was pretty much the same as at Hyde Park, and the Finns who showed up enjoyed the show.

Having warmed up in Scandinavia, the group headed for North America, and their U.S. tour opened in Newport, Rhode Island, on July 11, 1969.

Blind Faith were supported by Free and Delaney and Bonnie, the hotly tipped American outfit that would have a major effect on Clapton. The band's first show at Madison Square Garden was a sellout. But Blind Faith had to play Cream favorites such as "Sunshine of Your Love" to placate noisy audiences that were violent and vociferous in their demands. It was a pattern that was repeated across the country and into Canada. As a result, an increasingly disheartened Clapton spent more time away from Blind Faith, jamming with his newfound friends, the support group of Delaney and Bonnie.

Then trouble broke out over the controversial *Blind Faith* album cover. A garish design depicted a nude eleven-year-old girl photographed handling a solid-silver model airplane interpreted as a "winged phallus." Some stores refused to stock the LP, and the U.S. record company objected. It was eventually replaced by a more conservative design with a picture of the band.

Those around the group during that grueling tour could see that cracks were already appearing. Winwood's tour manager, Nobby Clarke, later said, "Blind Faith could have been a truly great band. But the pressure was far too great. There wasn't anybody strong enough to say, 'Wait a minute, this is what we want to do.' They got sucked into touring America far too soon. They only had one album of songs and the crowds immediately started yelling for Cream stuff. It became like Cream with Ginger playing all these huge solos. Yet the Blind Faith stuff they played was fantastic."

Plunged into the chaos was an eighteen-year-old road manager, Donal Gallagher, the brother of Irish guitarist Rory Gallagher, whose band Taste supported Blind Faith on some of the U.S. dates. Donal and Rory first met Clapton when Cream performed at the Star Club in Hamburg, Germany, back

Poster, Pacific Coliseum, Vancouver, British Columbia, August 9, 1969.

Blind Faith perform at the Los Angeles Forum on August 15, 1969. From left, keyboardist Steve Winwood, bassist Rick Grech, drummer Ginger Baker, and Eric Clapton. *John Olson/Time & Life Pictures/Getty Images*

in 1967. They met again when Cream came to Romano's Ballroom in Belfast, Northern Ireland, in November 2, 1967. Taste was the support act for that show, and the band also played at Cream's farewell Royal Albert Hall show.

Donal: "We saw the Cream guys socially when they came to Belfast. Eric was always very friendly and generous. He seemed like a sweet and level-headed guy. After the farewell concerts there was an idea to put Rory in a trio with Ginger Baker and Jack Bruce. Rory always got on really well with them, especially with Jack. Their Celtic spirit might have gelled nicely. But Rory felt teaming up with them was too obvious, you know?"

Donal and Rory then found themselves drawn into the Blind Faith circus. "I heard that Ginger just turned up at rehearsals with his drum kit," says Donal. "He was going to be the drummer, no argument. But when the group got to America, audiences were confused. Had it been a different drummer they might have accepted it as a new band. But the tag 'super group' had been attached, and they wanted the old Cream."

Donal Gallagher, traveling on a tourist visa, became one of the miniscule road crew overseeing a complex and demanding operation fraught with problems. Free played with Blind Faith for the first couple of weeks; then Taste took over as the support band. The Irish lads went to New York to pick up the tour as Blind Faith were opening at Madison Square Garden.

"We arrived at the venue just to watch the show," Donal recalls. "Blind Faith was performing on a rotating stage, spinning around in the middle of the hall and playing through a house PA system designed for boxing commentaries. As the stage rotated, the sound became a cacophony. It was also vulnerable to fans climbing up to pinch Ginger's drumsticks."

Donal also noted that the road crew included Mick Turner, who looked after Baker. Winwood had a keyboard technician called Albert. Clapton didn't appear to have anybody looking after him. "So everybody had to chip in, including me, and there were only four crew men for the whole tour."

Donal Gallagher saw that Baker's drum solo was the only recognizable item left over from the Cream days. All the rest of the new band's material was from an album few had heard. Kids were crying out "Dear Mr. Fantasy" at Winwood and "Crossroads" at Clapton. When they realized they weren't going to get them, they started chanting, and there were boos and catcalls.

"That's when Ginger played 'Do What You Like,' a magnificent drum solo similar to Cream's 'Toad,'" Donal continues.

View from the back of the stage at the Los Angeles Forum on August 15, 1969. *John Olson/Time & Life Pictures/Getty Images*

Advertisement, Fairgrounds Arena, Santa Barbara,
California, August 16, 1969. *Artist: Frank Bettencourt*

"In Seattle, his double bass drumming was so powerful he cracked the stage with the pressure."

The tour went on to the Spectrum in Philadelphia, and the backline equipment had to fit on a fifty-seat tour bus that was equipped with just one toilet. Clapton wanted everyone to travel on the same bus to preserve a communal spirit. Donal: "Eric was a very friendly guy, but there was no luxury about the bus whatsoever."

Departure depended on when the sleepy musicians turned up, and they were often late. Donal remembers Winwood's manager, Chris Blackwell, descending on the crew to find out what was wrong. "Stevie was up with the way things were going and Chris was angry with me. I got a bollocking. I was getting the blame for everybody being late and the show being a mess. But it wasn't *my* fault.

"Again we had a rotating stage at Philadelphia, and there was a meeting when some of the management finally turned up. Everyone assumed Eric was still managed by Robert Stigwood, but he certainly wasn't there during the gigs I saw. Eric was just left to get on with it." Heated exchanges ensued, and Blackwell urgently phoned the legendary Edward "Chip" Monck, a production man who put them in touch with a P.A. company. They provided a tractor trailer unit to stow all the backline gear. A car was hired for the crew to travel separately, and at last a system was developed. Donal: "Chip could organize most of the tour for us and things got much better. But there were some dates he couldn't do with us."

Monck was busy helping out at the Woodstock Festival in upstate New York, where he became famous as the master of ceremonies. Clapton wanted Blind Faith to play at Woodstock but was voted down. Delaney and Bonnie had heard bad reports about the traffic and weather and didn't want to go. Meanwhile, Rory Gallagher's Taste weren't on speaking terms with each other and were about to split up. Clapton couldn't understand what was going on with all these wrangling musicians.

The shows were also suffering. One of the worst was at Hartford, Connecticut. It was on a Sunday afternoon in a baseball stadium, and the promoter had provided a stage and P.A. system that was actually a trailer normally used by a preacher. Donal: "Steve Winwood took one look at this contraption

Program, U.S. tour, 1969.

BLIND FAITH

NOW ON **AMPEX** STEREO TAPE
8-TRACK CARTRIDGE, & CASSETTE

Promotional poster, *Blind Faith*, 1969.

Blind Faith's sole single was not an official release. The instrumental medley was cut by Ginger Baker, Steve Winwood, and Clapton in London in March or April 1969 and released on Chris Blackwell's Island label to promote Island's new office location. Only 500 copies of the 45 were believed pressed.

and refused to play. Eric, Rick Grech, and Ginger went on and did a couple of numbers, but it was abysmal. Mick Turner stayed with the drum kit because it was so vulnerable while I went back with Ginger to the dressing room. On the way, we ran into Janis Joplin, who lunged forward and said, 'Hi Ginger, how ya doing?' Ginger looked up and grunted at her. And she said: 'Oh, and by the way, Ginger, let me tell you about your new band. You really suck.' I remember his fist coming up and me holding it down. I don't think he would have hit her, but he made the gesture."

The tour went into Canada undergoing frequent customs and immigrations checks. "Certain substances would have to be left behind in case we got searched. We also had some extra hands on the bus who were guys dodging the Vietnam War," Donal explains. "Going into Canada was fine, but coming back into the States we were stopped at the border near Niagara Falls. We were told to wait on the bus, and the U.S. customs men were quite intimidating. They took away all our passports. After about twenty-five minutes, Ginger started to get angry, and so we all got taken off the bus. That was the scariest moment for me because of my visa. I thought I was going to be sent back home."

By now Donal couldn't help noticing that Clapton was hanging out with Delaney and Bonnie, Leon Russell, Dave Mason, and J. J. Cale. "He liked to jam with them more than playing with Blind Faith. It was like lifting the veil, having Eric come on stage before his own band. But that's what he wanted. In Chicago, he invited Rory and all the guest musicians to come up and jam with Blind Faith." Clapton even told Baker that Delaney and Bonnie should have been topping the bill.

Donal realized the whole Blind Faith concept was already doomed as far as Clapton was concerned: "The levels of expectation were too high, and having the tag 'super group' didn't help. The album was a slow burner, and the management should have put back the tour by six months until they were ready. You couldn't call the tour a disaster because the musicianship was second to none, but the audiences were confused, and traveling on that bus so was miserable Stevie decided to fly to the gigs."

As Blind Faith headed west to Los Angeles in August 1969, news of the Charles Manson murders reached the band and further blighted the mood. As panic spread, concerts were cancelled, including Blind Faith's, and the band's bus was diverted to Seattle. Donal missed out on a nineteenth birthday party, which would have been on August 9, the day of Sharon Tate's murder. Clapton tried to lighten the gloom: The following day in Seattle he personally delivered to Gallagher a special birthday treat with the message: "Shame about the party but here's the cake!"

Clapton with his grandmother Rose in the house he bought her in Surrey in 1970. *John Olson/Time & Life Pictures/Getty Images*

There would be no more treats for Blind Faith. After the final show in Honolulu, Clapton and Winwood broke up the band and laid off the bass player. The only member unaware of this shock decision was Ginger Baker. He was on a ten-week holiday with his family in Jamaica and took days to get home by sea.

When he visited Winwood back in England, Baker was horrified to learn Blind Faith had imploded during his absence and that Clapton was intent on touring with Delaney and Bonnie.

A restless Clapton was free to take the next big step in the endless quest for an ideal band. And it wouldn't be another super group—not if he could help it.

blind faith

Blind Faith was released in the United Kingdom and United States in August 1969. The album reached No. 2 in the U.K., No. 1 in the United States. This original issue of the album with the naked girl was excised.

An expectant world was breathing down their necks when the rock superstars gathered to make a record with fingers crossed and a great deal of blind faith. The result was an album that would divide fans and critics for years to come.

Blind Faith has many fine qualities, not the least being one of Clapton's most enduring composi- tions, "Presence of the Lord." The album's mood is mostly relaxed, pricked by moments of raw intensity and softened by Steve Winwood's poignantly wistful vocals. Yet there is a pervasive feeling it could all have been so much better, given time and a more disciplined approach.

The album came out in the same year that the first two Led Zeppelin LPs were shaking up the rock world, and it would have been difficult for any group to com- pete with Zep's exultant performances and dynamic production.

Yet it was clear Blind Faith was different from Cream, and if audiences expected a rerun of past glories, they hadn't read the signals emanating from the Clapton camp. The band had come together without any clear idea of what they were trying to achieve beyond a

desire to try out new material. The problem was that Blind Faith hadn't grown organically as its predecessor had, and the new songs hadn't been played in on the road.

In the face of intense pressure, the answer appeared to be "do what you like," a mantra that pervades the grooves of the LP finally released in August 1969. Initially, the trio of Clapton, Winwood, and Ginger Baker set to work at London's Morgan Studios, where the first rehearsals took place and several sessions were recorded.

Although Winwood could have played organ-pedal bass lines throughout, the band decided they needed a bass guitarist. Rick Grech was one of Clapton's pals who hung out with him at the Speakeasy Club. By April, the former Family member was thrust in at the deep end, contributing both bass and violin to the proceedings.

When the action transferred to Olympic Studios in Barnes, where the Rolling Stones and Zeppelin also recorded, Chris Blackwell and Robert Stigwood super- vised. But Baker allegedly ordered Blackwell out of the

The first album by

BLIND FAITH

is available on Atco Records
in two (2) different jackets

A   B

The record inside both
jackets is exactly the same

It's what's <u>inside</u> that counts

ATCO

Also available on 8 track stereo cartridges

'BLIND FAITH' IN CONCERT AT THE FORUM , FRI. EVE. AUG. 15th AT 8:30PM.
TICKETS $3.50 TO $6.50 AVAILABLE AT ALL MUTUAL AGENCIES , FORUM BOX OFFICE.

Even before *Blind Faith* was released, Atco ran this
advertisement on August 1, 1969, explaining that two
versions of the album cover art were available.

studio when he failed to roll the tapes for a particular take. Stones producer Jimmy Miller took over at the mixing desk.

The opening song "Had to Cry Today" sets a precedent, with plaintive vocals from Winwood often struggling to hit high notes in the key of C that doesn't suit him. Clapton's echoing guitar patterns are solid enough, but constant repetition and overlapping riffs leave little space for the number to breathe. "Can't Find My Way Home" is a beautiful Winwood composition, with Baker using brushes to complement the acoustic guitars. The same restraint is applied to the Buddy Holly tribute "Well All Right," but it's not until "Presence of the Lord" that Clapton stokes up the guitar fire in a rare burst of faith-filled energy.

The remaining tracks are indulgent and far too long. The graceful "Sea of Joy" is a pleasant enough Winwood showcase, but "Do What You Like" tries to build up tension as it sails toward one of Baker's least-effective drum solos. The whole thing collapses into a shambolic mess, in a way foretelling the ultimate fate of the group.

Many fans thought these performances were a letdown, and critics only grew to like them more with the passage of time. Yet Clapton has stoutly defended the album, saying, "I think *Blind Faith* is a lovely record. I like its looseness. It's like a super session but with something more. You can feel there is a lot of longing in the band."

9. Derek is Eric

Delaney and Bonnie, the Plastic Ono Band, Derek and the Dominos, and the Rainbow Concert, 1969–1974

ERIC CLAPTON LEARNED IMPORTANT LESSONS and made discoveries about himself during the Cream and Blind Faith era. He knew he was tired of being portrayed as a guitar hero and most of all wanted to make music that was more comfortable and less combative. But he was far from unhappy at the prospect of forging a new direction. "I was having a good time and feeling very secure. I was in a great frame of mind," he said later.

Among his most important influences was the relaxed sound of the Band and their 1968 album *Music from Big Pink* as well as the funky down-home drive of Delaney and Bonnie, who toured with Blind Faith. Once the Blind Faith dust settled, Clapton stayed in New York with the pair and later brought them to England where they stayed at his twenty-room mansion in Surrey.

"The most wearing thing for me at that time was my state of indecision," Clapton explains. "I could see a life after Cream and Blind Faith because I was listening to other kinds of music. I just wanted to do other things, even if it was to play straight rock.

Clapton performs with his friends, Bonnie and Delaney Bramlett of Delaney and Bonnie, drummer Jim Gordon, and George Harrison at the Beat 69 club in Copenhagen, Denmark, on December 10, 1969. *Jan Persson/Redferns/Getty Images*

Clapton, John Lennon, and Yoko Ono display their different views on how to say "peace." Clapton had joined Lennon and Yoko in the Plastic Ono Band, which headlined the Toronto Rock & Roll Revival at Varsity Stadium in Toronto, Ontario, on September 13, 1969.
Mark and Colleen Hayward/Getty Images

Poster, Toronto Rock & Roll Revival, Varsity Stadium, Toronto, Ontario, September 13, 1969.

BROWER-WALKER ENTERPRISES LTD. PRESENTS

VARSITY STADIUM SEPT. 13

WHISKY HOWL BO DIDDLEY CHICAGO TRANS
AUTHORITY JR. WALKER & THE ALL STARS
TONY JOE WHITE   ALICE COOPER
**KIM
FOWLEY (M.C.)
CHUCK BERRY
CAT MOTHER &
THE ALL NIGHT NEWSBOYS
JERRY LEE LEWIS   GENE VINCENT
LITTLE RICHARD   DOUG KERSHAW**
the doors

TORONTO ROCK & ROLL REVIVAL 1969

TICKETS NOW AVAILABLE AT SAM THE RECORD MAN, 347 YONGE ST. & GOLDEN MILE PLAZA
ATTRACTION TICKET OFFICE, EATON'S COLLEGE ST. (USE YOUR EATON'S CHARGE CARD.)

The Plastic Ono Band's *Live Peace in Toronto 1969* featured Clapton, as well as bassist Klaus Voorman and drummer Alan White.

Eventually I joined Delaney and Bonnie, which was really like a soul band. I lived with Delaney for a while and we started talking about me making a solo album with his band. We started out on a tour of England and Europe as 'Delaney and Bonnie and Friends with Eric Clapton.' He got me to start singing and tried to get me to compose as well. By the end of that tour I was ready to make the album."

The husband and wife team of Delaney and Bonnie Bramlett was one of the first white acts to be signed to Stax records. Delaney was born in Pontotoc County, Mississippi, on July 1, 1939; Bonnie in Action, Illinois, on November 8, 1944. Experienced session singers, they put together their constantly changing "Friends" group that would include Leon Russell, Dave Mason, Duane Allman, Carl Radle, and Bobby Whitlock.

In September 1969, Clapton found time to play with John Lennon, who he'd met during the Blind Faith tour. Clapton was invited to sit in with John and Yoko's Plastic Ono Band at a concert that yielded the *Live Peace in Toronto 1969* album. Clapton flew at the last minute to join the band, even rehearsing with them on the flight from London. They took part in Toronto's Rock 'n' Roll Revival festival held at the Varsity Stadium on September 13, 1969.

An all-star bill featured Chuck Berry, Bo Diddley, Gene Vincent, and Little Richard. Clapton hadn't been on stage since his last gig with Blind Faith, and Lennon hadn't played live since 1966 when he was with the Beatles. Lennon and Clapton were both nervous, but the Plastic Ono Band rose to the occasion, rocking out on "Blue Suede Shoes," "Money," and "Yer Blues," followed by a rousing "Give Peace a Chance," with Yoko cheerfully wailing in her inimitable fashion.

"Cold Turkey," the sole single released from *Live Peace in Toronto 1969*.

Clapton backed Leon Russell on his 1970 solo debut album.

Poster, Boston Tea Party, Boston, Massachusetts, February 8–9, 1970.

Poster, Electric Factory, Philadelphia, Pennsylvania, February 11, 1970.

Clapton's desire to adopt a lower profile and join in with such team efforts might be understandable, but were also damaging in the long term. The Clapton who walked away from top billing was the same Clapton who had quit Casey Jones and the Engineers as well as the Glands. He just needed to escape the spotlight and seek greater freedom. He garnered increased liberty when he toured Europe with Delaney and Bonnie and Friends in 1969.

The "Friends" included George Harrison, Rita Coolidge, and Dave Mason, and they were intent on a good time in accordance with the hippie spirit of the age. Alas, a few issues did not help their mood: Some German tour promoters billed them as Cream, and audiences were displeased to see Clapton standing at the back while Delaney and Bonnie took the glory. One concert in Cologne had to be abandoned after just four songs as a result of loud booing. Clapton was distraught, but they persevered.

The reception on their British tour dates proved more amenable. They opened at the London's Royal Albert Hall on December 1, 1969, supported by Ashton, Gardner and Dyke. They also played some dates in Scandinavia. Once touring was over, they flew to Los Angeles to start work on Clapton's first solo album, beginning recording in March 1970. Called simply *Eric Clapton*, it was produced by Delaney Bramlett and released in August.

The album had several Bramlett and Clapton originals, such as "Slunky," "Bad Boy," and "Bottle of Red Wine." A version of J. J. Cale's "After Midnight" laden with a horn section and backing vocals was released as a single in October 1970. Among the guest musicians were Stephen Stills and Leon Russell, who contributed the track "Blues Power," written with Clapton. The band adopted a rough and ready style with a boogie rock feel less focused than Cream, but certainly more relaxed. Clapton himself looked rather subdued in the album-cover photograph, sporting long hair and a beard.

Eric Clapton gave Clapton a chance to develop as a singer, and at one stage the album was going to be called *Eric Sings*. On "After Midnight" and "Blues Power," he showed the kind of restrained vocal style he would develop over the coming years. This was Clapton as singer/songwriter rather than guitar virtuoso. It was a role that hardcore fans took time to accept. Clapton would win them over in the end and gain a new audience in the process. But it would take pain, grief, and hard work to get there.

When Clapton took the plunge and formed his own band in 1970, he decided to call it Derek and the Dominos, relinquishing his own name. Eric thought it funny, and revealed later that the idea of a pseudonym had come from jovial keyboard player Tony Ashton of Ashton, Gardner and Dyke. Said Eric

Handbill, Fillmore West, San Francisco, California,
February 19–22, 1970. *Artist: David Singer*

later: "It wasn't a conscious attempt at anonymity. We presumed that everyone
would know what it was all about. It would be an open joke."

But promoters tended to look askance at the billing, and some audiences
were confused. The new band made their debut at a benefit concert at London's
Lyceum on June 14, 1970, just before the release of the *Eric Clapton* album.

Originally advertised as Eric Clapton and Friends, the band only became
Derek and the Dominos at the last minute. Clapton appeared clean shaven in
a smart suit, clutching a Fender Stratocaster, and looking happy. They played
songs from the new album and even added Cream's "Crossroads" to keep he
crowds happy.

Delaney & Bonnie & Friends' *On Tour with Eric Clapton* was released on May 29, 1970, in the United Kingdom and in June 1970 in the United States.

The all-American Dominos were keyboardist Bobby Whitlock, guitarist Duane Allman, bassist Carl Radle, and drummer Jim Gordon. Delaney Bramlett was not included, having apparently fallen out with his former bandmates. Despite their individual talents, the Dominos sounded rather dull to the ears of some when they embarked on a three-week small-club tour of the U.K. during August. Admission prices were kept to £1, and Eric's name wasn't allowed to be used on the posters. They played at London's Marquee Club, once the home of the Yardbirds, and at Birmingham Town Hall, where Robert Plant of Led Zeppelin wandered on stage, expecting to sing, only to be removed by security.

In the midst of these otherwise positive activities, Clapton was shocked by the sudden death of Jimi Hendrix. On September 18, 1970, Clapton bought a left-handed Fender Stratocaster he'd spotted in a London music store. He intended to give it to Hendrix at a concert by Sly Stone they were both due to attend that night. However, Hendrix didn't turn up, and Clapton later learned he had died during the night from suffocation after inhalation of vomit due to barbiturate intoxication. Only a few days earlier, Clapton had recorded a version of the Hendrix song "'Little Wing" for the forthcoming Derek and the Dominos album.

Hendrix' death at the age of twenty-five was a blow to Clapton. They had been friends since Jimi first arrived in London in 1966, and Hendrix always paid tribute to Clapton's achievements, even playing "Sunshine of Your Love" with his group the Experience in an unscheduled change of routine during a BBC TV show. Clapton later said that Hendrix' death had left him feeling "angry" at the loss of life and talent.

Some six weeks after Hendrix' death, Derek and the Dominos went on a U.S. tour. The record company had to launch a publicity campaign reminding potential concert-goers that "Derek is Eric" to end confusion over the identity of the bandleader. But the album still hadn't been released in America, and although the Dominos received a warm enough welcome at the Fillmore East in New York, other gigs were half empty. Press reviews were poor, suggesting that the shows were boring with muddy vocals battling with over loud volume levels. The tour ended, since Clapton had to fly back home to the U.K. on hearing that his sixty-year-old grandfather, John Clapp, was ill with cancer. He died shortly after Eric's return.

A suitably 1970s view of Clapton and George Harrison performing with Delaney and Bonnie in Copenhagen.
Jan Persson/Redferns/Getty Images

Clapton played this cherry finish 1959 Gibson Les Paul Standard guitar, nicknamed "Lucy," before giving it to his friend George Harrison in 1968. *Nigel Osbourne/ Redferns/Getty Images*

"[My sound] had really come about accidentally, when I was trying to emulate the sharp, thin sound that Freddy King got out of his Gibson Les Paul, and I ended up with something quite different, a sound that was a lot fatter than Freddy's. The Les Paul has two pickups, one at the end of the neck, giving the guitar a kind of round jazz sound, and the other next to the bridge, giving you the treble, most often used for the thin, typically rock 'n' roll sound. What I would do was use the bridge pickup with all of the bass turned up, so the sound was very thick and on the edge of distortion. I also always used amps that would overload. I would have the amp on full, with the volume on the guitar also turned up full, so everything was on full volume and overloading. I would hit a note, hold it, and give it some vibrato with my fingers, until it sustained, and then the distortion would turn into feedback. It was all of these things, plus the distortion, that created what I suppose you could call my sound."

—Eric Clapton, *Clapton: The Autobiography*, 2007

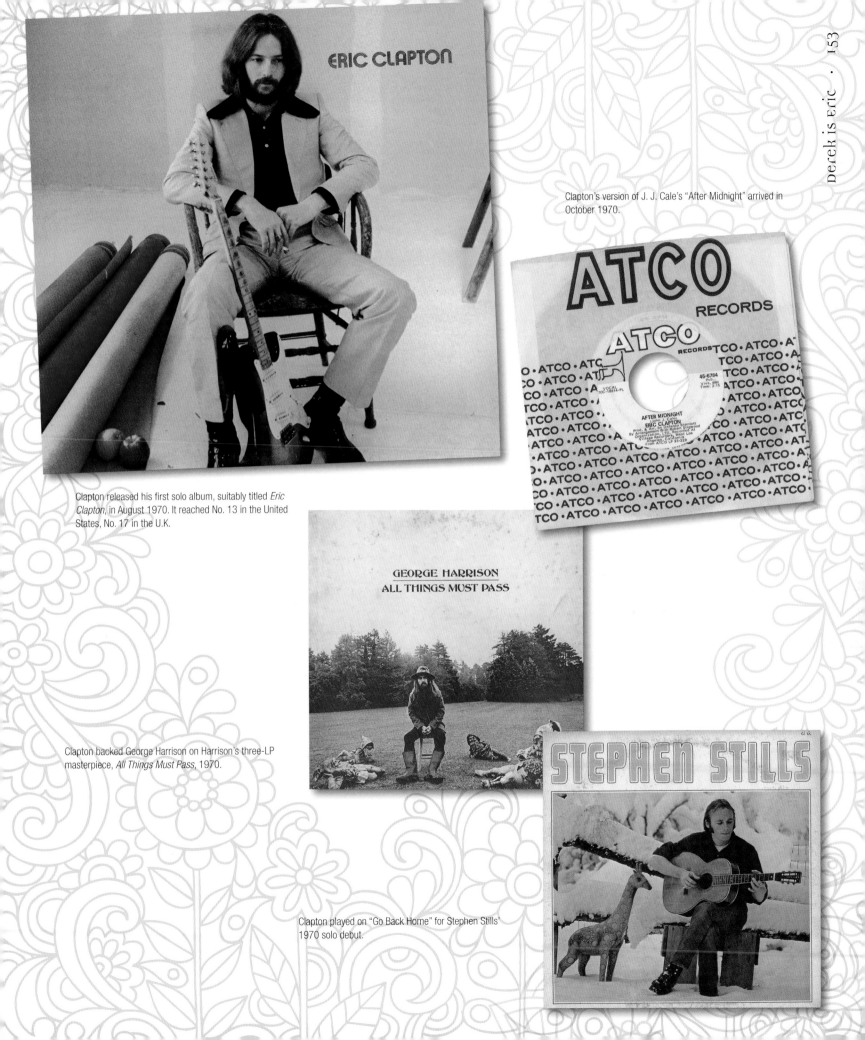

Clapton's version of J. J. Cale's "After Midnight" arrived in October 1970.

Clapton released his first solo album, suitably titled *Eric Clapton*, in August 1970. It reached No. 13 in the United States, No. 17 in the U.K.

Clapton backed George Harrison on Harrison's three-LP masterpiece, *All Things Must Pass*, 1970.

Clapton played on "Go Back Home" for Stephen Stills' 1970 solo debut.

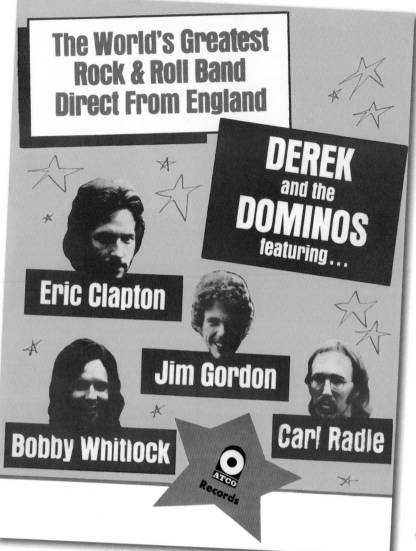

The World's Greatest
Rock & Roll Band
Direct From England

DEREK
and the
DOMINOS
featuring...

Eric Clapton

Jim Gordon

Bobby Whitlock

Carl Radle

ATCO
Records

After the Delaney and Bonnie tours, Clapton returned to
the stage with his new group, Derek and the Dominos,
playing their first concert on June 14, 1970, at the
Lyceum, London. Atco was quick to promote the band.

"Should I tell you where I got that riff? It's an Albert
King riff off an album *Born Under a Bad Sign* and
there's a song called 'There is Nothing I Can Do if
You Leave Me Here to Cry.' Duane Allman heard
that and just went!"

—Eric Clapton on the "Layla" guitar riff, *Creem*, 1977

Derek and the Dominos had finished recording their debut studio double album *Layla and Other Assorted Love Songs* before the tour. Work had begun in August 1970 at the Criteria Studios in Miami, Florida. Clapton had invited Duane Allman to play on the sessions, excited after seeing him play at a gig with the Allman Brothers. Allman made an inspirational contribution to an album that was completed in just ten days. As well as the assorted love songs, it showcased Clapton's master work and the song that would finally establish his credentials as a songwriter and a legend. "Layla" was inspired by Clapton's infatuation with Pattie Boyd, the former model who also happened to be the wife of his best friend, George Harrison.

The poignant lyrics were influenced by a seventh-century Arabian tale called *The Story of Layla and Majnun*, by Persian writer Nizami. It depicts a hopeless love affair with a girl called Layla. Prevented from marriage by her father, the young suitor Majnun is driven to madness. Identifying with Majnun, Clapton began writing his "Layla" with the help of Jim Gordon.

It was intended as a declaration of love for Pattie, his unobtainable dream girl. The result was a magnum opus that would be associated with Clapton for the rest of his career.

For her part, despite such blandishments, Pattie went back to Harrison and Clapton was further bereft.

The album was released in December 1970 without Clapton's name printed on an LP cover that was instead adorned with a mysterious painting of a girl's face. "Layla"/"Bell Bottom Blues" was also released as a single in November. The A-side was played nonstop at London night club the Speakeasy and was an underground hit. Allman's stirring guitar and Clapton's heartfelt vocals blended in an orchestral arrangement whose shifting moods proved irresistible.

Inexplicably, "Layla" failed to make the charts—a bitter blow for Clapton. It only became a hit after being reissued a couple of years later in the U.K. when it rose to No. 7 in August 1972. After struggling into the U.S. Billboard chart at No. 51 in 1971, "Layla" finally hit No. 10 on re-entry in May 1972. The album was also deemed a critical flop when it was first released and failed to hit the Top Ten in the United States or Britain.

"Bell Bottom Blues" was the first single from *Layla and Other Assorted Love Songs* in 1970.

"Layla" was released in early 1971, suitably backed with "I Am Yours."

"'Layla' . . . was actually about an emotional experience, a woman that I felt really deeply about and who turned me down, and I had to kind of pour it out in some way. So we wrote these songs, made an album, and the whole thing was great.

Interviewer: What did the woman in question think?

"She didn't give a damn."

—Eric Clapton, *Rolling Stone*, 1974

"I was incredibly proud of 'Layla,'" Clapton remembers. "It still knocks me out when I play it. But the funny thing was that once I'd got 'Layla' out of my system, I didn't want to do any more with the Dominos. I didn't want to play another note. I went home and stayed there and locked all the doors."

Clapton did have an early solo hit single with "After Midnight" that got to No. 18 in the United States in December 1970. But slowly his life began to unravel. The Dominos broke up in April 1971 after an attempt to record a second studio album was scrapped amidst rumors of internal strife. Their legacy was celebrated with the double live album *In Concert* recorded at the Fillmore East in New York in November 1970 but not released until March 1973.

A dark period in Eric Clapton's life began, and he succumbed to a serious heroin addiction. His drug dependency shocked friends and associates once they understood it was the cause of abrupt and mysterious isolation. For a year he became a recluse at his Surrey home, looked after by his girlfriend, Alice Ormsby Gore. Phone calls went unanswered, and Clapton barely touched his guitar.

In 1971, Clapton made just two public appearances, one at George Harrison's benefit Concert for Bangladesh at Madison Square Garden in New York on August 1, when he took part in an all-star jam session including Bob Dylan. He also turned up at London's Rainbow Theatre for a Leon Russell concert in December.

For most of the time it seemed Clapton was surrounded by drug users and his musical activities were put on hold. His true friends and admirers clearly could not allow the situation to continue, and they rallied around to try to get him help. Behind the scenes, those close to him put forth strenuous efforts to get him off drugs and back into shape.

His confidence also needed restoring, and Pete Townshend of the Who was determined to do something constructive on Clapton's behalf. He organized a special all-star concert held at London's Rainbow Theatre on January 13, 1973. There were two shows, and Clapton was backed by Townshend, Ronnie Wood, Rick Grech, Steve Winwood, and Jim Capaldi. The event was recorded and appeared later as the live album *Eric Clapton's Rainbow Concert*. A heavily bearded Clapton appeared in a white suit and played well enough.

Clapton: "Pete Townshend is great and I admire him. But I just don't know why he picked on me to do the Rainbow Concert. It could have been anybody, but I'm grateful he chose me. It had to be someone dragging me around by the scruff of my collar and making me do this and that. I thought the gig was okay, but when I listened to the tapes afterwards I realized I was under par. I wasn't really ready to go on stage. But the welcome really moved me."

Afterwards, however, he seemed to lapse back into addiction. It was only by sessions at a special clinic and a period of recuperation and rehabilitation on a farm in Wales that he felt able to restart his career properly.

The process of healing and restoration had been going on for years when suddenly Robert Stigwood called *Melody Maker* on April 4, 1974, to announce that "Eric is back."' A special press conference was held at the China Garden restaurant in Soho, London. Clapton was found sitting on the stairs looking confused and contrite. But he was ready to make his musical comeback and prepared to chat about plans for the future.

The restaurant was besieged with press, radio, and TV crews and bemused waiters were heard asking, "Who *is* Lobert Stigwood?" The party was organized by press agent Helen Walters at Stigwood's behest in a series of urgent phone calls. She'd only had a few hours to get it all together for Clapton. Many of the calls were made by radio telephone in Stigwood's car on the way to Soho.

"We just want to have a raving party to celebrate Eric's return to work," said Stigwood, "And we want everyone to enjoy themselves."

So how was Mr. Clapton?

"I'm fine!" he bawled. "Really great to be back!"

He certainly looked well with a rich brown suntan from his time working in the fields. His hair was short, but there was the trace of a beard and moustache. Clad in a Norwegian sweater, he bustled into the restaurant having arrived in a white Rolls-Royce, which itself drew admiring crowds in the street outside. As the photographers' flashguns pinged, a passing rock fan screeched to a halt. "Who's that going in there?" he asked. "What!" was his stunned response on hearing the glad tidings. Like many people, he thought Clapton had long since retired.

A crush of friends were there to greet Clapton, including Elton John in a white suit but *sans* platform shoes, which he complained made him feel smaller than usual. Pete Townshend reached out a welcoming hand to Clapton, while waiting in the wings were Long John Baldry, Dean Ford of the Marmalade, Rick Grech, and Ronnie Wood.

"I wish I'd known about this party earlier. I've got creases in my trousers," complained Townshend as lettuce leaves began to be thrown among the guests. Clapton raced around, greeting and shaking hands but not wanting to be pinned down on any specific subject, like his future plans. But why had he chosen now to renew his musical activity?

"I don't know why now, but I just felt the time was right. I'd been talking a lot to Robert Stigwood about the best way of doing things." Clapton explained he was going to Miami to record a new album and form a band with Carl Radle on keyboards and "a couple of guys" to play bass and drums. "It's all

Poster, Marquay Club, Town Hall, Torquay, England, August 21, 1970.

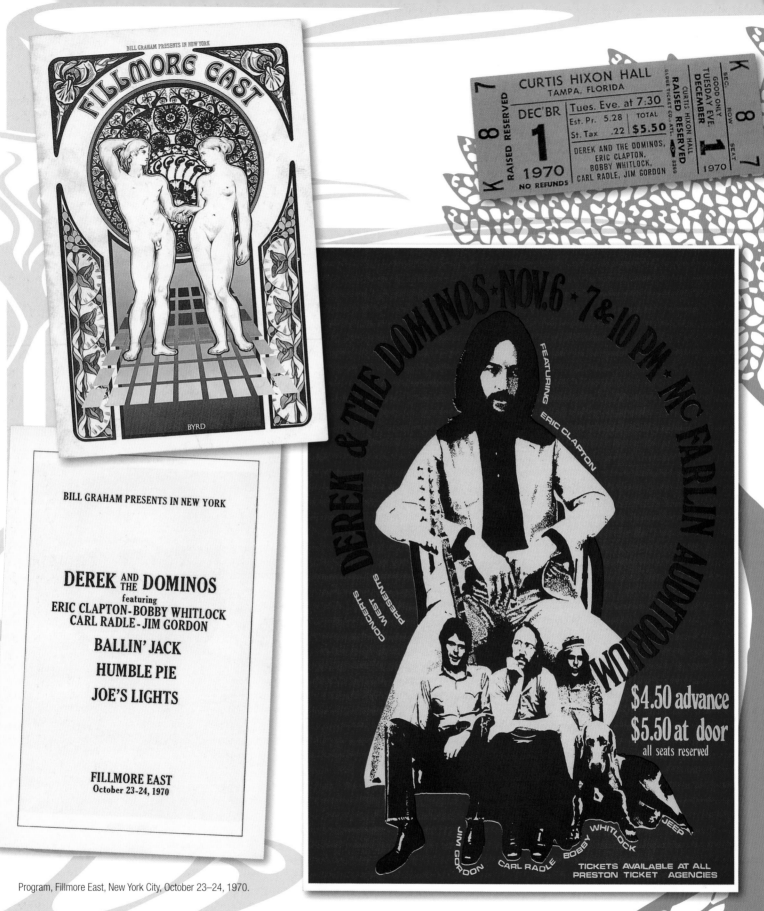

FILLMORE EAST

BILL GRAHAM PRESENTS IN NEW YORK

BYRD

BILL GRAHAM PRESENTS IN NEW YORK

DEREK AND THE DOMINOS
featuring
ERIC CLAPTON - BOBBY WHITLOCK
CARL RADLE - JIM GORDON

BALLIN' JACK

HUMBLE PIE

JOE'S LIGHTS

FILLMORE EAST
October 23–24, 1970

Program, Fillmore East, New York City, October 23–24, 1970.

CURTIS HIXON HALL
TAMPA, FLORIDA

DEC'BR
1
1970
NO REFUNDS

Tues. Eve. at 7:30
Est. Pr. 5.28   TOTAL
St. Tax .22 $5.50

DEREK AND THE DOMINOS,
ERIC CLAPTON,
BOBBY WHITLOCK,
CARL RADLE, JIM GORDON

GOOD ONLY
TUESDAY EVE.
DECEMBER
1
1970

DEREK & THE DOMINOS ★ NOV. 6 ★ 7 & 10 P.M. ★ MC FARLIN AUDITORIUM

FEATURING ERIC CLAPTON

CONCERTS WEST PRESENTS

$4.50 advance
$5.50 at door
all seats reserved

JIM GORDON   CARL RADLE   BOBBY WHITLOCK   JEEP

TICKETS AVAILABLE AT ALL
PRESTON TICKET AGENCIES

Poster, McFarlin Auditorium, Dallas, Texas, November 6, 1970.

Poster, Mammoth Gardens, Denver, Colorado, November 11, 1970.

Advertisement, Santa Monica Civic Center and Pasadena Civic Center, California, November 20 and 21, 1970.

Poster, Allen Theater, Cleveland, Ohio, November 28, 1970.

A Buffalo Festival Presentation
Derek & the Dominos
Wednesday, December 2nd 7 PM
Onondaga War Memorial Auditorium

DEREK & THE DOMINOS
CARL RADLE ERIC CLAPTON JIM GORDON BOBBY WHITLOCK
ELTON JOHN   TOE FAT

Tickets
$4.50, 5.50, 6.50
At the War Memorial Box Office, Sears and
the Syracuse University Book Store.

Poster, Onondaga War Memorial Auditorium, Syracuse,
New York, December 2, 1970.

just starting to happen but I want to record again and I'll also be doing a tour of America. And later on—yeah, I'll do some dates in England. There's no name for the band yet, but I don't think it will be Derek and the Dominos or anything like that. Basically I'm feeling very well. I'm a really happy man!"

Clapton's only associate from pre-Dominos days present was Rick Grech, recently arrived in town from Los Angeles. Rick expressed everyone's opinion when he said: "It's really nice that Eric's back and looking so well."

The China Garden celebration was transferred to Robert Stigwood's palatial mansion in North London, where the party raged on until 5 a.m. Few could remember what happened or exactly what Clapton was planning to do. Many doubted if he could remember himself. But the general verdict was that the Wanderer had returned to the fold.

Clapton, meanwhile, was quite hard on himself: "When I got out of hibernation I thought, look at the time I've wasted. I haven't really done anything with my life."

It was time to make amends.

"Clapton's comeback was a success in all ways and the consequences could be good. It's unlikely to be another eighteen months before he wants to gig again and other recent recluses, notably George Harrison, might be persuaded to do the same themselves. In Clapton's case the encouragement of Pete Townshend was crucial, as he admitted on Saturday night when he asked everyone to 'thank the man who got me to come up here, because I wouldn't have done it without him.'"

—John Pidgeon on the Rainbow Concert, *Let It Rock*, February 1973

Clapton performs with Derek and the Dominos during the 1970 U.S. tour, playing his Frankenstein's monster of a Stratocaster, nicknamed "Brownie." *Elliot Landy/Redferns/ Getty Images*

"Brownie"

Inspired by his love of American country, soul, and R&B music, Clapton purchased an old 1950s sunburst Fender Stratocaster. He began using the guitar with Delaney and Bonnie, and continued playing it for years after. Clapton nicknamed the Strat "Brownie," and it appeared with him on the cover of his first solo album and prominently across the back cover of *Layla and Other Assorted Love Songs*.

"My first Strat was 'Brownie,' and I played it for years and years, a wonderful guitar."

—Eric Clapton

"I still play a Les Paul. But with Delaney and Bonnie I use an old Stratocaster I've acquired which is really, really good—a great sound. It's just right for the kind of bag I was playing with them. . . . I just set the switch between the first and middle pickups. There is a little place where you can catch it so that you can get a special sound somehow. I get much more rhythm and blues or rock kind of sound that way."

—Eric Clapton in *Guitar Player* magazine, 1970

Clapton sold his Stratocaster "Brownie" at a charity auction on June 24, 1999, for his Crossroads Centre in Antigua, which he founded for the treatment of alcohol and drug dependency. *Getty Images*

Joining Bob Dylan and others, Clapton performed with George Harrison at his Concert for Bangladesh, Madison Square Garden, New York City, August 1, 1971.

Clapton and others backed Howlin' Wolf on *The London Howlin' Wolf Sessions*, 1971.

Derek and the Dominos' *In Concert* was released in 1973.

Clapton at his Rainbow Theatre comeback concert, with Pete Townshend, January 1973. *Chris Walter/WireImage/Getty Images*

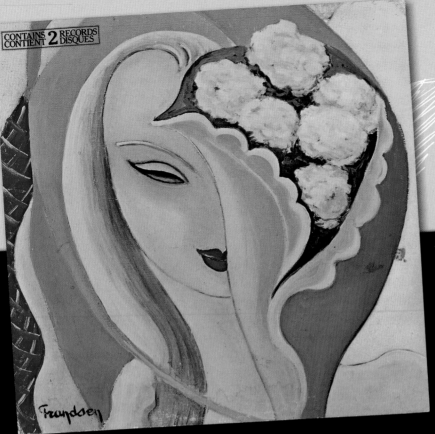

Layla and Other Assorted Love Songs was released in December 1970. It reached No. 16 in the United States, but didn't chart in the U.K.

Layla and other Assorted Love songs

Laze over a drink in the bar at London's Speakeasy Club any evening in the winter of 1970 and you'd hear a striking record that tugged at the heartstrings, played over and over again. The house DJ was determined to share his pleasure at discovering such a captivating ballad by none other than Eric Clapton, former star of Cream and Blind Faith. Only now Eric was Derek, performing a bunch of love songs with his new American band, the Dominos. "Layla" was the particular item that caught the DJ's ear, but the rest of the album, too, was packed with heartfelt performances.

Music biz habitués of the "Speak" loved Derek's double LP, in its gatefold sleeve adorned by an unusual cover painting that made no reference to the star's name.

The trouble was the rest of populace didn't get it, at least not right away. While the now-familiar guitar introduction, performed by Derek with his special guest Duane Allman, prefaced an extraordinarily good song,

the single culled from the album was not the instant hit everyone expected.

The Southern country rock sound of the Dominos came in sharp contrast to the more direct linear attack associated with Clapton's previous recordings. A loping beat whipped up by the Carl Radle and Jim Gordon rhythm team, married to Bobby Whitlock's organ and piano, propels a mesh of overlaid guitar tracks in which Clapton's guitar identity is submerged. This was no doubt exactly what Clapton was looking for in his need to downplay his starring role.

However, there is no disguising the passion with which Clapton sings and plays, especially on the excellent "Bell Bottom Blues," another anguished portrayal of unrequited love. "Give me one more day please . . . I don't want to fade away."

Those yearning to hear Clapton in jamming mode would be rewarded by "Keep On Growing," although the barrage of duelling between Clapton and his mate from the Allman Brothers makes it difficult to distinguish who is playing what. Clapton plays his Fender Stratocaster "Brownie" while Allman uses a Gibson Les Paul to get a "full-tilt screech." It's a fun track and belies the belief that the Dominos was a band somehow associated with gloom and grief.

Even so, Clapton is in a mellow mood when he makes his first attempt at tackling a venerable standard with his version of "Nobody Knows You When You're Down and Out." Such delving into the archives would be revisited many years later on 2010's Clapton, when he delivered a solemn "Autumn Leaves."

Many more fine performances illuminate Derek's masterpiece, notably "Tell the Truth" and "Why Does Love Got to Be So Sad" that became regular features at gigs. A tribute to the late Jimi Hendrix with Clapton's interpretation of "Little Wing" is especially moving.

When "Layla" finally appears as the penultimate song, the searing pain of Clapton's vocal delivery is paradoxically joyful. "Layla, you've got me on my knees," sings the troubled troubadour in a series of telling phrases that would echo down the years.

A year after the release of *Layla*, Duane Allman died in a motorcycle accident, on October 29, 1971, and in many respects the album became his memorial.

The fortieth anniversary of *Layla and Other Assorted Love Songs* was celebrated by the release in March 2011 of Deluxe and Super Deluxe multi-format editions of the album. The package included new and long-unavailable music, notably six performances intended for a second Dominos album, remixed by Andy Johns.

The double disk was made available in vinyl and digital formats with four audio performances from Derek and the Dominos' only TV appearance, on the Johnny Cash Show in November 1970, plus a concert recorded at New York City's Fillmore East re-mastered from the original master tape.

SD2-704
2 LP Set
LAYLA
DEREK AND THE DOMINOS
Eric Clapton
Jim Gordon
Bobby Whitlock
Carl Radle
Duane Allman

On Atco Records & Atco Tapes (Tapes Distributed by Ampex)
A Product of Polydor-England

Frandsen

DEREK AND THE DOMINOS NOW ON TOUR

featuring . . .
Eric Clapton
Jim Gordon
Bobby Whitlock
Carl Radle

Dallas—Nov. 6, McFarlin Aud.
Houston—Nov. 7, Sam Houston Music Hall
Denver—Nov. 11, Mammouth Gardens
Sacramento—Nov. 12, Mem. Aud.
Reno—Nov. 13, Univ. of Nevada
San Bernardino—Nov. 14, Swing Aud.
Honolulu—Nov. 15, HIC Convention Center
Berkeley—Nov. 18 & 19, Community Theater
Santa Monica—Nov. 20, Civic Aud.
Pasadena—Nov. 21, Civic Center
Chicago—Nov. 25, Auditorium Theater
Cincinnati—Nov. 26, Music Hall
St. Louis—Nov. 27, Kiel Aud.
Cleveland—Nov. 28, Allen Theater
Detroit—Nov. 29, Masonic Temple
Tampa—Dec. 1, Curtis Hixon Aud.
Syracuse—Dec. 2, War Mem. Aud.
Boston—Dec. 3, Music Hall
Portchester, N.Y.—Dec. 4 & 5, Capitol Theater

Sole Representation: Robert Stigwood Organisation, London, England • Booking Agency: Chartwell, New York, N.Y.

ATCO

10. "i play the guitar . . ."

Solo Career, 1974–1982

A SIGH OF RELIEF RESONATED AROUND the rock world when Eric Clapton returned to center stage and relaunched a career many feared had come to an untimely end. His drug addiction abated, he was finally united with Pattie Boyd once she left George Harrison, and his beloved "Layla" became a hit record at last.

Clapton was able to put his experience with the Dominos behind him and look forward to working with a more compatible band. All he needed was another hit record to replenish his confidence. Miraculously, he would achieve all these aims as he returned to the United States and faced the new challenges of the 1970s.

At first, Clapton beat himself up, convinced he had wasted three years of his life in dissolute idleness. But then he discovered a hoard of forgotten home tape recordings that revealed he hadn't lost his touch. He was pleasantly surprised to hear that even when singing and playing guitar by himself, he had retained his technique and feeling for the blues. The cassettes told him he could still cut it and had no need to worry.

Clapton performs at Nassau Coliseum, Long Island, New York, on June 30, 1974.
Steve Morley/Redferns/Getty Images

Layla: Pattie Boyd with Clapton, 1975. *Graham Wiltshire/ Redferns/Getty Images*

As 1974 dawned, Clapton's first thought was to reform the Dominos. But he was daunted by the task of ringing round musicians or checking out the "Gigs Wanted" advertisements. In the end, former Dominos colleague Carl Radle sent him a telegram advising he had a band all set up and ready. Would Clapton like to play with them? The answer came back, "Sure thing."

The Eric Clapton Band would include Clapton on guitar and vocals backed by guitarman George Terry, keyboardist Dick Sims, bassist Radle, and drummer Jamie Oldaker together with pianist Albhy Galuten and vocalist Yvonne Elliman. They set to work with producer Tom Dowd at Criteria Studios in Miami, Florida. The result was Clapton's all important "comeback" album, *461 Ocean Boulevard*, released in August 1974.

At first it seemed like a shot in the dark. Clapton had only a couple of songs ready to record, including Charles Scott Boyer's "Please Be With Me." Clapton: "I really had no ideas for *461* before I went to Miami. I just jammed and put it together as I went along. I played everything I could think of." He claimed to have tried out a hundred songs, feeling unsure about using any of the material he had written during the previous three years. And he felt shy in the presence of his new bandmates. "So we just made things up. I left the tapes with Tom Dowd and said 'Pick out what you think is best and put it on the album.'"

Dowd worked miracles and came up with a well-rounded and classy production packed with good performances. The tracks included Eric's "Give Me Strength" and a cheerful version of the Johnny Otis rock 'n' roll standard "Willie and the Hand Jive." There was less emphasis on Clapton as a virtuoso guitarist and greater expansion of his role as a singer.

The choice of material and mellow delivery helped him reach a much wider public. The confirmation came when his version of Bob Marley's "I Shot the Sheriff" became a major hit single. Clapton's jaunty cover shot to No. 1 in the Billboard Top 40 in August. It was his first U.S. hit since "Layla" peaked at No. 10 in 1972. "Willie and the Hand Jive" was also a hit, reaching No. 26 in November 1974.

Clapton first heard "I Shot the Sheriff" when George Terry played him Bob Marley and the Wailers' *Burnin'* album. "It took me a while to get into it," Clapton remembers. "I was coming from a different place and had to break my inherent musical tightness down into this really loose thing. It was difficult for me to assimilate. The only way I could stamp my personality on it was

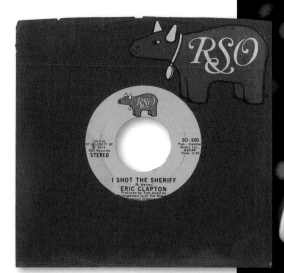

to sing and just play the occasional lick. It was a complete hybrid."

Not long after the single charted, Clapton received a phone call from Marley himself, and they had a friendly chat during which Clapton tried to find out if it was true the reggae star had actually shot a sheriff. Marley wouldn't confirm the story even when they later met face to face during a Wailers' tour of England. Clapton went to the Wailers' dressing room at the Odeon Hammersmith and met Marley. Clapton: "He was a great guy. So warm. A beautiful man."

In the United Kingdom, Clapton singles did less well, but "I Shot the Sheriff" peaked at No. 9. It was good news for the man who had feared his fans had forgotten him. *461 Ocean Boulevard* (named after the Miami studio address) would top the U.S. album chart for four weeks and rose to No. 3 in the U.K. The successful team Radle had brought together would stay with Clapton for the next four albums.

Clapton's version of the Bob Marley reggae single "I Shot the Sheriff," 1972.

"Willie and the Hand Jive," 1974.

"Swing Low Sweet Chariot," 1974.

Clapton returned to playing live before *461 Ocean Boulevard* was released and headed for European dates that included a memorable trip to Denmark where it became clear that he hadn't lost his love for partying. He may have been cured of his narcotics addictions, thanks to the power of acupuncture, but he still liked a drink or three.

A *Melody Maker* correspondent visited him in Copenhagen and filed a report on Clapton's merrymaking. He was discovered enjoying himself in a raunchy nightspot with the rest of the band after a gig shouting, "We want Buddy Holly! I *am* Buddy Holly!"

As *Melody Maker* noted in June 1974: "Blowing defiance on a honking duck-call, the figure wearing a misshapen trilby hat, lens-less glasses, and oversized dungarees, crashed full-length down the aisle of a Danish sex club, and lay semi-conscious before a disbelieving erotic dancer, her nakedness no match for this alternative spectacle. . . .

"Eric Clapton, once voted England's Best Dressed Man, was celebrating his return to active service. Of all the many roles Eric has played over the years, this was undoubtedly the most bizarre. Gone was the white suit of yesteryear, and the super cool image. In its place, a lurching raver, dressed like a scarecrow. And yet it symbolized Eric's apparent determination to break out of the self-imposed hibernation of the last few years.

"Since Derek and the Dominos folded-up, Clapton has withdrawn from the world. But now he is back and although a little nervous and shy, he is out to enjoy himself and prove that the Clapton guitar magic is still there."

The tour had kicked off in Stockholm, Sweden, with the same band that recorded *461*. A surprise addition was former Bonzo Dog Band singer and tap dancer "Legs" Larry Smith, fresh from a tour with Elton John and now working as Clapton's compere and court jester.

The *Melody Maker* writer described their Copenhagen show as: "Fun, overlong, occasionally sloppy but promising. By the time they get into their twenty-six week American tour, they should be either completely exhausted from excessive raving, or the tightest, hottest band on the circuit. And Eric? Well, it was worth the trip to Copenhagen just to hear him dig into the blues again on 'Have You Ever Loved a Woman?'"

The previous night's debut concert at Stockholm's Tivoli Gardens had been something of a riot. The show was attended by fifteen thousand and the Clapton Band enjoyed themselves so much they kept on playing well over their allotted time. The promoter was displeased and complained he was losing thousands in takings at the adjacent funfair. Attempts were made to pull the P.A. plugs and silence the musicians. Clapton's manager, Robert Stigwood, had to keep the promoter out of harm's way by engaging him in time-consuming conversation.

Several early tracks by Vivian Stanshall and the Sean Head Showband, including Clapton, appeared on *The History of the Bonzos*, 1974.

Clapton made a guest appearance in the film version of the Who's rock opera *Tommy*, playing the Preacher. *Moviestore Collection Ltd/Alamy*

There had been another even more serious problem, as Clapton revealed during a chat at his hotel: "The van with all the equipment crashed on its way from Stockholm. That's why we're sitting around here. We should be having a soundcheck down at the hall."

When the equipment finally turned up, the band convened in a large, hot, and airless concert hall more suitable for basketball than music. It was packed with Danish youths in blue denim and all smoking dope, without fear of fine or arrest.

Melody Maker noted: "Legs Larry Smith—dubbed for the occasion, Legs Christian Anderson—induced the Scandinavians to roar with mirth, blowing kisses, bowing, and clutching a guitar the size of George Formby's ukulele. It was the final outrage when the tapes switched to Pete Townshend's 'Pinball Wizard' and Larry cavorted like the phantom guitar smasher from Shepherd's Bush.

"'And now from l'il old England, just across the sea, it's my privilege to introduce you to the one and only—Eric Clapton!'

"A roar of real applause wafted up through the smoke laden air, and then faltered. For who was this baffling figure, disguised like a down and out? But as

461
TOUR
1974

FESTIVAL EAST CONCERTS
PART I — SATURDAY
"SUMMERFEST"
Abbott Road
"ERIC CLAPTON"
Also . . . . "RO
NOTICE—This ticket is a revocable
related or terminated at any time.
injury and all responsibility for pro
and release Festival East Concerts
and their agents and employees from
No bottles or cans are allowed on
search all packages brought into the St

ENTER TOWER | GATE | 25 | GATE
C | 25
2nd PROMENADE $6.50
340 C 4
SEC. ROW SEAT
SAT. EVE. JULY 13 1974
ERIC CLAPTON
8:00 P. M.

Eric took off his hat, even the baggy dungarees that billowed around his haunches, failed to completely disguise the man who had come thus far, all the way from Yardbirds, John Mayall, and all-stations to Cream, Blind Faith, and the Dominos. 'Tell the Truth' was the aptly-titled tune, and Clapton the musician shone through his subterfuge."

It was reported that many of the songs were taken at a slow tempo and there was a lot of riffing and jamming. Clapton occasional sang in the wrong key, and time changes and codas were delivered with a degree of uncertainty.

"But it was funky, fun, and in the most part, satisfying," *Melody Maker* stated. "And most importantly, it was a vehicle for a guitarist who can still raise goose pimples and send a shiver through the bones. A lot of the time, Eric was content to chord, while George Terry offered some excellent slide guitar work. 'Layla' was welcome, but ragged, followed by the best song, 'Please Remember,' a fine ballad with the drums laying out giving us a chance to recall how well Eric can sing when he has the urge.

"The first shiver down the spine came when Eric played a stop-time intro to 'Blues Power,' and his guitar stood out at last from the churning ensembles. 'Loved a Woman' followed, with churchy organ backing from Dick Sims that brought to mind Billy Preston. Here Clapton excelled, turning the legend into reality.

"'Willie and the Hand Jive' was a bit of a bore, throbbing along to a Bo Diddley beat for about ten minutes and 'I Can't Find My Way Home' was a trifle laborious and failed to earn much applause. Hastily the band snapped into a fast boogie blues, which turned out to be 'Little Queenie,' with Eric offering a few arm-swoops a la Townshend, and climaxing on the time-honoured cry of 'Good evening, friends.'"

"After two hours plus of continuous blowing, the band quit the stage, to be ordered back for an encore on a slow raunchy 'Crossroads' and a final jam. Neither was particularly inspired, but the audience were happy and so were the musicians. For this was an event to be entered into the scrapbooks, the night Eric the Ready came back."

After the show, the band hastened to a restaurant for a party and a proposed banquet.

Melody Maker: "Local record executives offered hearty congratulations, one going so far as to tell Robert Stigwood: 'Tonight I heard the greatest music I haff heard in my entire life.' Eric could match that. As he sat with Yvonne Elliman at a corner table he announced: 'Eric Clapton is the greatest thing—in the entire world!' and proceeded to order and down, two tumblers of Bacardi and orange."

Clapton talked to the reporter about the band and the night's performance, explaining they'd not had much time to rehearse: "Nobody knows what we are going to play next. We just fall into each number, depending how we feel. Our drummer Jamie is only twenty-two. He was recommended to me by Carl, who got the guys together in America. We've recorded quite a few new things for the album, but tonight we did mainly the old favourites because they come out best and it's what people want to hear."

The proposed banquet was abruptly cancelled and instead the party proceeded in a fleet of taxis to the Eden Club, a forty-minute drive away. The raucous British

Road-crazy: Clapton poses with his suitcases and a banana somewhere on tour, 1974. *Jan Persson/Redferns/Getty Images*

and American musicians were seated in a luxurious theater and amidst much laughter, hooting, and catcalls, a troupe of local glamor girls attempted to give them a private show.

"'Please, listen, if you do not want to watch the show, then we shall leave,' said one nude performer, uncertain how to cope with these foreign hooligans. The reply was short and sharp: 'Go 'ome then you old ****!'

"While classical music and soap bubbles filtered from the roof, Eric set up a barrage of duck-calls, usually delivered at the most dramatic moment of erotic play. 'Shudda your mouth!' stormed the artistes. 'You don't know how to enjoy yourselves! And take your hand away from there. That is not allowed here.'

"'Listen, love,' said Legs Larry Smith, seated in the front row, 'After the drive out to this place, my hand is frozen stiff!' A roar of applause greeted this, and shortly after Eric made his Buddy Holly declaration.

"'Eric, I think you should get some rest,' said a concerned Robert Stigwood. 'Rest?' roared Eric. 'I'm too tired to rest!'"

Clapton got into his stride after the huge success of "I Shot the Sheriff" and *461 Ocean Boulevard*. A succession of albums lit up his career during the 1970s, notably *No Reason to Cry* (1976), *Slowhand* (1977), and *Backless* (1978). His business affairs were now managed by Roger Forrester, who took a paternal interest in ensuring Clapton kept both busy and healthy.

The guitarist's somewhat slapdash performances were still evident during the period when drinking had taken over from drugs, but during the 1974 U.S. tour he began to regain confidence and a renewed sense of professionalism. The revitalized Clapton was greeted as a prodigal son when his band played at New York's Madison Square Garden, the scene of former triumphs by Cream and Blind Faith.

But it wasn't always an easy ride, especially when audiences began to adopt a less reverential attitude to rock stars. The Eric Clapton Band played two shows at London's Odeon Hammersmith on December 4, 1974, their first in the United Kingdom. Guitarist Ronnie Wood, then still with the Faces, made a surprise guest appearance for the encore number. Clapton and Woody played a brief duet on "Little Queenie" that went down a storm. However, the atmosphere at the Odeon was rather strange and there was some heckling from hard-to-please Londoners.

Clapton adopted a Cockney accent to mollify the locals, but even this was greeted with derisive shouts. "Gah, you old bankrupt!" was one less-than-charitable catcall from somewhere in the circle. Another yelled, "Get on with it, you old ****." Clapton was moved to respond, "What a rowdy punch of idiots," and mimicked their cries for "Layla," giving the impression he was more than peeved.

Singers Yvonne Elliman and Marcia Levy backed Eric's vocals as the band played on regardless, unleashing "Badge," "Let It Rain," "I Shot the Sheriff," and inevitably, "Layla." The applause, when it eventually came, was deafening and Ronnie Wood's appearance, resplendent in natty suit, won an ovation.

"What a marvellous band," Wood said encouragingly, paying his respects to the Guv'nor, who had seemed upset by unfriendly elements in the crowd. They confirmed Clapton's worst suspicions about "home" audiences, who he felt were the toughest to entertain. Maybe their presence inspired the title of Clapton's next album.

461 Ocean Boulevard

THE CLASSIC ALBUMS

461 Ocean Boulevard was released in 1974, peaking at No. 1 in the U.K., No. 3 in the United States; it went gold in both countries.

Eric Clapton's comeback album proved a bestseller and provided him with two of his biggest hits of the 1970s: "I Shot the Sheriff" and "Willie and the Hand Jive." The 1974 LP is a well-balanced selection of songs, devoid of great drama or instrumental panache but rich in tasteful and personal performances. Clapton reveals his growing confidence as a singer and composer, taking a step onward from Layla with such songs as the poignant "Give Me Strength." Here, he intones "Dear Lord, give me strength to carry on," delivering a plea of heartbreaking intensity. The mood is complemented by the distinctive tone of his resonator acoustic guitar.

There is guitar power aplenty as Clapton is teamed with George Terry on opening track "Motherless Child" that reveals a happy band at work, energized by Jamie Oldaker's spirited drumming. The sessions recorded in a relaxing atmosphere at Miami's Criteria Studios seemed to put Clapton into a positive and constructive frame of mind after his much publicized fight with drugs. Even so he takes it easy a lot of the time. The rhythmic Johnny Otis hit "Willie and the Hand Jive" is taken at a surprisingly slow pace yet seems to benefit from a slow burn.

Other ditties, such as "Get Ready" sung with Yvonne Elliman, are almost too relaxed for their own good, but it's reassuring to hear Clapton's laughter as the track fades out in desultory fashion. "I Shot the Sheriff" was the surprise choice of a classic Bob Marley song. The reggae pulse gave Clapton a new direction and a smash hit that became a staple of his live shows for many years. In direct contrast, he harked back to R&B days with "I Can't Hold Out." It slots comfortably into the organ and guitar groove British bands loved to play at London's Flamingo Club in the 1960s.

Clapton seemed to be trying to please all aspects of his fan base by mixing and matching styles, but ultimately the prevailing impression of 461 Ocean Boulevard is of a man intent on taking care of himself and treating everything with caution. His interpretation of Charles Scott Boyer's "Please Be With Me" is gentle and lilting, a clear description of his own state of mind. While audiences out in the wilds of rock may have carelessly bellowed for "Steppin' Out," the man in touch with his feminine side was more concerned with delicacy and personal affairs.

Another steady-paced Clapton composition, "Let It Grow," reveals a deep vocal tone as he sings at his best, moving away from the rather nasal drawl he sometimes affected. This excellent song was good enough to be covered by other artists.

In the midst of such balladeering came "Steady Rollin' Man," a Robert Johnson blues tune that provided a much needed emotional lift with Jim Fox' upbeat drive on the drums. The final jam session "Mainline Florida" is a celebration of an album well done and a location that provided the best possible vibes for music making and mind healing.

Clapton coaxes a blue note from "Blackie," 1978.
Richard E. Aaron/Redferns/Getty Images

2090 166

ERIC CLAPTON

KNOCKING ON HEAVEN'S DOOR

"Knocking on Heaven's Door," French issue, 1975.

There's One in Every Crowd was produced by Tom Dowd and released in April 1975. It powered up to No. 15 in the U.K. and No. 21 in the United States It also yielded another U.K. hit single with Clapton's version of the spiritual "Swing Low Sweet Chariot."

After their earlier success with "I Shot the Sheriff," Dowd suggested the band go to Jamaica to record to soak up the vibes and experience the true source of reggae. The band convened at Dynamic Sounds Studio in Kingston. Said Clapton: "When we got there, people were just wandering in and out of the studio, lighting up these massive joints. After a while I didn't know who was in the studio, there was so much smoke in the room."

In the end, it was decided to back track on the reggae influence, especially when Clapton realized he didn't really know what he was singing about or what the Jamaican musicians they met were talking about, due to their heavy accents. The band wasn't overly keen on the reggae direction either.

Clapton found his new status as a chart star a surprise that put him under pressure: "Going out on my own was a massive step which really shook me. I had to come to terms with the fact I was regarded as a pop musician as well as a rock 'n' roll musician and a blues musician. So I had to contrive an image that suited all these categories without disowning any part of my audience."

Meanwhile Clapton still wasn't quite getting his live performances properly balanced. At some shows, he'd tentatively kick off with an acoustic set, delivering low-key songs and accompanying himself on an acoustic Martin guitar. Then he'd turn up the heat with rock tunes and blues. "All the seventies were like that. I was trying to find my way. Later I went through a period of thinking I'd just do blues and R&B all night. But you can't satisfy everybody, or even yourself. If you do all blues, you'd still like to play 'Let It Rain' or 'Badge' because they are fun to play. For most of the seventies I was content to lay back and do what I had to do with the least amount of effort. I was grateful to be alive. I didn't want to push it."

Clapton also avoided trying to join in with the new wave of guitar players who wanted to play as loud and fast as possible, ironically inspired by his own example with Cream and by his old mate Jimmy Page with Led Zeppelin.

"The more I heard that style, the more I wanted to back off," said Clapton. Instead he developed his own relaxed and comfortable way of playing, saving any fireworks for the occasional heavy blues number and mostly singing the melodic hit songs that appealed to so many of his new fans.

Even so, he often seemed to be coasting rather than just relaxing. It was his way of coping with an increasing workload. There were extensive tours of Australia, Hawaii, and the United States scheduled during summer 1975. "I was underplaying a lot and I guess the band was still trying to get to know one another. I just wasn't keen to project myself as a guitarist because there were too many others who could top me. There is always someone faster, isn't there? I'm not a competitive guitarist and if I have to change my ways to top a poll, I'd rather not play at all."

Whether trying hard or not, the hits kept coming. A version of Bob Dylan's "Knocking on Heaven's Door" reached No. 38 in the U.K. Top 40 in August 1975. "Hello Old Friend" got to No. 24 in the U.S. Billboard chart in December 1976.

Keeping up the output, his record company also released a live album, *E.C. Was Here*, compiled from recordings made at Long Beach Arena, Long Beach, California, in July 1974, from London's Odeon Hammersmith in December 1974, and during the 1975 U.S. tour.

Explained Clapton: "I didn't really want to put it out, but the record company was worried about the sales of *There's One in Every Crowd*. They thought if they put out a live album to coincide with a tour it would help it sell."

There's One in Every Crowd, 1975.

Clapton rolls with the Rolling Stones onstage at Madison Square Garden on June 27, 1975. From left, Billy Preston, Clapton, Mick Jagger, Ron Wood, Keith Richards, and Charlie Watts. *Waring Abbott/Michael Ochs Archives/ Getty Images*

"I spend my time listening to people and being heavily influenced by them. Then when it comes time to record, I go down to the studio, try something new, and it comes out as me again."

—Eric Clapton, *Creem*, 1977

As well as touring with his own band, Clapton resumed his penchant for sitting in with fellow superstars and in March 1976 jammed with Rick Danko of the Band, Elton John, and Stevie Wonder at Los Angeles' Roxy. The jam took place while Clapton was working on his next album, *No Reason to Cry*, at Shangri-Las Studios near Malibu. Clapton and Carl Radle produced it, as Dowd was unable to work with them due to a contractual dispute. The regular musicians were augmented by percussionist Sergio Pastora Rodrigez, who joined the band during the 1975 U.S. tour and would stay with them until 1977.

Several of Clapton's heavy friends guested on the sessions, including Ronnie Wood, Bob Dylan, Georgie Fame, and the Band. Among the tracks was the new Clapton hit "Hello Old Friend" and some written with Danko, such as "All Our Past Times." Clapton had clearly begun to move away from the reggae feel toward American country rock, heavily influenced by the Band and his new favorite country singer, Don Williams.

With a plethora of lead guitarists taking care of business, Clapton stretched out only on an Otis Rush slow blues, "Double Trouble."

E.C. Was Here, 1975.

"Hello Old Friend," 1976.

Most of the time he was content to deliver a few slide guitar solos. Dylan's contribution was the song "Sign Language," which he claimed to have written after getting out of bed one morning. Clapton thought it was quite a surreal piece and proclaimed he'd thoroughly enjoyed all the sessions. His faith in the project was confirmed when *No Reason to Cry* got to No. 15 on the U.S. album chart and was a U.K. Top Ten hit. This was good timing, as Clapton was about due to tour the United Kingdom for the first time since the days of Derek and the Dominos.

Clapton played a warm-up show on July 29, 1976, at the Pavilion, Hemel Hempstead. He performed for an ecstatic audience while chain smoking and swigging from cans of beer, adopting his down-to-earth Cockney demeanor. It seemed like he was trying to find his way back to his English working-class roots after being caught up in the world of American rock 'n' roll for so long. At his next gig, he played South London's Crystal Palace Bowl and shared the stage with guest guitarists Freddie King, Larry Coryell, and Ronnie Wood.

During the latter half of 1976 and into 1977, Clapton spent more time relaxing at home, although he played a fun charity gig, raising funds for a hospital. He appeared incognito at a St. Valentine's Day dance at his local village hall with an outfit dubbed Eddie Earthquake and the Tremors. It actually comprised members of Ronnie Lane's band, Slim Chance. There was nothing Clapton liked more than getting away from all the razzmatazz of the rock circus and the scrutiny of the media. He'd sooner play under a pseudonym than be the guitar hero.

Andy Murray, an executive of Stiff Records, recalled seeing Clapton play a secret gig at a holiday camp at Hayling Island on the English south coast. "He played 'Layla' for all the mums, dads, and kids, and nobody seemed to recognize it. But when he played 'I Shot the Sheriff' they knew it was a hit. He was going to play at another Butlin's holiday camp, but they had seven thousand applications for tickets. The management panicked and cancelled the show."

Clapton set out on a U.K. tour in April 1977 supported by Ronnie Lane and Slim Chance. There was much merrymaking on the road. It got to the point where the drinking and heavy touring schedule began to make Clapton ill. When they appeared at London's Rainbow Theatre, Clapton had to walk off stage at the end of a number. Manager Roger Forrester took him outside for breath of fresh air. It seemed like Clapton would have to abandon the show, until Pete Townshend came into his dressing room and dragged him back on stage insisting the show had to go on. Clapton dutifully responded, summoning up all his strength to play "Crossroads" and "Layla."

To celebrate the finale of the Band, Clapton performed as part of *The Last Waltz* at San Francisco's Winterland Ballroom on November 25, 1975. From left, Robbie Robertson, Eric Clapton, Paul Butterfield, and Bobby Charles. *Ed Perlstein/Redferns/Getty Images*

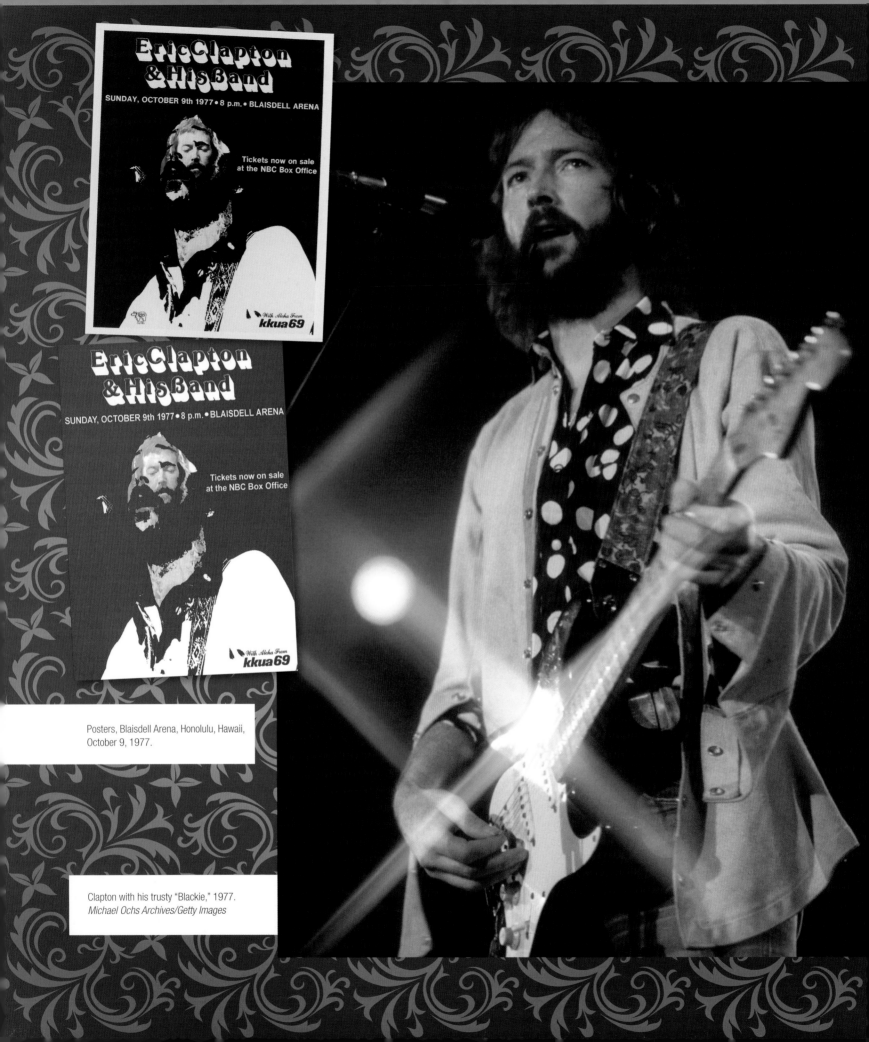

Eric Clapton & His Band

SUNDAY, OCTOBER 9th 1977 • 8 p.m. • BLAISDELL ARENA

Tickets now on sale
at the NBC Box Office

With Aloha From
kkua 69

Eric Clapton & His Band

SUNDAY, OCTOBER 9th 1977 • 8 p.m. • BLAISDELL ARENA

Tickets now on sale
at the NBC Box Office

With Aloha From
kkua 69

Posters, Blaisdell Arena, Honolulu, Hawaii,
October 9, 1977.

Clapton with his trusty "Blackie," 1977.
Michael Ochs Archives/Getty Images

After an exhausting tour, Clapton went into the studios to record his next album, *Slowhand*. Produced by Glyn Johns at Olympic Studios in Barnes, England, it was the first time Clapton had recorded in a U.K. studio since *Fresh Cream*. Released in November 1977, the new LP reflected his continued interest in country music, epitomized by Don Williams, whose work he much admired. It was a taste he shared with Ronnie Lane, who also sang the praises of the mild-mannered American singer.

Clapton found Glyn Johns a tougher producer than Tom Dowd. But the album was a success, and included "Wonderful Tonight," one of Clapton's best songs since "Layla." The opening track, "Cocaine," by J. J. Cale, would become a concert favorite.

The new year began well, as Clapton hit the charts with "Lay Down Sally," a track from *Slowhand* that reached No. 3 on the U.S. Billboard charts. The album peaked at No. 2, just behind *Saturday Night Fever*. In July, the moving "Wonderful Tonight," written for his wife, Pattie, reached No. 16 in the U.S. By now Clapton had earned his reputation as an important and gifted composer, far from the "stumbling writer" he'd once described himself as in Cream.

In November 1978, Clapton set out on a two-month European tour, with the ever-loyal Carl Radle, Jamie Oldaker, and Dick Sims, but without George Terry, who had quit after the recording sessions for the latest album, *Backless*.

Like *Slowhand*, the new LP was recorded at Olympic with Glyn Johns in the control room. Released in November, it would be Clapton's last album with his all-American band. The title was an in-joke, derived from Bob Dylan's habit of facing his own band and glaring at them when the backing music was going awry. Clapton had an association with Dylan going back to the 1960s; in 1978, he was even called up to work with Dylan on the bard's European tour.

"It was an inspiration working for Bob," Clapton says. "Sometimes he'd turn round and it would be like, 'Okay, you're not listening,' and he knew all the time if you were paying attention or not. He knew what everyone was doing behind him. The best gig we did was in Nuremberg. It was the place where Adolf used to hold the rallies. The place where he used to come out and stand on his podium was directly opposite us. It was a black doorway. And Bob had come out to an incredible atmosphere. The atmosphere was there, again but this time it was for a Jewish songwriter. And Bob didn't even *know*. I get on with Bob very well. I love him, he's a fantastic guy.

"The first time I worked with Bob was when I was with John Mayall. He came to London and liked John, who had made a record called 'Crawling Up a Hill.' Bob was very freaked out by this. After calling up London Zoo and asking if he could have a giraffe delivered to his hotel room, he called up John and we did a session at Chappell's in Bond Street. Tom Wilson was the producer and there was a huge entourage. People were telling me, 'Don't play country style—play city, go electric, don't play acoustic.'

"Bob gets on the piano and starts playing. The next thing you know, there's nothing happening. Silence. And I said, 'What's happening? Where's he gone?' And he'd gone to Madrid! This was back in 1965. It's never been a serious friendship. We just jive. It's like working with Muddy Waters, you know? We don't talk seriously. That's forbidden."

SLOWHAND
TOUR
1978

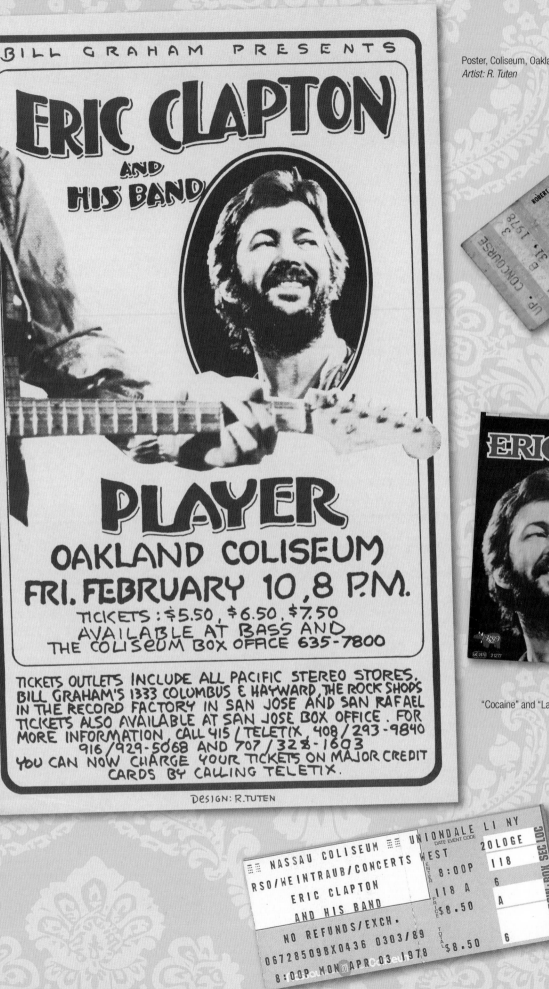

BILL GRAHAM PRESENTS

ERIC CLAPTON
AND HIS BAND

PLAYER
OAKLAND COLISEUM
FRI. FEBRUARY 10, 8 P.M.
TICKETS : $5.50, $6.50, $7.50
AVAILABLE AT BASS AND
THE COLISEUM BOX OFFICE 635-7800

TICKETS OUTLETS INCLUDE ALL PACIFIC STEREO STORES,
BILL GRAHAM'S 1333 COLUMBUS & HAYWARD, THE ROCK SHOPS
IN THE RECORD FACTORY IN SAN JOSE AND SAN RAFAEL
TICKETS ALSO AVAILABLE AT SAN JOSE BOX OFFICE. FOR
MORE INFORMATION CALL 415 / TELETIX, 408 / 293-9840
916 / 929-5068 AND 707 / 328-1603
YOU CAN NOW CHARGE YOUR TICKETS ON MAJOR CREDIT
CARDS BY CALLING TELETIX.

DESIGN: R.TUTEN

Poster, Coliseum, Oakland, California, February 10, 1978.
Artist: R. Tuten

"Cocaine" and "Lay Down Sally," French issue, 1978.

In December, the Clapton band played United Kingdom dates while Clapton had to fend off rumors of a proposed Cream gig. Ginger Baker had wanted to bring Clapton and Jack Bruce together again at his polo club to play a special concert. Unfortunately word leaked to the national press and the polo fraternity panicked, expecting an invasion of rockers on their hallowed ground. The Cream reunion was hastily cancelled.

Although Clapton had cut back on his drinking, he was still up for partying until five a.m. after a concert at the Gaumont Southampton, England. He went to a local disco keen to celebrate and found that the local girls were unimpressed by Eric's John Travolta–style routines. To his chagrin they refused to join him on the floor. In the end he put a bandana round his head and danced alone.

After years of avoiding publicity and trying to shake off his fame, Clapton, now in his thirties, went unrecognized by the younger generation. When he attempted to chat to a pair of girls sitting at his hotel bar, they had not the faintest idea who he was. He was shocked to discover they'd never heard of Cream nor Bob Dylan, for that matter.

"What do you work at?" asked one girl, puzzled by this dishevelled man surrounded by a posse of photographers and reporters.

"Musician," he responded as if he were saying "bricklayer" or "industrial cleaning contractor."

"What sort?"

"A rock 'n' roll musician."

The girls persisted with their probing questions. What was he doing here in Southampton, they wanted to know.

"I've come to do a gig here, haven't I," said Eric. "We played the Gaumont. Last night." He began to sound testy. "Last night was a gas! Not many. Dear o' Lor'. It steamed along. My band is incredibly tight."

Clapton was proud of his band and annoyed at complaints that they sometimes seemed sloppy. As far he was concerned, they were firing on all cylinders, especially since they had cut down to a four-piece. It was his most comfortable mode of working since the Dominos.

As Clapton would explain: "When we had the two girl singers and George Terry on guitar, I was always looking from one side of the stage to the other to check out what was going on. Two of the girls would be redundant a lot of the time, just sitting in chairs. That saps your energy and I don't think it was good for anybody. Trouble is, I can't fire people. Yvonne Elliman finally left because she wanted to pursue a solo career. The Dominos was a four-piece, and I enjoyed that. It's the whole thing about having a Booker T–type feel. I have to work more, it's true, and that's what I really enjoy doing. Everybody has to work. We started out trying too hard and over-compensating. Now it's a lot more simplified."

No snow, no show: Clapton on stage at the Oakland Coliseum on February 10, 1978. *Ed Perlstein/Redferns/Getty Images*

Despite this simplification, the rigors of touring were still taking their toll, and Clapton summed up his feelings at this halfway stage in his career: "I'm tired, man, really tired. I went to a disco last night, and there were some really ugly birds there. There were about twenty bouncers to every fella. I spent most of my time chatting up the bouncers, so I wouldn't get hit. I was going to have a dance competition last night. I was all wound up and going to give it plenty, but no chance. None of the girls wanted to dance. I've always been a dancer. I've been a dancer all me life. But the best dancer in the world is Bob Marley."

At the hotel bar, one of the girls plucked up courage and finally asked him the ultimate question that would solve the mystery.

"What do you do in your group?" she asked sweetly.

"I play guitar and sing," said Eric Clapton pleasantly.

Clapton settled into a productive routine in the 1970s during which he toured assiduously, dutifully releasing an album every year. The high musical dramas of the Cream years were far behind him, however, and his albums, while pleasant enough, veered toward middle-of-the-road rock rather than cutting-edge innovation.

Perhaps it was enough that Clapton had simply survived and was still capable of writing and performing. There were sparks of genius when he was in the right mood and his popularity remained steady. He maintained that equilibrium by adopting a down-to-earth attitude toward fame and work.

He confessed that he did as little of the latter as possible. When asked about his approach to guitar playing, he replied, "Nah, I don't practice, I get my inspiration from the band. That's where it comes from. They're the source. If I'm on my own in a room, who have I got to play for? I'll write a song maybe, if it's there to write. I like to play for other people. It's always for someone else. You don't do anything for your own pleasure, do you? There is a point where you've got something almost right, and you don't want to present it to anybody, unless it's absolutely right. But I'm not a perfectionist. Unskilled labor and hard work. That's all it is."

Clapton seemed to have recovered from his years of drug and alcohol dependency, but there was a residual sense of disorientation in the aftermath and his health had been undermined.

Looking back to his mid-1970s revival, he said, "I was worried. I just didn't know where I was going. I didn't know whether I should carry on, or whether I should pack it in altogether. And then a song came along. It was 'Dear Lord, Give Me Strength.' It just kept coming back to me like a dream. I thought if I didn't do something, then I would be letting people down. That gave me the strength to carry on being a musician."

There were practical considerations as well, and these sustained Clapton's need to work in the post-Dominos years. As he explained in 1978, "I couldn't knock it on the head, anyway. Businesswise I was in breach of contract, because I hadn't done anything for three years. My contract said I had to make at least two albums a year and go on the road. So I *had* to and it was in the back of my mind.

"It was also a matter of loyalty and word of honor. Robert Stigwood would never have come down on me, but I had given my word, whether it was written on paper or a handshake. That was a strong factor in pulling me through too. Now I'm enjoying playing and there's nothing in the way."

Like many rock musicians, he still had to endure noisy mavericks in audiences who showed little respect toward the artist on stage. More than most, Clapton seemed to spark shouts and bizarre requests while he was trying to play. He learned to adopt a resolutely protective, insular attitude.

"I don't take any notice. I just look at the exit signs. I can just about see the kids coming in and going out. At one gig kids started shouting at me, 'Duane Allman!' and 'Jack Bruce!' They actually stood up and shouted in a roar. They didn't even seem to realize that Duane had been dead for four years and Jack had his own band. So when that happens I just show them the back of my guitar and walk off, after doing my allotted time, of course."

It might seem that Clapton's past hung over him like a cloud, but he felt this was more of a problem for others than himself. "It doesn't hang over me. I can handle it. But I feel for my band. There are three other people playing on stage with me and they get hurt by all that. It incenses me, it really does. But then you don't always know what's going through that guy's mind, when he shouts for Duane Allman. He might just be saying 'Great, do you remember Duane Allman?'

"But Cream, with Jack and Ginger, that was *years* ago. And I've been back on the road now, longer than I was ever off the road. I'm still a road musician and I can see that going on forever. I'm a wanderer, a gypsy. I get three days off, I go home and I have a row with everybody. I wander about and complain about things. Get back on the road, and I'm as happy as a sandboy. I've been on the road too long, man, I can't give it up. I'll stay on the road until I drop, mate. Until I drop."

Whatever the competition from new waves of guitar heroes and changing fashions, Clapton had his innate ability to maintain his popularity and status. And he did it without relying on high-speed pyrotechnics and special effects.

"What comes out of the guitar is the most important thing. I can still blow myself away. But if you are being watched and examined to see whether or not you can pull it off and you blow it, people come down hard on you. They expect so much."

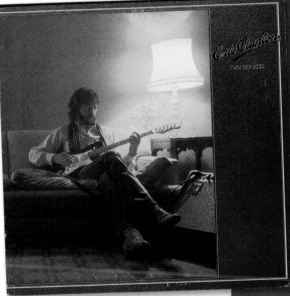

Backless was released in 1978, going silver in the U.K. and platinum in the United States.

In March 1978, Clapton began his *Backless* world tour with a new, all-British band. He had decided to dispense with his American mates, including Carl Radle, who had helped get his career back on track. Drummer Jamie Oldaker also declared he wanted to settle down and take a rest. Clapton's new recruits included Albert Lee, a self-effacing, much-admired lead guitarist who had formerly played with R&B group Chris Farlowe and the Thunderbirds. The others were keyboardist Chris Stainton, bassist Dave Markee, and drummer Henry Spinetti. Stainton had been a member of Joe Cocker's Grease Band while the latter two had played as studio musicians with Roger Daltrey, Joan Armatrading, and Leo Sayer.

Poster, Forest-Vorst Nationaal, Brussels, Belgium, November 19, 1978.

DIMANCHE ZONDAG **19 NOVEMBRE**RER **20h** **FOREST - VORST NATIONA[A]L**

ERIC CLAPTON

and special guest
MUDDY WATERS

LOCATION:
EST-VORST NATIONA[A]L 02/345.90.50   CAROLINE MUSIC 02/512 60 21

MARSHBROOK LTD in conjunction with HARVEY GOLDSMITH ENTERTAINMENTS LTD

WOULD LIKE TO THANK

ERIC CLAPTON
AND HIS BAND

FOR A SELL-OUT EUROPEAN TOUR '78

NOVEMBER
5th PABELLON DEPORTIVO DEL REAL MADRID
6th CLUB JUVENTUD, BARCELONA
8th PALAIS DES SPORTS, LYON
10th SAARLANDHALLE, SAARBRUCKEN
11th FESTHALLE, FRANKFURT
12th OLYMPIA HALLE, MUNICH
14th PHILLIPSHALLE, DUSSELDORF
15th CONGRESSCENTRUM, HAMBURG
16th CONGRESSCENTRUM, HAMBURG
18th LE PAVILLION, PARIS
19th FOREST NATIONAL, BRUSSELS
20th JAP EDENHAL, AMSTERDAM
24th APOLLO THEATRE, GLASGOW
25th CITY HALL, NEWCASTLE UPON TYNE
26th APOLLO THEATRE, MANCHESTER
28th VICTORIA HALL, HANLEY
29th GALA BALLROOM, WEST BROMWICH
DECEMBER
1st GAUMONT THEATRE, SOUTHAMPTON
2nd CONFERENCE CENTRE, BRIGHTON
5th ODEON THEATRE, HAMMERSMITH
6th ODEON THEATRE, HAMMERSMITH
7th CIVIC HALL, GUILDFORD

SPECIAL GUEST STAR MUDDY WATERS.

Marshbrook Limited
67 Brook Street, London W1Y 1YE. Telephone (01) 629 9121. Telex: 264267.

Harvey Goldsmith Entertainments Limited
7 Welbeck Street, London W1M 7PB. Telephone (01) 487 5303/6. Telex: 22721.

Advertisement, European tour, 1978.

Clapton's presence in the U.S. Top 40 singles chart was maintained by "Promises," which got to No. 9 in January 1979, followed by the B-side "Watch Out For Lucy," which reached No. 40 in March.

The *Backless* tour began on March 8 with dates in Ireland followed by a full U.S. tour.

In the midst of all this work came a dramatic development. After pressure from his manager, Clapton decided to marry his long-term girlfriend, Pattie Boyd, at a ceremony in Tucson, Arizona, on March 27, 1979. The reception held in their honor at a nearby hotel ended in a typically Clapton-inspired cake fight. The next night, he and the band commenced the tour in Tucson and carried on until on June 24 with a show at the Seattle Coliseum. This exhausting expedition crisscrossed the States, visiting nearly every major city and included guest appearances by Muddy Waters.

Back in England after the tour, Clapton and his new wife held a wedding celebration party with celebrity guests including Mick Jagger, Jeff Beck, Jack Bruce, and Lonnie Donegan. There was even a jam session with the amazing lineup of Paul McCartney, George Harrison, and Ringo Starr. John Lennon later said he would have come over from New York to join his former Beatle mates if he'd been invited.

After a brief rest, it was back to work on a European tour commencing on October 6, 1979, in Austria, followed by shows in Germany, Yugoslavia, Croatia, and Poland—Eric's first appearance behind the Iron Curtain. While he had grown used to noisy audiences and people shouting for requests, nothing prepared him for the scenes that greeted them during the Polish dates in October.

The country, then still under Soviet domination, was virtually a police state. The band played without incident in Warsaw, but when they arrived at the Hala Sportowo in Katowice on October 17, the police reacted violently when

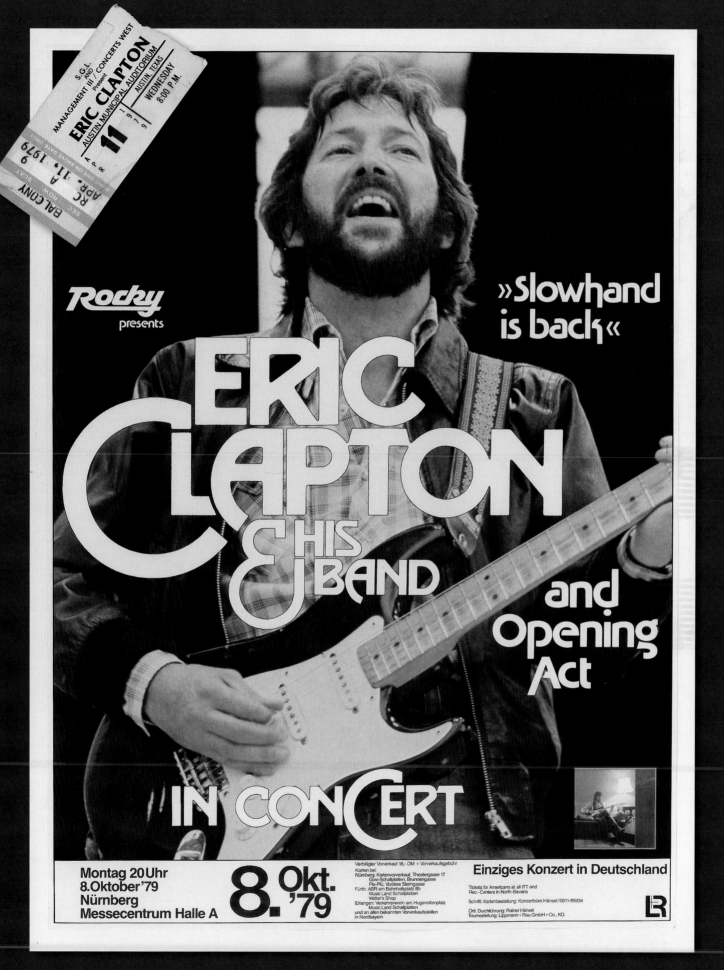

Poster, Messe Centrum, Nuremberg, Germany, October 8, 1979.

the young audience became overenthusiastic. The police sprayed exuberant fans with mace to calm them down, and the subsequent mêlée wrecked the P.A. system. The band was blamed by the authorities and had to flee the country without being paid.

The tour moved on to Israel, and then in November commenced a string of dates in the Far East, visiting Thailand, the Philippines, and Hong Kong. On November 23, they arrived in Japan, and after visiting varies cities, they recorded tracks for a live double set, *Just One Night*, at the Budokan, Tokyo, on December 3 and 4. The album was produced by British recording engineer Jon Astley and released in May 1980. It was the first recording by Clapton's new band.

Astley, who enjoyed his own career as a singer in the 1980s, has fond memories of his time working with Clapton. He recalls that Tokyo's Budokan was a favorite venue among visiting Western rock stars: "Both Cheap Trick and Bob Dylan had recorded live records there, and I thought if we could use the same Japanese guys who recorded them, it would be great. They actually built us a control room in one of the dressing rooms, rather than set up a mobile studio. And it worked a treat. It was all based on one performance by Eric on his first night. The second night at the Budokan wasn't as good. Critics said it was an 'over produced and over corrected album,' but it really wasn't. There was just one bass note we had to repair out of the whole record. Everything else was exactly as it was recorded that night.

"But Eric wasn't supposed to know I was there. I was smuggled in and out by his manager Roger Forrester. He was worried Eric would get nervous. Roger said I'd have to take all the microphones down from the auditorium in case Eric saw them. But really, I think Eric knew damn well I was there!"

Just One Night included "Tulsa Time" and versions of "Lay Down Sally" and "Wonderful Tonight." After working on the album, Astley says that he introduced Clapton to the next big passion in his life.

"Trout fishing. I took him down to Roger Daltrey's place where he had a fish farm and said, 'Have a go.' He loved it and now he's got his own beautiful piece of trout river. He's even been salmon fishing on helicopters in Russia and loves game fishing in Siberia. It's not putting a worm on a hook and sitting beside the canal bank these days. He and Steve Winwood are like country gents together. 'Let's go shooting this weekend. No, let's go fishing!' They get into their four-by-fours and go off for the weekend's sport wearing all the right gear."

As the new decade dawned, the Eric Clapton Band set off on a thirteen-date U.K. tour in May 1980, augmented by new recruit Gary Brooker, former keyboard player and vocalist with Procol Harum. That same month, *Just One Night* shot to No. 3 on the U.K. album chart. It seemed a time for celebration—until Clapton learned the sad news that his former American bandmate Carl Radle had fallen ill and then succumbed to a kidney infection.

Clapton first met Radle in the days when Delaney and Bonnie supported Blind Faith on tour. The bassist later helped put the Dominos together and worked on the *Layla* album. When Clapton made his comeback with *461 Ocean*

Boulevard, Radle was there as a friend and adviser and remained a part of his band for another five years. Known as a musician's musician, Radle died at age thirty-seven on May 30, 1980.

More such personal losses and tragedies affected Clapton over the coming decades, and there were times when he responded by falling off the wagon.

The year 1981 began well when his latest album, *Another Ticket*, released in February, shot into the U.S. and U.K. charts. It was produced by old associate Tom Dowd and recorded at Compass Point studios in the Bahamas. It featured his latest band together with new member Gary Brooker. Among the outstanding tracks were Clapton originals "Something Special" and "I Can't Stand It," which was a Top Ten U.S. hit. The album itself topped the U.S. album charts for two weeks.

In March 1981, Clapton was taken ill, suffering from bleeding ulcers. This was simply the result of years of eating rich food and drinking too much. He collapsed during a show in Madison, Wisconsin, and was rushed to a hospital. The rest of a major sixty-date U.S. tour was cancelled. Clapton spent his thirty-sixth birthday in St. Paul's United Hospital in Philadelphia.

Just four days after leaving the hospital, he was involved in a car crash in Seattle. The car he was riding in shot a red light and hit another car before colliding with a telephone pole. As result of these disasters, future tours of Japan and South America were cancelled.

Clapton had a history of unpleasant experiences on the road in the States. He recalled a particularly hectic interlude during the Cream years. "I once spent the night in the L.A. County jail. I was busted for being in a place where smoke was being used.

"I was hanging out with Buffalo Springfield and they all got 'done.' Neil Young had a fit, because he had a history of epilepsy. In jail, we had to take all our clothes off and line up for mug shots. Then they hosed us down and sprayed us with insecticide and took our clothes away. While they were doing all this Neil just went, 'Wh-o-o-a-!'

"They took him out of the room, and it was the last I saw of him. I spent the night in a cell with three Black Panthers and I had to convince them that I was a blues guitarist.

"When I look back, it was a good experience. I know never to get busted. No way. One night of that was hell. It's a good idea when they take young offenders to a prison and show them what it's like, because it's not like joining the Army. And I had *pink* boots on and a frizzed-out Afro hairstyle. I was wearing all my psychedelic gear."

The wardens took all his bracelets and chains away, and he had to wear blue denims with "L.A. County Jail" written on them. "But they left me in my pink boots and threw me in a cell with three Black Panthers. It was like I was a punk, you know? I just had to keep talking and tell them I was English and didn't really understand what was going on. I told them I played blues guitar and dug Willie Dixon, Muddy Waters, Bo Diddley, and Chuck Berry. It worked.

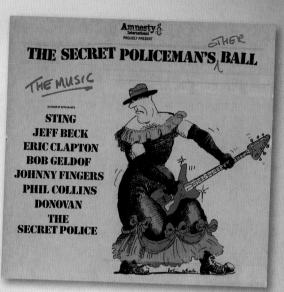

Clapton joined Jeff Beck and others for Amnesty International's *The Secret Policeman's Other Ball*, 1981.

"Blues Power," 1980.

"BLUES POWER"

☆ **ERIC CLAPTON** ☆

"EARLY IN THE MORNING"
RSO 1051

It cooled them out—just about. I think they had been in for about three or four years. Eventually I applied for bail. There was one guy there who had been applying for bail every day for seven years, but nobody had put the money up for him."

In 1982, Clapton ended his long association with Robert Stigwood and his RSO label. With Roger Forrester, he created his own Duck record label distributed by Warner Bros. However, there was no Clapton album released in 1982. In the midst of much personal turmoil, he suffered a relapse into drinking and decided to check into Hazleden Treatment Center in Center City, Minnesota, where he was treated for alcoholism.

The beneficial results were that Clapton was better able to refocus his mind and reorganize his life. The rest of the 1980s and 1990s became the era when he forged new friendships, made better albums, and adopted a smarter, cooler image. He wore Armani suits and drove a Ferrari while hobnobbing with the rich and famous. After all, Clapton had become rich himself, with an estimated net worth of some £120,000,000, putting him among the musical elite's top earners. He was no longer "Derek" or a "musical laborer." He was a celebrity and hailed as a rock 'n' roll elder statesman.

Just One Night, 1980.

At the end of 1982, Clapton's all-British backing band was broken up. Henry Spinetti and Dave Markee left the group and were replaced by an American rhythm section consisting of famed Booker T and the MGs bassist Duck Dunn and drummer Roger Hawkins. In 1983, Clapton celebrated his twentieth year as a professional musician by releasing *Money and Cigarettes*. It had been two decades since he first joined Casey Jones and the Engineers.

The new album was produced by Tom Dowd and recorded in the Bahamas. Clapton's band was augmented by guest artist Ry Cooder on slide guitar, and the album was hailed as one of his best in years. It got to No. 16 in the United States and No. 13 in the U.K. The tracks included "I've Got a Rock 'n' Roll Heart," which peaked at No. 18 in the United States in February 1983, and a satisfying version of the Sleepy John Estes song "Everybody Oughta Make a Change," which seemed an appropriate message from the reforming Mr. Clapton.

Amidst all the excitement over *Money and Cigarettes*, a song was brought out of the archives and re-issued: this new version of "Layla" became a No. 4 hit single in the U.K. in April.

It was a time to feel generous, and in March that year Clapton took part in a unique benefit concert at London's Royal Albert Hall, organized to raise money for Ronnie Lane, former bassist with the Small Faces and the Faces who had succumbed to crippling multiple sclerosis. The show took place on September 20, and among the highlights was the historic spectacle of Eric

Timepieces: The Best of Eric Clapton, 1982.

Clapton, Jimmy Page, and Jeff Beck performing together on stage for the first time. Steve Winwood, Andy Fairweather Low, Charlie Watts, Bill Wyman, and Kenny Jones were among the other musicians who took part. The old guitar heroes delighted the audience by playing their own spots. Beck performed "Hi Ho Silver Lining" and Page played an instrumental version of "Stairway to Heaven." Then came the great moment when Beck, Page, and Clapton joined forces for the ultimate ex-Yardbirds lineup, playing "Tulsa Time," "Louise," and "Layla" to emotional cheers.

The concert was such a success that the concept was repeated with an eight-date ARMS (Action for Research into Multiple Sclerosis) tour of the United States with extra guests Paul Rodgers and Joe Cocker. It concluded with a sellout concert at Madison Square Garden on December 8, 1983.

The year 1984 was quieter, but it was a time when Clapton could revive an old friendship and start a new one. He joined Bob Dylan on stage at a concert at London's Wembley Arena. And he began recording yet another album. It would be a new challenging time for Clapton with more upheavals in his personal life to come. The rock 'n' roll gypsy still had a long road to travel.

Brothers in arms: Jimmy Page, Clapton, and Jeff Beck perform at the ARMS Charity Concert at London's Royal Albert Hall in September 1983. *Larry Hulst/Michael Ochs Archives/Getty Images*

Amidst a kaleidoscope of lights, Clapton plays "Blackie," 1984.
Michael Ochs Archives/Getty Images

Behind the Sun, 1985.

Slowhand, 1977.

Hailed as one of Eric Clapton's best, 1977's *Slowhand* is a great improvement on the star-studded *No Reason to Cry* released the previous year. It certainly became a big commercial success. The reasons were partly due to the fact that Clapton had eschewed guest musicians and concentrated his writing and performing in closer contact with his regular band.

The result is a tight, well-recorded set where many of the imperfections of the past, such as jumbled mixes and overlapping layers of guitar, are firmly radicated. The clean sound obtained at London's Olympic Studios can be credited to producer Glyn Johns, who kept a tight rein over proceedings.

Slowhand has a number of palpable hits, including "Wonderful Tonight," "Lay Down Sally," and J. J. Cale's controversial "Cocaine." When Clapton performed "Cocaine" live at an English concert, some thuggish youths yelled out in protest. This was, of course, in the era before the local working class adopted cocaine as their drug of choice, having previously stayed loyal to beer and potato chips.

Clapton the lyricist and singer surpasses himself on "Wonderful Tonight" as he describes the cosmetic preparations of his beloved before heading off to dance at a party. Tiptoeing along to a delicate but firm beat, his lyrics captivate the imagination. You can visualize the bearded guitarist surveying the object of his affection with a beating heart: "Darling, you look wonderful tonight." One can see her twirling around to tell her rock 'n' roll suitor to have a shave and straighten his tie.

There is still a country rock mood that pervaded Claptonia during the 1970s, and "Lay Down Sally" is a typical example. Written with Marcia Levy, it flows along with the effortless virtuosity only experienced, mature musicians can achieve. The hoedown riff doesn't want to stop, so they just fade it out. Hard to believe such all-American rural feeling was achieved on the banks of the river Thames and not the Mississippi.

Not all the songs are brilliant. "Next Time You See Her" has a rather weak vocal, and the lyrics are simplistic to the point of banality. Yet being Clapton, it is a forgivable offense and the tune has the nagging ability to penetrate the memory and stay there, as does the more serious "We're All the Way."

When Clapton and the band finally get into cooking mode, "The Core" provides a neatly arranged ensemble piece with lots of breaks and tricky tags. One wonders if Clapton learned to read musical scores to help interpret such demanding charts or whether he relied on scribbled notes on the backs of cigarette packs.

Those still seeking the blues were no doubt pleased with the inclusion of "Mean Old Frisco," one of the album's sturdiest tracks. Taken at a measured pace, it is filled with glorious lowdown licks.

If all this was too earthy for his more romantically inclined admirers, *Slowhand* climaxes with the beautifully conceived instrumental piece "Peaches and Diesel," which is full of pregnant pauses and graceful melodies.

Quite where Clapton was going with *Slowhand* is difficult to judge from this distance in time, but the album shows a man taking one step at a time in the search for peace and satisfaction.

"Blackie"

There are few guitars anywhere so famous. Perhaps B. B. King's "Lucille." Or Stevie Ray Vaughan's "No. 1." But "Blackie"—the well-traveled, well-used, and much-loved black Fender Stratocaster that Clapton used through much of his career—has become an icon of the guitar world.

"I was in Nashville at a store called Sho-Bud, as I recall, and they had a whole rack of old '50s Strats in the back, going secondhand. They were so out of fashion you could pick up a perfectly genuine Strat for two hundred or three hundred dollars—even less! So I bought all of them. I gave one to Steve Winwood, one to George Harrison, and one to Pete Townshend, and kept a few for myself. I liked the idea of a black body, but the black one I had was in bad condition, so I took apart the ones I kept and assembled different pieces to make 'Blackie,' which is a hybrid, a mongrel."

—Eric Clapton

Clapton's hybrid Fender Stratocaster "Blackie."
Robert Knight Archive/Redferns/Getty Images

Clapton's hybrid Fender Stratocaster "Blackie."
Robert Knight Archive/Redferns/Getty Images

"'Blackie' has become part of me."
—Eric Clapton

Working closely with Clapton, Fender created a replica run of "Blackie" Stratocasters, complete with authentic Duck Bros. case and other accoutrements.
Fender Musical Instruments Corporation

Money and Cigarettes, 1983.

Money and cigarettes

A Salvador Dali-esque image depicting a guitar melting over an ironing board makes a striking image for Clapton's 1983 offering *Money and Cigarettes*. He had returned to Compass Point in Nassau to make the new album. But the heat of the electric iron and the weather in the Bahamas was not necessarily matched by the temperature raised in the studio. Some felt that the music was bland and claimed that Clapton was on autopilot while playing through a brace of allegedly lukewarm tracks.

And yet Clapton came equipped with a hot new band for the occasion, including bassist Donald "Duck" Dunn of Booker T and the MGs and drummer Roger Hawkins. Albert Lee guested on guitar and vocals together with the much-respected Ry Cooder on slide guitar.

Although critics were harsh in their verdicts, in retrospect *Money and Cigarettes* (Clapton smoked sixty a day at this time) has much to recommend it. Not least the hit track, "I've Got a Rock 'n' Roll Heart," which once again showed Clapton's unerring ability to flip out a zippy pop tune at the drop of a guitar pick. "I get off on screaming guitars . . ." he sings with rare irony.

"Everybody Oughta Make a Change" is the swinging opening number, credited to bluesman Sleepy John Estes. It offers a sound piece of advice that many people of his generation subconsciously took to heart, thanks to Clapton's example. He emphasizes the point with a series of tips such as the need to change suits, shirts, money, and people.

Clapton, of course, changed his appearance drastically over the years, and the cover of the album shows a smart-suited dude gazing confidently at the camera and holding a cigarette twixt be-ringed fingers. The money was presumably being well cared for in the nearest bank.

As well as changing his shirt and tie, Clapton was also subtly changing the way he made records, keeping a calmer profile as he was comfortable about projecting himself as the main man, taking charge and making decisions. That confidence is expressed on "The Shape You're In," a lively tune with nifty guitar licks and solos that push the beat as he sings, "Take it easy, take it slow"— fine advice on health and sobriety. "Ain't Going Down" is a bright, assertive piece that builds a head of steam over a pulsing bass riff. Clapton wails forth a howling solo before the final chorus. This is another of those exhilarating sequences no musician ever wants to end.

There's good time rock 'n' roll a plenty on "Slow Down Linda," while "Pretty Girl" is a cut-glass ballad that sways with the comforting rhythm of a rocking chair. It is one of Clapton's most perfectly formed songs delivered with a rare sense of dynamics. If critics and fans thought this was all getting too soft, "Crosscut Saw" injects funk and blues into the mix.

Money and Cigarettes proved a highly successful album and has much to recommend it, despite the reservations of sceptics. As with much of Clapton's work, it matures with age.

11. Autumn Leaves

Crossroads Foundation, Cream Reunion, and Touring with Steve Winwood, 1983–2010

D. A. PENNEBAKER'S 1965 FILM OF BOB DYLAN carried a message in its title of *Don't Look Back*. Yet Eric Clapton began the process of looking back just when his career was reaching a pinnacle. He had enjoyed unprecedented success and was showered with accolades during the twenty-five years that followed the Clapton revival of the 1980s.

His motivation had always been to push forward, to keep on working in the hope he'd find peace of mind and please those who supported him loyally through good and bad times. In those days, there were ambitions left to fulfill and fresh challenges to meet. But as he matured into middle age, the once-reckless Clapton attained a dignity more appropriate to a revered rock icon. Now he could afford to slow down and take stock.

As a guitarist, his playing became ever more sophisticated and technically polished. When pushed he could respond with all of his old fire and feeling for the blues. But where he once sought oblivion, he now enjoyed a life without stimulants. He could see and think more clearly. As happiness and contentment came, he considered his good fortune and felt the need to give thanks and make reparations.

Clapton plays the blues, 1990. *Terry O'Neill/Getty Images*

Clapton set up the Crossroads Foundation to help other victims of the drugs and alcohol culture that had nearly wrecked his own life. He'd always been a generous man; now he could find more practical ways to help. He also wanted to heal the wounds of the past and bring closure to unfinished business.

Hence the surprise decision to reunite with former colleagues Jack Bruce and Ginger Baker and revive Cream in 2005. It was a reunion dreamt about by fans but always deemed unlikely. It was all part of the process in which Clapton was happy to look back—and be proud.

In 1983, he had spent some time recording with former Pink Floyd composer and singer Roger Waters for a project called *The Pros and Cons of Hitch Hiking*. Clapton later performed on stage with Waters at London's Earls Court in June 1984 and joined him for tour dates in Europe and the United States.

Clapton supported Roger Waters on his 1984 solo debut album, *The Pros and Cons of Hitch Hiking*.

After this diversion, he concentrated on recording his next album, *Behind the Sun*, at George Martin's Air Studios in Montserrat during the summer of 1984. It was produced by Phil Collins, the Genesis drummer and singer who had enjoyed great solo success with his album *Face Value*. Clapton and Collins were neighbors in Surrey and formed a close friendship. It was Collins' intention to update Clapton's sound and improve on the rather jaded approach evident on albums such as *Money and Cigarettes*. Clapton bought a Roland guitar synthesizer and found working with Collins an invigorating experience.

Many of Clapton's songs written for *Behind the Sun* reflect his marital problems with Pattie Boyd, notably "She's Waiting," "Same Old Blues," and "Just Like a Prisoner." The title song came from a line in Muddy Waters' song "Louisiana Blues."

Completed in a month, the album was rush-released in March 1985. Critics acclaimed Clapton's best guitar playing on record since his days with Cream, especially on "Forever Man," which became a Top 40 hit single in the United States and was featured in a popular MTV video.

In 1985, there was fresh turmoil in Clapton's private life. Returning home from tour dates in Australia and Hong Kong, he discovered that Boyd had left home and moved into a London flat; he was left alone in his mansion. During that year's world tour, he met and began an affair with Lori Del Santo, a photographer and TV actress who he met at a party in Italy. This led to Del Santo becoming pregnant and giving birth to their son,

Surrounded by his Marshall amps, Fender guitars, and Duck Bros.–stenciled flight cases, Clapton poses for a portrait backstage before a performance, 1985.
David Montgomery/Getty Images

August, 1986.

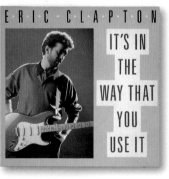

Conor, on August 15, 1986. Clapton and Pattie Boyd were divorced the following year.

Clapton took center stage once more when he was invited to appear on the world's largest ever rock event, Live Aid, which was performed simultaneously at the JFK Stadium in Philadelphia and Wembley Stadium in London. Millions watched around the world on TV on July 13, 1985, as organizer Bob Geldoff raised money for the starving in Ethiopia. Clapton's performance in Philadelphia turned out to be a difficult gig. Lacking rehearsal time, he chose to play Cream's "White Room," a song he hadn't performed in years. He got an electric shock off the microphone, which unsettled him even more. But when Phil Collins joined Jamie Oldaker on the drums and Clapton launched into "Layla," their performance was greeted with thunderous applause. Live Aid proved to be a key element in boosting Clapton's career.

During 1986, Clapton and American movie music composer Michael Kamen wrote a score for the BBC TV drama series *Edge of Darkness*. Writing for TV and films was a welcome departure. Back on stage, Clapton took part in a Prince's Trust show with Phil Collins, Elton John, Paul McCartney, and Rod Stewart at Wembley Arena. Then in October, he joined Julian Lennon and Keith Richards at the Fox Theatre in St. Louis, Missouri, to celebrate Chuck Berry's sixtieth birthday.

Clapton's album *August* was released in November 1986, named in honor of the month his son, Conor, was born. Produced by Phil Collins and Tom Dowd, it featured one of Clapton's best bands, with keyboardist Greg Phillinganes, bassist Nathan East, and Collins on drums and backing vocals. The tracks included the outstanding funky riff on "Tearing Us Apart" with Tina Turner singing lead. The album was a bestseller despite reservations by critics who thought Clapton was edging too much toward pop.

One of Clapton's favorite venues was London's Royal Albert Hall, and in 1987 he performed there for three nights, stints that became an annual residency and evolved into a marathon. In January 1990, he played there for eighteen nights with three different bands, one with blues guitarists Robert Cray and Buddy Guy and backed by a sixty-piece orchestra.

An even grander twenty-four-night stand was staged in February 1991 when Clapton played in a four-piece band with Phil Collins and three other lineups, one with Albert Collins, Robert Cray, and Buddy Guy together with a nine-piece band and the National Philharmonic Orchestra conducted by Michael Kamen. Both seasons were recorded for the live album *24 Nights*.

Following the release of *August*, Clapton departed on yet another world tour, jammed with the Rolling Stones at New York's Shea Stadium, and wrote more film music. He attended copious rock awards ceremonies and in 1989

continued on page 212

Armed with appropriate Gibson archtop guitars, Clapton, Chuck Berry, and Keith Richards pose for a photograph at Berry's Los Angeles home during the filming of Taylor Hackford's documentary film *Hail! Hail! Rock 'n' Roll*, 1986.
Terry O'Neill/Getty Images

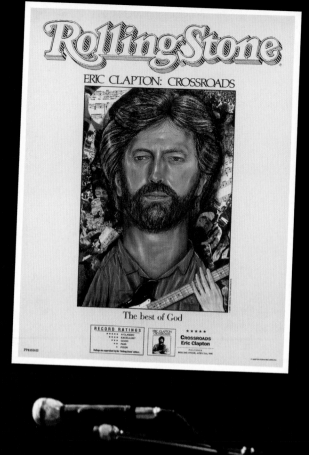

Poster advertising the *Crossroads* box set, 1988.

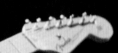

Clapton joins Dire Straits onstage, 1988. From left, bassist John Illsley, Mark Knopfler, keyboardist Alan Clark, and Clapton. *Ebet Roberts/Redferns/Getty Images*

ERIC CLAPTON
TOUR '88
AFTER SHOW ONLY

MICHELOB PRESENTS
ERIC CLAPTON
BUCKWHEAT ZYDECO
MEADOWLANDS ARENA
EAST RUTHERFORD, NJ
TUE SEP 6, 1988 8:00PM

HARVEY GOLDSMITH ENTS BY ARRANGEMENT WITH ROGER FORRESTER presents

ERIC CLAPTON
AND HIS BAND
PLUS
SPECIAL GUESTS

SHEFFIELD CITY HALL
TEL: 0742-735-295
MON 16th JAN
NEWCASTLE CITY HALL
TEL: 091-261-2606
TUES 17th JAN
EDINBURGH PLAYHOUSE
TEL: 031-557-2590
WED 18th JAN
ROYAL ALBERT HALL
TEL: 01-589-8212
FRI 20th SAT 21st
SUN 22nd JAN

TICKETS FROM £11.50 AVAILABLE THROUGH BOX OFFICES & USUAL AGENTS (max 4 tkts per person)
CREDIT CARD BOOKINGS: 748-1414. 240-7200. 818-6131 (subject to bkg. fee)

Advertisement, U.K. tour, 1988.

Clapton performs at London's Hammersmith Odeon in February 1987. *David Redfern/Redferns/Getty Images*

The Eric Clapton Signature Model Stratocaster

In 1988, Fender Musical Instruments Corporation introduced the Eric Clapton Signature Model Stratocaster, built to Clapton's specifications. Through the years, the guitars have undergone several changes in specs, as Clapton's own requirements varied. Still, they remain *the* Strat endorsed by Mr. Clapton.

2010 Fender Eric Clapton Signature Stratocaster.
Fender Musical Instruments Corporation

Advertisement, Eric Clapton Signature Model Stratocaster.
Fender Musical Instruments Corporation

FOREVER MAN

Poster from the concert after which Stevie Ray Vaughan died in a helicopter crash, Alpine Valley Music Theatre, East Troy, Wisconsin, August 25–26, 1990.

continued from page 204

released a new studio album, *Journeyman.* It was as if being clean of drugs and drink had unleashed a wholly new and invigorated artist. Clapton was destined, however, to receive more shocking blows to upset his newfound happiness.

On August 27, 1990, four of his colleagues were killed in a helicopter crash following an Alpine Valley Music Theatre concert in East Troy, Wisconsin. Clapton traveled safely in the first of four flights. The morning after the concert, he awakened in his hotel room to a call from Roger Forrester telling him that the helicopter carrying Stevie Ray Vaughan had crashed in fog, killing him as well as Clapton's agent, tour manager, and bodyguard. Stevie, an old friend, had been jamming on stage with Clapton just the night before.

On March 20, 1991, Clapton was further devastated by the tragic death of his four-year-old son, Conor. Following the February concerts at the Royal Albert Hall, Clapton had flown to New York to meet Conor and his mother Lori Del Santo, planning to spend holiday time together. Arriving on March 19, he took Conor to a circus at Nassau Coliseum before returning him to his mother's condominium on East 57th Street. Clapton then went to stay at the nearby Mayfair Regent hotel.

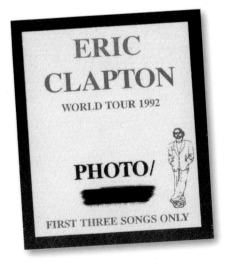

Playing with heroes: Clapton invited a grand lineup of fellow guitar greats to Royal Albert Hall in 1991. Buddy Guy takes the spotlight, backed by harpman Jerry Portnoy, Albert Collins, Robert Cray, Jimmie Vaughan, and Clapton.
Mick Hutson/Redferns/Getty Images

The following morning came the shocking news. Conor, who had been play-ing at home on a day off from school, ran across a room toward an open window and plunged from the fifty-third floor some 750 feet to his death, landing on the roof of an adjacent building. The window had been left open by a cleaner, but a subsequent inquest held that nobody was to blame for the accident.

Clapton and Del Santo were devastated and sought to comfort each other. Many wondered whether the shock might tip Clapton over the edge once more. Friends and fans rallied around him and thousands of letters and messages of condolence arrived, including one from Prince Charles.

Clapton found the strength to carry on and cope with the crisis. To assuage his grief, he wrote one of the finest and most moving songs of his life—the tribute to Conor titled "Tears in Heaven," written in collabora-tion with Texan songwriter Will Jennings. Released in March 1992, it shot to No. 2 in the United States and was a hit around the world.

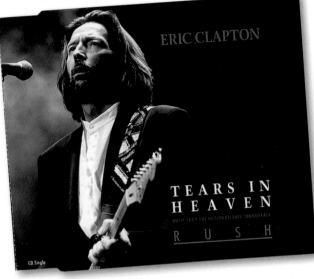

"Tears in Heaven," 1992.

Also in 1992 he revitalized his old hit "Layla" with a new acoustic version that appeared on his highly successful *Unplugged* album. It was a bold move to tamper with an old favorite, but it worked. That year, Clapton received six Grammy awards.

The work schedule remained as heavy as ever and more albums fol-lowed, including 1994's *From the Cradle* followed by 1998's *Pilgrim*, with its moving ballad "My Father's Eyes," which became another huge Clapton hit.

One of his most positive achievements out of the recording studios was to set up the Crossroads Foundation in Antigua in 1997. The charity provided help for those suffering from alcohol and drug dependencies. Clapton also finally found domestic bliss when he married Melia McEnery and started a family. They met in 1999 at a party in Los Angeles thrown by Giorgio Armani, who was a partner in the Crossroads Centre.

Melia, a twenty-three-year-old graphic designer, worked for Armani and had been told not to fraternize with the guests. But when she asked Clapton for his autograph, they hit it off and became an item. They married in 2002, and have since had three daughters: Ella May, Julie Rose, and Sophie.

The new millennium saw Clapton end his association with long-term man-ager Roger Forrester as he began to assert more control over his own life and decisions. As Clapton says, "I missed him. He was my father, brother, and best pal. But I needed the separation."

In 2000, Clapton was settled enough to contemplate his musical roots. He teamed up with B. B. King for *Riding with the King* and another solo album, *Reptile*, followed in 2001. The return to the blues was celebrated with 2004's *Me and Mr. Johnson*, a selection of covers of songs by Robert Johnson. Clapton followed this up with *Sessions for Robert J.*

In 2004, Clapton was awarded the CBE (Companion of the British Empire) in the annual New Year's Honour List. Just nine years earlier, he had been awarded an OBE (Order of the British Empire) in recognition of his charitable work. It showed how well he was regarded by the establishment and in royal circles.

Overwhelmed by awards: Clapton grapples with his six Grammys won at the 35th annual Grammy Awards on February 24, 1993. "Tears in Heaven" won both as record and song of the year, while *Unplugged* won as album of the year. *STR/AFP/Getty Images*

Unplugged: Clapton performs at Royal Albert Hall with the spotlight on just himself and his Martin acoustic guitar. *Mick Hutson/Redferns/Getty Images*

Following the success of the MTV *Unplugged* performance, Martin Guitars worked with Clapton in creating the Martin 000-42EGB and 000-28EC Eric Clapton Signature Model acoustic guitars. *Nigel Osbourne/Redferns/Getty Images*

In 2004, he also began recording *Back Home*, an album that had taken him three years to write. Among the songs was "So Tired," a wry ditty about coping with being a father and being kept up all night feeding babies. The title track was an acoustic guitar tribute to his domestic bliss. Many of the songs also paid tribute to Melia, the source of his newfound contentment. The album was released in February 2005.

In October 2004, Clapton decided he'd like to re-form the band that meant so much to him in the 1960s and sold 35 million records. Former bandmate Jack Bruce had been suffering from ill health, and Ginger Baker had been through a succession of different groups, traveling the world without ever really settling. Both of them yearned for the chance to get back together with Clapton, and he finally decided it was time for a Cream reunion.

The seeds for the reunion were sown when Cream were inducted into the Rock and Roll Hall of Fame in Los Angeles in January 1993, where the trio played a short set.

The trio reunited for rehearsals and then performed at Royal Albert Hall, scene of their final concerts in 1968. They played brilliantly on May 2, 3, 5, and 6, 2005, although Clapton, now aged sixty, succumbed to a bout of influenza during the first three shows.

Cream were filmed for a DVD release. Later in the year, they went to New York to play Madison Square Garden. Their concerts in October 2005 were hailed a success by fans, although there were disagreements between Bruce and Baker over volume levels on stage. This scrapped any plans for further U.S. Cream shows, although they could easily have sold out a full tour.

"We had stayed in touch over the years and when we were inducted into the Rock and Roll Hall of Fame, that was a big factor," says Clapton. "It was such an instant groove when we got together again. We were inside this little rehearsal room the day before the event. We were being inducted, but they also expected us to play. We were also supposed to make acceptance speeches. I found myself becoming overwhelmed, and as I was talking I found tears coming into my eyes. I had not realized how much that whole thing had meant to me. It was an early part of my musical experience and very powerful. That stuck with me apart from the fact we played so well. We rebounded and the magic was still there. Even then we hadn't played together for twenty-five years so that was a leap frog toward our reunion in 2005.

"At the time I wasn't ready for a full reunion then until I became better equipped to handle it later. I had a lot of my own fish still to fry and now I'm scratching around for ambitions and they don't come as thick and fast as they used to. I had more time to look at reviving Cream.

"I knew that Jack had been pretty seriously ill and had a year to convalesce. But the idea came up in the middle of 2004, and we started to assemble it

"I just don't find it very inspiring to play the guitar on my own. Playing the guitar is a very sacred experience, and I feel kind of lonely doing it with no-one around. Music's got to be a shared experience and if I don't play onstage or on tour I don't play at all. It's my only way of disciplining myself. I never play at home. I don't have the necessary self-control and discipline to sit down and practise. Which is perhaps just as well because if I did I would probably develop a style which is totally unsuited to live music and quite alien to an improvised situation."

—Eric Clapton, *Q*, 1990

gradually. We talked to one another, and the more I thought about it, I realized it was a pretty strenuous gig. I hadn't played in a trio for years. The closest I had got to it was in Derek and the Dominos, which was a quartet. I was young then and it was really hard work. Until we got our feet in Cream and we were touring, it was hard work. So I thought we'd need about a month's rehearsal.

"The way my life has evolved I was starting to feel a little more generous toward my own past and I wanted to get in touch with it again. I did a reunion gig with John Mayall and we didn't even rehearse for that at all. We talked through that one on the phone. He told me what he wanted to do and we just got up and did it.

"The Royal Albert Hall Cream shows were incredibly well received. I remember the first night we walked out it didn't seem like they would stop cheering. There was a big ovation and we could have just stood there for ages. I had dreamed about us getting a big reaction, but the reality was pretty overwhelming.

"We had a great time doing the Albert Hall. We rehearsed for a month because I knew we'd all have to get back up to speed. I was fit as a fiddle and then the night before the first show I came down with something the kids had. It was a really nasty virus, which knocked me for six. I was on antibiotics and I didn't get well until the last gig. The only one I remember was the last one."

Cream reunite—for just one night. After being inducted into the Rock and Roll Hall of Fame, Jack Bruce, Ginger Baker, and Clapton performed at the ceremony in Los Angeles in January 1993. *Jeff Kravitz/FilmMagic/Getty Images*

Poster, Lincoln Center, New York City, May 2, 1994.

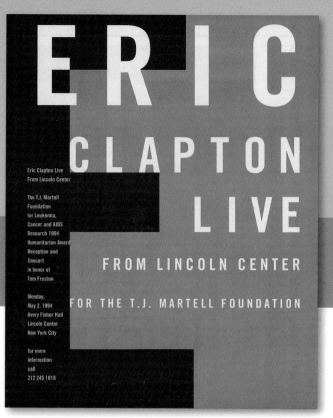

Poster advertising *From the Cradle*, 1994.

"I see myself as kind of being like a lone guy on a quest."

—Eric Clapton, *Larry King Live* interview, 1998

The 2005 Cream reunion soon became yet another memory, a stepping stone in the incredible journey of Eric Clapton.

Yet there was more excitement to come. In February 2008, he teamed up with his old friend, Steve Winwood, for the first time since their days in Blind Faith forty years ago. The pair performed three historic concerts at New York's Madison Square Garden that were filmed for a special DVD. This proved so successful that Clapton and Winwood then embarked on a full U.S. tour in 2009 that concluded with a night at the Hollywood Bowl on June 30.

They also visited the United Kingdom and Europe in 2010, performing Blind Faith classics, personal hits, and their own personal favorite tunes, notably "Presence of the Lord," "Layla," "Little Wing," and "Dear Mr. Fantasy." Their backing band included keyboardist Chris Stainton, bassist Willie Weeks, and drummer Abe Laboriel Jr.

In May and June 2011, Clapton and Winwood scheduled five concerts at London's Royal Albert Hall that sold out as soon as tickets went on sale. As if that wasn't enough, the Eric Clapton Band also embarked on a world tour in Spring 2011 with concerts in the Far East, United States, Europe, and the United Kingdom with another six nights at the Royal Albert Hall in May.

In 2010, he unleashed another new studio album, called simply *Clapton*, on which he elegantly performed songs he'd grown to love with the passage of time. Among the fourteen tracks was a haunting rendition of "Autumn Leaves," the classic Johnny Mercer/Joseph Kosma ballad. The nostalgic lyrics seemed even more effective when dreamily intoned by a man who had lived such an extraordinary life and created so much great music.

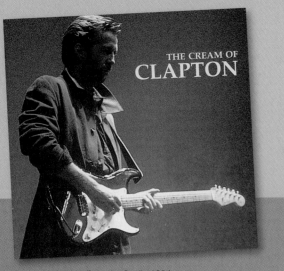

Poster advertising *From the Cradle*, 1994.

Pilgrim, 1998.

Handbill, Palace, Auburn Hills, Michigan,
September 23, 1995. *Artist: Mark Arminski*

"Change the World" single from the film
Phenomenon, 1996.

Bob Dylan and Clapton share the spotlight at the Crossroads Benefit on June 30, 1999. *Kevin Mazur/WireImage/Getty Images*

B. B. King and Clapton swap licks at Jazz at Lincoln Center's Blowin' the Blues Away gala at the New York City's Apollo Theater on June 2, 2003. *Kevin Mazur/WireImage/Getty Images*

Poster, Reunion Arena, Dallas, Texas, May 10, 2001.
Artist: David Dean

Me and Mr. Johnson, 2001.

One More Car, One More Rider, 2002.

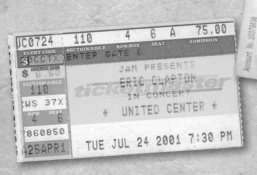

Opera singer Luciano Pavarotti and Clapton join forces for the Pavarotti and Friends concert in Modena, Italy, on May 26, 2003. The gala raised money to help Iraqi children. *United Archives GmbH/Alamy*

Clapton worked with Italian pop singer Zucchero Fornaciari on several projects and concerts, including *Zucchero & Co.*, 2003.

Clapton displays his CBE in front of Buckingham Palace in November 2004, accompanied by his pregnant wife, Melia McEnery. *Trinity Mirror/Mirrorpix/Alamy*

Clapton performs at the One Generation 4 Another show at Royal Albert Hall on March 15, 2004. The special for the Lord's Taverners provided financial backing for sport-related requirements for children with special needs.
Jo Hale/Getty Images

Tribute to Buddy Holly: Clapton joins members of Holly's original band, the Crickets, including guitarist Sonny Curtis and drummer Joe B. Mauldin, along with Albert Lee.
Jeffrey Mayer/WireImage/Getty Images

Poster, Seoul, Korea, March 23, 2004.

Cream reunion: Jack Bruce, Ginger Baker, and Clapton reunite at Royal Albert Hall on May 5, 2005. *Graham Wiltshire/Hulton Archive/Getty Images*

Program, ticket, and handbill, Cream Reunion,
Royal Albert Hall, London, October 24–26, 2005.
Handbill artist: John Van Hamersveld

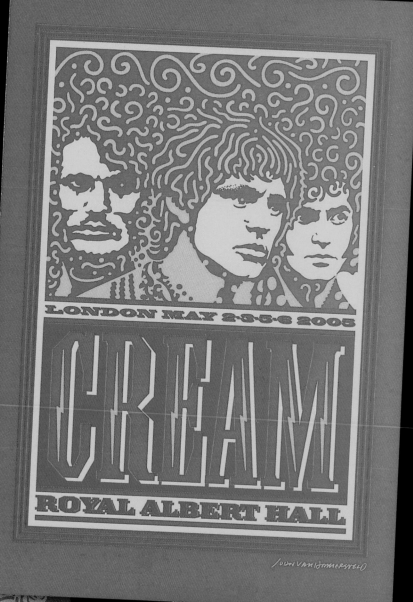

"We used to take a lot of risks and that's what makes it really interesting. It gets very intense. Although we had our problems, when we play there's magic there."

—Jack Bruce on the Cream reunion, 2008

Queen Elizabeth II greets Jeff Beck, Clapton, Jimmy Page, and Brian May at the Music Day at the Palace event at Buckingham Palace on March 1, 2005. The Royal reception was held to recognize the excellence of British music and the contribution it makes to the culture and economy of the United Kingdom. *Fiona Hanson/Tim Graham Picture Library/Getty Images*

Carl Perkins & Friends Blues Suede Shoes: A Rockabilly Session, 2006.

Back Home, 2005.

Otis Rush & Friends Live at Montreux 1986 featured Clapton and Luther Allison, 2006.

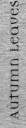

Autumn Leaves

15 January 2007   Doors open 7:00 p.m.
Impact Arena, Muang Thong Thani

Conditions
- No Cameras / Video Cameras / Audio - Visual Recorders Allowed
- This Ticket is Non Refundable / Non Refundable
- This Ticket is Valid For Date of Show Only

15/01/2007 09:02 27/10/06
20:30

4   L   P   19   1000-
0934

-TIME COLLABORATION FROM
AR GREATS ON ONE NEW ALBUM.
'RIDE THE RIVER' AND 'DANGER'

V. 7

.com   jjcalemusic.com
...rchandise always available at ericclapton.com/store.
official Eric Clapton fan club. Visit ECAccess.cc to join.

ESCONDIDO

©2006 Reprise Records, A Warner Music Group Company.
For Promotional Use Only. Not For Resale. Made in USA.

...ster advertising *The Road to Escondido* with Clapton
...d J. J. Cale, 2006.

...apton performs on the Shanghai Grand Stage on January 20, 2007
...Shanghai, China. *China Photos/Getty Images*

Poster, Schleyer-Halle, Stuttgart, Germany, June 4, 2006.

UNITED PROMOTERS AG PRESENTS

Eric Clapton
RTL

Back Home Tour

Sonntag, 20:00 Uhr
4. Juni '06   STUTTGART   SWR
SCHLEYER-HALLE

Karten an allen bekannten Vorverkaufsstellen. Tel. Kartenservice: SKS Russ: Tel. 0711-163 53 21
Easy Ticket: Tel. 0711-255 55 55 · Örtliche Durchführung: SKS Michael Russ GmbH
Bundesweite Ticket-Hotline: 01805-570 000 (12 Cent/Min.) oder unter www.eventim.de

TOYOTA
CENTER

SEC
C108

ROW
8

SEAT
9

Eric Clapton & Steve Winwood

CROSSROADS
GUITAR FESTIVAL
2007

c Clapton
2008

MAY 2008

SH
/HOUSE/PROMOTER

Clapton defends the wicket during an annual celebrity charity cricket match at Cranleigh School, Surrey, England, on July 12, 2009. *Carl de Souza/AFP/Getty Images*

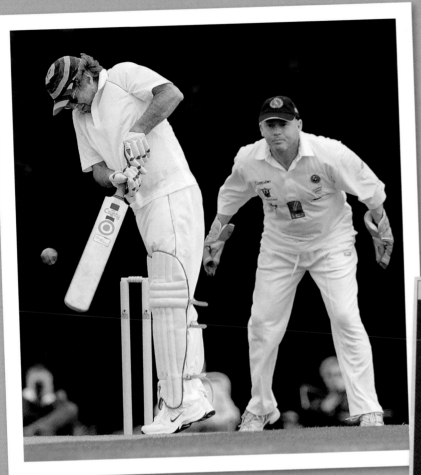

Clapton is God: The Cream of Early Eric, 2007.

Poster, Madison Square Garden, New York City, February 18–19, 2010.

A longtime fan of Ferrari automobiles, Clapton has owned several new and classic models over the years, including this 1964 Ferrari 250 GT Lusso Berlinetta. *Motoring Picture Library/Alamy*

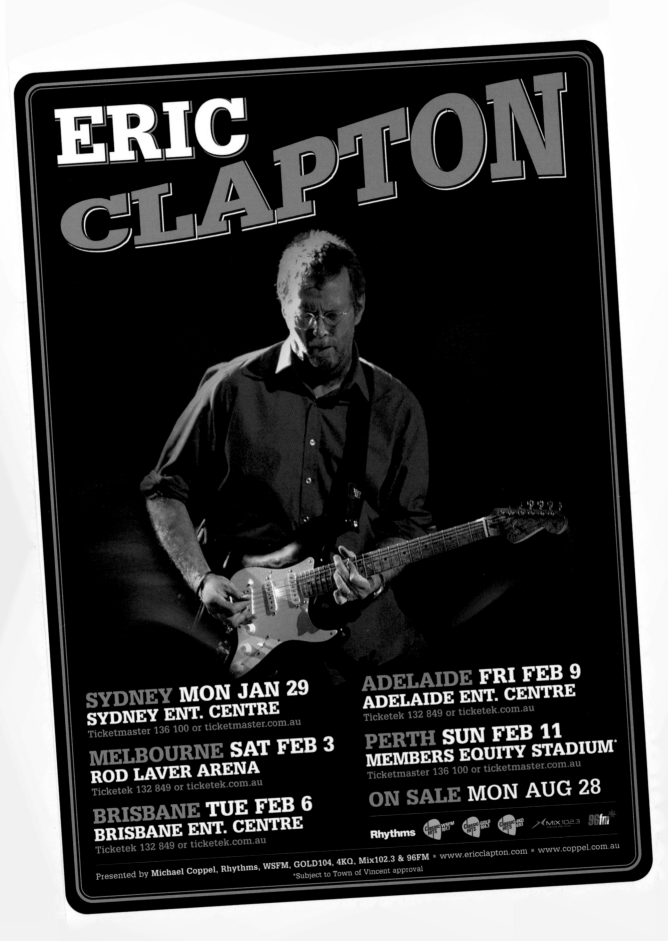

Steve Winwood and Clapton reunite to perform at London's Wembley Arena on May 20, 2010. *Christie Goodwin/Getty Images*

Clapton and Steve Winwood, *Live from Madison Square Garden*, 2009.

ERIC ~AND~ STEVE
CLAPTON WINWOOD

LIVE
FROM MADISON SQUARE GARDEN

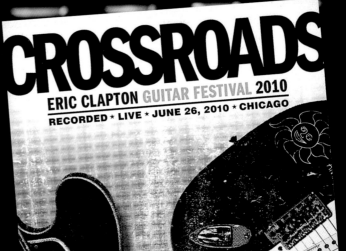

Clapton and Jeff Beck perform onstage during the 2010 Crossroads Guitar Festival at Toyota Park in Bridgeview, Illinois, on June 26, 2010. *Kevin Mazur/ WireImage/Getty Images*

All-star finale to the 2010 Crossroads Guitar Festival. From left: Derek Trucks, Warren Haynes, James Burton, Jimmie Vaughan, Susan Tedeschi, Keb Mo, Clapton, Buddy Guy, and Johnny Winter. *Barry Brecheisen/WireImage/Getty Images*

Steve Winwood, Clapton, and Willie Weeks play at
Königsplatz in Munich, Germany, on June 5, 2010.
Stefan M. Prager/Redferns/Getty Images

Clapton, 2010.

Autumn leaves: Clapton fingerpicks a grand Gibson L-5CESN archtop guitar at the Prince's Trust Rock Gala at Royal Albert Hall on November 17, 2010. *Chris Jackson/Getty Images*

unplugged

THE CLASSIC ALBUMS

Unplugged, 1992.

When MTV launched their *Unplugged* acoustic shows, it was an inspired move that helped musicians present their repertoire in a relaxed and friendly atmosphere. Clapton recorded his contribution to the series, performing many of his best songs, just singing along and playing acoustic guitar. He was backed by a superb band also utilizing acoustic instruments and avoiding the bombast of rock production. They too seemed to enjoy the simple act of playing unfettered by the edicts of record producers.

Clapton's show was recorded in front of an audience at Bray Film Studios in Windsor, England, on January 16, 1992. The band included former Amen Corner singer Andy Fairweather Low on acoustic guitar, percussionist Ray Cooper, acoustic bassist Nathan East, drummer Steve Ferrone, keyboardist Chuck Leavell, and backing vocalists Katie Kissoon and Tessa Niles. Clapton played a Martin acoustic guitar and introduced a lilting version of "Layla," saying impishly, "See if you can spot this one."

The re-working of "Layla" was a rare example of an old standard (as it had become by the 1990s) actually benefiting from being tampered with, slowed down and reverse-engineered. It was so successful it became a hit single, following "Tears in Heaven" into the U.S. Billboard chart to peak at No. 12 in October 1992.

Oddly enough, it was said that Clapton could not see any merit in releasing an album from the show and actually fought the idea. He was convinced it would only sell a minimal number of copies. In fact, *Unplugged* went to No. 1 in the United States and sold a staggering ten million copies, going platinum. Clapton also earned six Grammy awards, including Record of the Year, Album of the Year, Song of the Year, Best Male Pop Vocal Performance, Best Rock Male Vocal Performance, and Best Rock Song. "Tears in Heaven" earned three of the awards.

Clapton's delivery of "Tears in Heaven" on the show was restrained and yet so moving in its simplicity that it touched the hearts of millions of viewers and record buyers in a way that few pop songs had done in decades. It was this sincerity that shone through the whole record and led many critics to conclude that *Unplugged* was one of Clapton's best ever records. It clearly rose above all the heavily produced and carefully contrived albums of the past and made a nonsense of much received wisdom about rock.

While "Tears in Heaven" and "Layla" are highlights, there are plenty of other great moments, including versions of Bo Diddley's "Before You Accuse Me," Robert Johnson's "Walkin' Blues," and Muddy Waters' "Rollin' and Tumblin'."

In a way, *Unplugged* was almost back to where Clapton came in, playing acoustic blues with an "unplugged" Cream at their first rehearsals way back in 1966. All that volume, noise, and chaos was done away with at a stroke. And the music still rocked and the blues remained blue. What would Jimi Hendrix have done with his own *Unplugged* show, one wonders?

One of Clapton's vintage Martin acoustic guitars.
Robert Knight Archive/Redferns/Getty Images

Poster advertising *Unplugged*, 1992.

THE CLASSIC ALBUMS

from the cradle

Riding with the King, 2000.

It was an important moment when Eric Clapton decided to make the all-blues record that been at the back of his mind for decades. He'd started his career as a young man devoted to studying, absorbing, and then playing and singing the blues. But he had traveled a long, hard road before coming to grips with the music in all its forms on one dedicated album.

As it turned out, From the Cradle was and remains one of Clapton's most ambitious and successful albums and more than rewarded the care and devotion he put into the project. It was recorded in 1994 at Olympic Studios in Barnes, London, and produced by Clapton and Russ Titelman. A team of like-minded musicians was assembled including guitarist Andy Fairweather Low, keyboardist Chris Stainton, bassist Dave Bronze, and drummer Jim Keltner. Jerry Portnoy added harmonica, and a brass section helped fill out the sound where appropriate.

Clapton planned to record all sixteen tracks live in the studio, and there were only a couple of overdubs added later. He chose a range of material, including songs by Elmore James, Muddy Waters, Willie Dixon, and Lowell Fulson. The styles encompass country, rural, and big city blues all played at authentically slow tempos or at a breezily upbeat pace. The rather shocking "Blues Before Sunrise" by Elmore James shows Clapton's determination to get down to the nitty-gritty. He adopts an unusually gruff and throaty vocal attack to match the greasy slide guitar licks and boogie piano.

From here on, Clapton relaxes his vocal approach and his guitar work just gets better. On Willie Dixon and Eddie Boyd's "Third Degree," his vocal delivery is more natural as he protests that he's been charged with murder and even forgery "When I can't write my name . . . bad luck is killing me."

On such tracks as "Reconsider Baby," "Hoochie Coochie Man," and "Five Long Years," Clapton adapts his guitar phrasing, tones, and picking styles to suit the mood. It shows just how deeply he had immersed himself in the tradition of America's musical legacy. "Going Away Baby" displays the jollier face of the blues with a two-beat rhythm that suggests going on a hayride rather than laboring in a cotton field.

One of the most outstanding performances is "Motherless Child," on which Clapton switches to acoustic guitar and the mood harks to skiffle days. The tempo slows down for "Someday After a While (You'll Be Sorry)," where his electric guitar becomes angry and intense before giving way to the lowdown and dirty "Standin' Round Crying" and "Groanin' the Blues," where the drums hammer out a beat behind Clapton staccato guitar.

It could be argued that From the Cradle is overladen with the blues and needs more variety and the interjection of a few Clapton-esque popular songs. But that would be missing the point and would have completely undermined the intentions behind the project. The CD was a No. 1 hit in 1994. The success of the album encouraged Clapton to stick with his personal blues revival, and he went on to record Riding with the King with B. B. King and Me and Mr. Johnson, his tribute to Robert Johnson.

After all the toils and troubles Clapton had been through in his life, it is fair to say that he'd earned his right to sing the blues.

Posters advertising *Riding with the King*, 2000.

12. sock it to me one more time

Jamming with the Stones; Touring with Jeff Beck; and the Deaths of Jack Bruce, J. J. Cale, and B. B. King, 2010–2015

IN 2013, AT THE AGE OF SIXTY-EIGHT, Eric Clapton celebrated his fiftieth anniversary as a professional musician. The following year, Clapton intimated that he wanted to retire from touring due to ongoing health issues and an increasing dislike of the rigors of travel. And yet the old master still had plans to complete and ambitions to fulfill. It seemed the public didn't want him to stop, and he couldn't resist any opportunity to pick up his guitar and play.

As well as enjoying sold-out shows with old friend Steve Winwood, Eric found himself jamming with the Rolling Stones and playing alongside former Yardbirds alumni Jeff Beck. These were the sorts of gigs audiences in the past could only have dreamt about. Now they were coming true for new generations of fans.

Yet there was sadness, too, when Clapton lost three of his oldest friends and musical mentors. J. J. Cale died in July 2013; Jack Bruce died in October 2014; and B. B. King, the king of the blues, passed away in May 2015. When Clapton attended Bruce funeral, the

Guitarists Eric Clapton and B. B. King on stage during the 2010 Crossroads Guitar Festival at Toyota Park on June 26, 2010, in Bridgeview, Illinois. *Barry Brecheisen/Getty Images*

Above inset: Eric Clapton & Friends' *The Breeze: An Appreciation of JJ Cale*, 2014.

Jeff Beck and Eric Clapton perform on stage at Madison Square Garden on February 18, 2010, in New York City. *Roger Kisby/Getty Images*

gray-haired, unshaven mourner wearing dark glasses seemed far removed from the glamorous guitar hero of Cream's heyday.

Looking back, Clapton had such a surge of activity in his sixth decade as a traveling bluesman it seems as if he was trying to pack in as many of the opportunities he'd missed out on in his younger years.

On November 29, 2012, Clapton played with the Rolling Stones on stage at London's O2 Arena, a band he might once have joined if the dice had tumbled in his favor. The grand meeting of rock 'n' roll minds took place during the second of the Stones' five shows devised to celebrate their fiftieth anniversary. Keith Richards and Clapton happily joined forces on the great Muddy Waters' classic "Champagne and Reefer," a truly low-down and dirty blues.

With Jagger prancing up front, Clapton, Ronnie Wood, and Richards formed a phalanx of rock warriors, ready to win their battle honors as soloists. *"Play your guitar!"* urged Jagger as Clapton stepped out and the pair exchanged delighted smiles, subconsciously reliving their youth. Perhaps they were sharing memories of the sixties and the Soho clubs, where they had all performed to somewhat smaller crowds.

More great moments ensued when Clapton flew to New York a few days later to appear at a special charity concert for the Hurricane Sandy Relief Fund at Madison Square Garden on December 12.

The hurricane had laid waste to a swath of the East Coast, so naturally Bruce Springsteen and Jon Bon Jovi—both from New Jersey—headlined a

Steve Winwood and Eric Clapton perform at Wembley Arena on May 20, 2010, in London, England.
Matt Kent/Getty Images

Guitarists Sonny Landreth and Eric Clapton perform on stage during the 2010 Crossroads Guitar Festival at Toyota Park on June 26, 2010, in Bridgeview, Illinois.
Barry Brecheisen/Getty Images

Eric Clapton, Mark King, and Jools Holland (left to right) perform at Prince's Trust Rock Gala 2010 at the Royal Albert Hall on November 17, 2010, in London, England.
Ian Gavan/Getty Images

Fans await the start of Eric Clapton's performance on October 6, 2011, in Porto Alegre, Brazil. *AFP Photo/ Jefferson Bernardes/Getty Images*

Mick Jagger, Eric Clapton, Ronnie Wood, Charlie Watts, and Keith Richards perform at the O2 Arena on November 29, 2012, in London, England. *Dave J. Hogan/Getty Images*

show that welcomed many British artists, among them Sir Paul McCartney, the Rolling Stones, Roger Waters of Pink Floyd, and Chris Martin of Coldplay. Clapton's spot featured him playing an acoustic version of "Nobody Knows You When You're Down and Out." He snatched up an electric guitar for a more upbeat "Crossroads" and "Got to Get Better in a Little While" backed only by bass and drums.

Rolling Stones celebration jams and charity guest spots were all fun, but perhaps the most satisfying musical moments during these hectic years were his collaborations with Steve Winwood. The former singer and multi-instrumentalist with the Spencer Davis Group and Traffic had once teamed up with Clapton in the short-lived Blind Faith project. Even before that, Clapton had occasionally sat in with Winwood at club gigs. Now the talented mates could pick up where they left off in 1969 with some serious touring and their first full concerts together in forty years.

The reunion began when they played together at the Crossroads Guitar Festival in 2007. Clapton gleefully told the audience, "I'm bringing somebody on I've been dying to play with for the last twenty-five years. It's finally come to pass. Please welcome Steve Winwood."

As they played songs from the Blind Faith era such as "Presence of the Lord," Clapton enthused about "the romance and beauty of stuff we'd played in the past that sparked something off," adding, "It felt like we had never really resolved what we had started, until now." Winwood also recalled that from the earliest days of his career, Clapton had taken a "brotherly" interest in him, supporting his musical ambitions.

In the meantime, Clapton was reunited with another old pal when he teamed up with former Yardbirds guitarist Jeff Beck for two shows at London's O2 Arena (February 13 and 14, 2010). While they had never played together in the Yardbirds, they had a mutual respect and complementary styles that resulted in a special kind of guitar magic whenever they shared the stage. (It happened back in 2007 when Beck appeared at the Crossroads Guitar Festival and while Clapton sat in at London's Ronnie Scott's that same year. Beck played five nights at the packed-out jazz club and when Clapton came on stage to play "Little Brown Bird" and "You Need Love" with Beck, there was a standing ovation from a crowd that included Jimmy Page and Robert Plant.)

More shows with Beck in the United States and Canada during 2010 included Madison Square Garden, New York; the Air Canada Centre, Toronto; and Bell Centre, Montreal. They also played at the Crossroads Guitar Festival in Illinois on June 26.

Old Sock, 2013.

Clapton's appetite for touring was further whetted when he embarked on a round of dates in eleven U.S. cities during February and March that year, with Roger Daltrey of the Who appearing as his opening act.

He returned to his favorite venue, the Royal Albert Hall, on November 17, 2010, as a guest on Prince's Trust Rock Gala, performing with a "house" band comprising Jools Holland, Midge Ure, and Mark King.

The year 2011 was just as busy, with Clapton playing to fifteen thousand people at a stadium concert in Italy in June and with a trip to South America in October where he gave his first shows there in ten years. There was also an extra thirteen-date tour of Japan with Steve Winwood in November and December.

On December 4, 2011, the revered blues man Hubert Sumlin died at the age of eighty. Famed for his guitar work, Sumlin had first come to attention while performing with his mentor, the late Howlin' Wolf, as well as fellow blues legend Muddy Waters. In his honor, a special Howlin' for Hubert Tribute concert was held on February 24, 2012, at the Apollo Theater in New York headed by Clapton and Keith Richards.

Hosts Dan Aykroyd and Eric Clapton speak on stage during the 2013 Crossroads Guitar Festival at Madison Square Garden on April 13, 2013, in New York City. *Larry Busacca/Getty Images*

On March 12, 2013, Clapton released a new album, *Old Sock* (Surfdog Records), that like its predecessor, *Clapton*, featured more poignant versions of popular standards, notably Jerome Kern's "The Folks Who Live on the Hill," once a hit for Peggy Lee.

Clapton also sang Gershwin's "Our Love Is Here to Stay" and another 1930s favorite "All of Me." Clapton offered brief but illuminating commentaries on selected tracks and told a revealing anecdote about why he really left the Yardbirds in 1965. It seems he was quite amenable to their manager Giorgio Gomelsky's idea that they should try to get a chart-hit single to break out of the club scene, and he joined in a band member's poll to find a suitable song.

He liked the Otis Redding track "Your One and Only Man" that Gomelsky played him, even though he'd never heard of Redding at the time. He suggested the Yardbirds record it for their single but was overruled by Paul Samwell-Smith who wanted to do "For Your Love" instead. "You know who won and I was out!" laughed Clapton. "I thought, 'One day I'm gonna do that song, and then they'll be sorry.'"

Eric Clapton performs during the 2014 New Orleans Jazz & Heritage Festival at Fair Grounds Race Course on April 27, 2014, in New Orleans, Louisiana. *Erika Godring/ Getty Images*

Clapton also explained that as he neared his seventieth birthday, songs he'd once rejected as a youth, believing they belonged to an older generation, had taken on a new meaning for him. In his maturity, he had begun to appreciate the craft of such artists as Billie Holiday and Peggy Lee. He also felt that songs like "Our Love Is Here to Stay" should be treated in a different way from the Rod Stewart smooth approach, with "a bit of funk and scratch and not too glossy."

In the wake of *Old Sock*, a series of concerts in the United States, United Kingdon, and Europe was scheduled that would last from March 14 to June 19, 2013, celebrating his fiftieth anniversary. But around the same time, in February, he warned that he would stop touring in 2015. In June 2014 he repeated his retirement announcement, citing that traveling had now become "unbearable" and that he might even have to stop playing guitar altogether on health grounds.

One of Clapton's biggest influences from the seventies was John J. Cale, the singer, guitarist, and composer from Oklahoma City. Better known as J. J. Cale, he'd written the Clapton hits "After Midnight" and "Cocaine." When he died on July 26, 2013, Clapton was moved to prepare a tribute album. Eric Clapton & Friends' *The Breeze: An Appreciation of JJ Cale* was released on July 29, 2014. A selection of Cale songs was performed by Clapton, Mark Knopfler, John Mayer, Tom Petty, Willie Nelson, and Don White, commencing with a jaunty version of Cale's 1972 single "Call Me the Breeze."

Although Clapton was still performing regularly, the strain of endless touring began to show during a concert at the brand-new £125 million Glasgow SSE Hydro music venue on June 21, 2014. Clapton abruptly walked off stage during the show, and upset fans began booing. He returned for a final song but the concert ended forty minutes early.

The official explanation was that technical difficulties at the venue had made conditions too difficult for Clapton to perform. He described the sound on stage as "unbearable."

Then came the death of his old friend Jack Bruce, aged seventy-one, from liver disease on October 25th. Clapton had last played with Bruce during the Cream reunion shows in 2005. The funeral was held on November 5 at Golders Green Crematorium and was attended by Clapton with fellow Cream partner Ginger Baker, along with Gary Brooker, Phil Manzanera, and Nitin Sawhney. The mourners joined in renditions of "Morning Has Broken," "Strawberry Fields Forever," and Bruce composition "Theme for an Imaginary Western."

Clapton was back at work ready to celebrate his seventieth birthday with two shows at New York's Madison Square Garden on May 1 and 2, 2015. It was the forty-sixth anniversary of his first appearance there with Cream on November 2, 1968, and it was noted that he had played the Garden more than any other U.S. venue, forty-five times in all.

Eric Clapton attends the funeral of Jack Bruce at Golders Green Crematorium on November 5, 2014, in London, England. *John Phillips/Getty Images*

There were no "unbearable" sound problems when he completed a seven-night residency back at the Royal Albert Hall (May 14 to 23). These shows marked the fiftieth anniversary of the first time he'd played at the prestigious London venue, back in December 1964, when he was with the Yardbirds, an event televised by BBC Two for one of the channel's early pop shows.

A satisfyingly funky backing band at the RAH included Chris Stainton (keyboards), Paul Carrack (organ, vocals), Nathan East (bass), and Steve Gadd (drums). They stormed through "Hoochie Coochie Man," "I Shot the Sheriff," and "Crossroads," as well as the ballads "You Are So Beautiful," and "Tears in Heaven." On the final night, Clapton played "Rock Me Baby" in tribute to B. B. King, who had died on May 14, aged eighty-nine.

A glowing review in London's *Metro* newspaper was headed "Thank you, Eric, you were wonderful tonight" and pronounced "Clapton is a master and knows how to meet expectations. It is all part of his enduring appeal."

When Clapton left the stage at the Royal Albert Hall that year, he waved to fans and said, "See you down the road somewhere." We surely will. In the fall of 2015, work began on the production of a career-spanning *Eric Clapton Visual Anthology,* a full-length documentary film intended to represent a comprehensive study of Clapton's fifty-year musical journey. And who knows what's down the road after that. . . .

Clapton performs live on stage at Royal Albert Hall on May 14, 2015, in London, England.
Brian Rasic/Getty Images

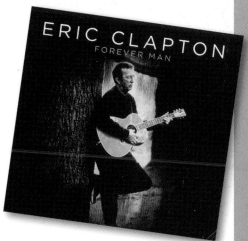

Forever Man, 2015.

Discography

The following discography is not meant to be a complete, exhaustive list of all of Clapton's recordings and appearances. Such a discography could comprise a book in itself when including variations in releases by different nations, reissues, expanded editions, greatest hits collections, and so on.

Instead, this discography focuses on Clapton's main album releases during the period of a band's main activity or his own solo career.

The track list is based on the original LP release.

the yardbirds

Five Live Yardbirds

Label: Columbia

Released February 1965

Track List

"Too Much Monkey Business"

"Got Love if You Want It"

"Smokestack Lightning"

"Good Morning Little Schoolgirl"

"Respectable"

"Five Long Years"

"Pretty Girl"

"Louise"

"I'm a Man"

"Here 'Tis"

john mayall's blues breakers

Blues Breakers

Label: Deram/London

Released July 1966

Track List

"All Your Love"

"Hideaway"

"Little Girl"

"Another Man"

"Double Crossing Time"

"What I'd Say"

"Key to Love"

"Parchman Farm"

"Have You Heard"

"Ramblin' on My Mind"

"Steppin' Out"

"It Ain't Right"

cream

Fresh Cream

Label: Polydor

Released December 1966

Track List

"I Feel Free"

"N.S.U."

"Sleepy Time Time"

"Dreaming"

"Sweet Wine"

"Spoonful"

"Cat's Squirrel"

"Four Until Late"

"Rollin' and Tumblin'"

"I'm So Glad"

"Toad"

"The Coffee Song"

"Wrapping Paper"

"Born Under a Bad Sign"
"Deserted Cities of the Heart"
"Crossroads"
"Spoonful"
"Traintime"
"Toad"

Disraeli Gears
Label: Polydor/PolyGram
Released November 1967
Track List
"Strange Brew"
"Sunshine of Your Love"
"World of Pain"
"Dance the Night Away"
"Blue Condition"
"Tales of Brave Ulysses"
"SWLABR"
"We're Going Wrong"
"Outside Woman Blues"
"Take It Back"
"Mother's Lament"

Goodbye
Label: Polydor/PolyGram
Released March 1969
Track List
"I'm So Glad"
"Politician"
"Sitting on Top of the World"
"Badge"
"Doing that Scrapyard Thing"
"What a Bringdown"
"Anyone for Tennis"

Live Cream
Label: Polydor
Released April 1970
Track List
"N.S.U."
"Sleepy Time Time"
"Sweet Wine"
"Rollin' and Tumblin'"
"Lawdy Mama"

Live Cream Volume II
Label: Polydor
Released March 1972
Track List
"Deserted Cities of the Heart"
"White Room"
"Politician"
"Tales of Brave Ulysses"
"Sunshine of Your Love"
"Steppin' Out"

Wheels of Fire
Label: Polydor/PolyGram
Released August 1968
Track List
"White Room"
"Sitting on Top of the World"
"Passing the Time"
"As You Said"
"Pressed Rat and Warthog"
"Politician"
"Those Were the Days"

Best of Cream
Label: Atco/Polydor
Released June 1969
Track List
"Sunshine of Your Love"
"Badge"
"Crossroads"
"White Room"
"SWLABR"
"Born Under a Bad Sign"
"Spoonful"
"Tales of Brave Ulysses"
"Strange Brew"
"I Feel Free"

Blind Faith

Blind Faith
Label: PolyGram/Polydor
Released August 1969
Track List
 "Had to Cry Today"
 "Can't Find My Way Home"
 "Well All Right"
 "Presence of the Lord"
 "Sea of Joy"
 "Do What You Like"

Delaney and Bonnie and Friends

On Tour with Eric Clapton
Label: Atco/Atlantic Records
Released June 1970
Track List
 "Things Get Better"
 "Poor Elijah—Tribute to Johnson
   (Medley)"
 "Only You and I Know"
 "I Don't Want to Discuss It"
 "That's What My Man Is For"
 "Where There's a Will, There's
   a Way"
 "Coming Home"
 "Little Richard Medley"

Derek and the Dominos

Layla and Other Assorted Love Songs
Label: Polydor/PolyGram
Released December 1970

Track List
 "I Looked Away"
 "Bell Bottom Blues"
 "Keep on Growing"
 "Nobody Knows You When You're
   Down and Out"
 "I Am Yours"
 "Anyday"
 "Key to the Highway"
 "Tell the Truth"
 "Why Does Love Got to Be So Sad"
 "Have You Ever Loved a Woman"
 "Little Wing"
 "It's Too Late"
 "Layla"
 "Thorn Tree in the Garden"

In Concert
Label: RSO/Polydor
Released March 1973
Track List
 "Why Does Love Got to Be So Sad"
 "Got to Get Better in a Little
   While"
 "Let It Rain"
 "Presence of the Lord"
 "Tell the Truth"
 "Bottle of Red Wine"
 "Roll It Over"
 "Blues Power"
 "Have You Ever Loved a Woman"

solo career

Eric Clapton
Label: RSO/Polydor
Released August 1970
Track List
 "Slunky"
 "Bad Boy"
 "Lonesome and a Long Way
    From Home"
 "After Midnight"
 "Easy Now"
 "Blues Power"
 "Bottle of Red Wine"
 "Lovin' You Lovin' Me"
 "Told You for the Last Time"
 "Don't Know Why"
 "Let It Rain"

Eric Clapton's Rainbow Concert
Label: RSO/Polydor
Released September 1973
Track List
 "Badge"

 "Roll It Over"
 "Presence of the Lord"
 "Pearly Queen"
 "After Midnight"
 "Little Wing"

461 Ocean Boulevard
Label: RSO/Polydor
Released August 1974
Track List
 "Motherless Children"
 "Better Make It Through Today"
 "Willie and the Hand Jive"
 "Get Ready"
 "I Shot the Sheriff"
 "I Can't Hold Out"
 "Please Be With Me"
 "Let It Grow"
 "Steady Rollin' Man"
 "Mainline Florida"
 "Give Me Strength"

There's One in Every Crowd
Label: RSO/Polydor
Released April 1975

Track List
 "We've Been Told (Jesus
    Coming Soon)"
 "Swing Low Sweet Chariot"
 "Little Rachel"
 "Don't Blame Me"
 "The Sky is Crying"
 "Singin' the Blues"
 "Better Make It Through Today"
 "Pretty Blue Eyes"
 "High"
 "Opposites"

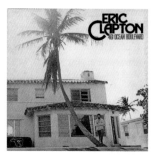

E.C. Was Here
Label: RSO/Polydor
Released August 1975
Track List
 "Have You Ever Loved a Woman"
 "Presence of the Lord"
 "Drifting Blues"
 "Can't Find My Way Home"
 "Rambling on My Mind"
 "Further on up the Road"

No Reason to Cry
Label: RSO/Polydor
Released August 1976
Track List
 "Beautiful Thing"
 "Carnival"
 "Sign Language"
 "County Jail Blues"
 "All Our Past Times"
 "Hello Old Friend"
 "Double Trouble"

"Innocent Times"
"Hungry"
"Black Summer Rain"
"Last Night"

"I'll Make Love to You Anytime"
"Roll It"
"Tell Me That You Love Me"
"If I Don't Be There By Morning"
"Early in the Morning"
"Promises"
"Golden Ring"
"Tulsa Time"

"Another Ticket"
"I Can't Stand It"
"Hold Me Lord"
"Floating Bridge"
"Catch Me if You Can"
"Rita Mae"

Slowhand

Label: RSO/Polydor
Released November 1977
Track List
  "Cocaine"
  "Wonderful Tonight"
  "Lay Down Sally"
  "Next Time You See Her"
  "We're All the Way"
  "The Core"
  "May You Never"
  "Mean Old Frisco"
  "Peaches and Diesel"

Just One Night

Label: Polydor
Released May 1980
Track List
  "Tulsa Time"
  "Early in the Morning"
  "Lay Down Sally"
  "Wonderful Tonight"
  "If I Don't Be There by Morning"
  "Worried Life Blues"
  "All Our Past Times"
  "After Midnight"
  "Double Trouble"
  "Setting Me Up"
  "Blues Power"
  "Rambling on My Mind"
  "Cocaine"
  "Further on up the Road"

Money and Cigarettes

Label: Reprise/Warner Bros.
Released February 1983
Track List
  "Everybody Oughta Make a Change"
  "The Shape You're In"
  "Ain't Going Down"
  "I've Got a Rock 'n' Roll Heart"
  "Man Overboard"
  "Pretty Girl"
  "Man in Love"
  "Crosscut Saw"
  "Slow Down Linda"
  "Crazy Country Hop"

Backless

Label: Polydor
Released November 1978
Track List
  "Walk Out in the Rain"
  "Watch Out for Lucy"

Another Ticket

Label: RSO/Polydor
Released February 1981
Track List
  "Something Special"
  "Black Rose"
  "Blow Wind Blow"

Timepieces Volume II: Live in the Seventies

Label: RSO/Polydor
Released May 1983
Track List
  "Tulsa Time"
  "Knockin' on Heaven's Door"
  "If I Don't Be There by Morning"
  "Rambling on My Mind"
  "Presence of the Lord"
  "Can't Find My Way Home"
  "Smile"
  "Blues Power"

"Take a Chance"
"Hold On"
"Miss You"
"Holy Mother"
"Behind the Mask"
"Grand Illusion"

Behind the Sun
Label: Reprise/Warner Bros.
Released March 1985
Track List
"She's Waiting"
"See What Love Can Do"
"Same Old Blues"
"Knock on Wood"
"Something's Happening"
"Forever Man"
"It All Depends"
"Tangled in Love"
"Never Make You Cry"
"Just Like a Prisoner"
"Behind the Sun"

August
Label: Reprise/Warner Bros.
Released October 1986
Track List
"It's in the Way That You Use It"
"Run"
"Tearing Us Apart"
"Bad Influence"
"Walk Away"
"Hung Up on Your Love"

Journeyman
Label: Reprise/Warner Bros.
Released November 1989
Track List
"Pretending"
"Anything for Your Love"
"Bad Love"
"Running on Faith"
"Hard Times"
"Hound Dog"
"No Alibis"
"Run So Far"
"Old Love"
"Breaking Point"
"Lead Me On"
"Before You Accuse Me"

24 Nights
Label: Reprise
Released October 1991
Track List
"Badge"
"Running on Faith"
"White Room"
"Sunshine of Your Love"
"Watch Yourself"
"Have You Ever Loved a Woman"
"Worried Life Blues"
"Hoodoo Man"
"Pretending"
"Bad Love"
"Old Love"
"Wonderful Tonight"
"Bell Bottom Blues"
"Hard Times"
"Edge of Darkness"

Unplugged
Label: Reprise
Released August 1992
Track List
"Signe"
"Before You Accuse Me"
"Hey Hey"
"Tears in Heaven"
"Lonely Stranger"
"Nobody Knows You When You're
    Down and Out"
"Layla"
"Running on Faith"
"Walkin' Blues"
"Alberta"
"San Francisco Bay Blues"
"Malted Milk"
"Old Love"
"Rollin' and Tumblin'"

From the Cradle
Label: Reprise/Warner Bros.
Released September 1994
Track List
"Blues Before Sunrise"
"Third Degree"
"Reconsider Baby"
"Hoochie Coochie Man"
"Five Long Years"
"I'm Tore Down"
"How Long Blues"
"Goin' Away Baby"
"Blues Leave Me Alone"
"Sinner's Prayer"
"Motherless Child"

"It Hurts Me Too"
"Someday After a While"
"Standin' Round Crying"
"Driftin'"
"Groaning the Blues"

Crossroads 2: Live in the Seventies
Label: Polygram/Polydor
Released April 1996
Track List
"Walkin' Down the Road"
"Have You Ever Loved a Woman"
"Willie and the Hand Jive"/"Get Ready"
"Can't Find My Way Home"
"Driftin' Blues"/"Rambling on My Mind"
"Presence of the Lord"
"Rambling on My Mind"/"Have You Ever Loved a Woman"
"Little Wing"
"The Sky is Crying"/"Have You Ever Loved a Woman"/"Rambling on My Mind"
"Layla"
"Further on up the Road"
"I Shot the Sheriff"
"Badge"
"Driftin' Blues"
"Eyesight to the Blind"/"Why Does Love Got to Be So Sad"
"Tell the Truth"
"Knockin' on Heaven's Door"
"Stormy Monday"
"Lay Down Sally"
"The Core"
"We're All the Way"
"Cocaine"
"Goin' Down Slow"/"Rambling on My Mind"
"Mean Old Frisco"
"Loving You Is Sweeter Than Ever"
"Worried Life Blues"
"Tulsa Time"

"Early in the Morning"
"Wonderful Tonight"
"Kind Hearted Woman"
"Double Trouble"
"Crossroads"
"To Make Somebody Happy"
"Cryin'"
"Water on the Ground"

Pilgrim
Label: Reprise/Warner Bros.
Released March 1998
Track List
"My Father's Eyes"
"River of Tears"
"Pilgrim"
"Broken Hearted"
"One Chance"
"Circus"
"Going Down Slow"
"Fall Like Rain"
"Born in Time"
"Sick and Tired"
"Needs His Woman"
"She's Gone"
"You Were There"
"Inside of Me"

Riding with the King
B. B. King and Eric Clapton
Label: Reprise/Warner Bros.
Released June 2000
Track List
"Riding with the King"
"Ten Long Years"
"Key to the Highway"
"Marry You"
"Three O'Clock Blues"
"Help the Poor"
"I Wanna Be"
"Worried Life Blues"
"Days of Old"
"When My Heart Beats Like a Hammer"
"Hold On I'm Coming"
"Come Rain or Come Shine"

Reptile
Label: Reprise/Warner Bros.
Released March 2001
Track List
"Reptile"
"Got You on My Mind"
"Travelin' Light"
"Believe in Life"
"Come Back Baby"
"Broken Down"
"Find Myself"
"I Ain't Gonna Stand for It"
"I Want a Little Girl"
"Second Nature"
"Don't Let Me Be Lonely Tonight"
"Modern Girl"
"Superman Inside"
"Son and Sylvia"

Me and Mr. Johnson

Label: Reprise/Warner Bros.
Released March 2004
Track List
 "When You Got a Good Friend"
 "Little Queen of Spades"
 "They're Red Hot"
 "Me and the Devil Blues"
 "Traveling Riverside Blues"
 "Last Fair Deal Gone Down"
 "Stop Breakin' Down Blues"
 "Milcow's Calf Blues"
 "Kind Hearted Woman Blues"
 "Come on in My Kitchen"
 "If I Had Possession Over
    Judgement Day"
 "Love in Vain"
 "32–20 Blues"
 "Hell Hound on My Trail"

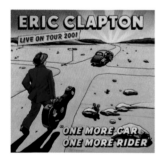

One More Car,
One More Rider

Label: Reprise
Released November 2002
Track List
 "Key to the Highway"
 "Reptile"

"Got You on My Mind"
"Tears in Heaven"
"Bell Bottom Blues"
"Change the World"
"My Father's Eyes"
"River of Tears"
"Goin' Down Slow"
"She's Gone"
"I Want a Little Girl"
"Badge"
"Hoochie Coochie Man"
"Have You Ever Loved a Woman"
"Cocaine"
"Wonderful Tonight"
"Layla"
"Sunshine of Your Love"
"Over the Rainbow"

Sessions for Robert J

Label: Reprise/Warner Bros.
Released December 2004
CD Track List
 "Sweet Home Chicago"
 "Milcow's Calf Blues"
 "Terraplane Blues"
 "If I Had Possession Over
    Judgement Day"
 "Stop Breakin' Down Blues"
 "Little Queen of Spades"
 "Traveling Riverside Blues"
 "Me and the Devil Blues"
 "From Four Until Late"
 "Kindhearted Woman Blues"
 "Ramblin' on My Mind"

DVD Track List
 "Kindhearted Woman Blues"
 "They're Red Hot"
 "Hellhound on My Trail"
 "Sweet Home Chicago"
 "When You Got a Good Friend"
 "Milkcow's Calf Blues"

"If I Had Possession Over
   Judgement Day"
"Stop Breakin' Down Blues"
"Terraplane Blues"
"Me and the Devil Blues"
"From Four Until Late"
"Love in Vain"
"Ramblin' on My Mind"
"Stones in My Passway"

Back Home

Label: Reprise/Warner Bros.
Released August 2005
Track List
 "So Tired"
 "Say What You Will"
 "I'm Going Left"
 "Love Don't Love Nobody"
 "Revolution"
 "Lost and Found"
 "Heaven"
 "Love Comes to Everyone"
 "One Day"
 "One Track Mind"
 "Run Home to Me"
 "Back Home"

Road to Escondido

 J. J. Cale and Eric Clapton
Label: Reprise/Warner Bros.
Released November 2006
Track List
 "Danger"
 "Heads in Georgia"
 "Missing Person"

"When This War Is Over"
"Sporting Life Blues"
"Dead End Road"
"It's Easy"
"Hard to Thrill"
"Anyway the Wind Blows"
"Three Little Girls"
"Don't Cry Sister"
"Last Will and Testament"
"Who Am I Telling You"
"Ride the River"

Live from Madison Square Garden

Eric Clapton and Steve Winwood
Label: Reprise/Warner Bros.
Released May 2009
CD Track List
 "Had to Cry Today"
 "Low Down"
 "Them Changes"
 "Forever Man"
 "Sleeping in the Ground"
 "Presence of the Lord"
 "Glad"
 "Well Alright"
 "Double Trouble"
 "Pearly Queen"
 "Tell the Truth"
 "No Face, No Name, No Number"
 "After Midnight"
 "Split Decision"
 "Rambling on My Mind"
 "Georgia on My Mind"
 "Little Wing"
 "Voodoo Chile"

"Can't Find My Way Home"
"Dear Mr. Fantasy"
"Cocaine"

DVD/Blu-ray Track List
 "Had to Cry Today"
 "Them Changes"
 "Forever Man"
 "Sleeping in the Ground"
 "Presence of the Lord"
 "Glad"
 "Well Alright"
 "Double Trouble"
 "Pearly Queen"
 "Tell the Truth"
 "No Face, No Name, No Number"
 "After Midnight"
 "Split Decision"
 "Rambling on My Mind"
 "Georgia on My Mind"
 "Little Wing"
 "Voodoo Chile"
 "Can't Find My Way Home"
 "Dear Mr. Fantasy"
 "Cocaine"
 "The Road to Madison Square Garden" (documentary)
 "Rambling on My Mind"
 "Low Down"
 "Kind Hearted Woman Blues"
 "Crossroads"

Clapton

Label: Reprise/Warner Bros.
Released September 2010
Track List
 "Travelin' Alone"
 "Rocking Chair"
 "River Runs Deep"
 "Judgment Day"
 "How Deep Is the Ocean"
 "My Very Good Friend the Milkman"
 "Can't Hold Out Much Longer"
 "That's No Way to Get Along"
 "Everything Will Be Alright"
 "Diamonds Made from Rain"
 "When Somebody Thinks You're Wonderful"
 "Hard Times Blues"
 "Run Back to Your Side"
 "Autumn Leaves"

Old Sock

Label: Bushbranch/Surfdog
Released March 2013
Track List
"Further on Down the Road—Commentary"
"Further on Down the Road"
"Angel—Commentary"

"Angel"
"The Folks Who Live on the Hill—
    Commentary"
"The Folks Who Live on the Hill"
"Gotta Get Over—Commentary"
"Gotta Get Over"
"Till Your Well Runs Dry—
    Commentary"
"Till Your Well Runs Dry"
"All of Me—Commentary"
"All of Me"
"Born to Lose—Commentary"
"Born to Lose"
"Still Got the Blues—Commentary"
"Still Got the Blues"
"Goodnight Irene—Commentary"
"Goodnight Irene"
"Your One and Only Man—
    Commentary"
"Your One and Only Man"
"Every Little Thing—Commentary"
"Every Little Thing"
"Our Love Is Here to Stay—
    Commentary"
"Our Love Is Here to Stay"

The Breeze:
An Appreciation of JJ Cale

Eric Clapton & Friends: Mark
    Knopfler, John Mayer, Willie Nelson,
    Tom Petty, and Don White
Label: Bushbranch/Surfdog
Released July 2014
Track List
"Call Me the Breeze"
"Rock and Roll Records"
"Someday"

"Lies"
"Sensitive Kind"
"Cajun Moon"
"Magnolia"
"I Got the Same Old Blues"
"Songbird"
"Since You Said Goodbye"
"I'll Be There (If You Ever Want Me)"
"The Old Man and Me"
"Train to Nowhere"
"Starbound"
"Don't Wait"
"Crying Eyes"

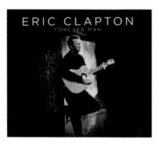

Forever Man

Label: Reprise
Released April 2015
Track List

Disc 1—Studio
"Gotta Get Over"
"I've Got a Rock 'n' Roll Heart"
"Run Back to Your Side"
"Tears in Heaven"
"Call Me the Breeze"
"Forever Man"
"Believe in Life"
"Bad Love"
"My Father's Eyes"
"Anyway the Wind Blows"—with
    J. J. Cale
"Travelin' Alone"
"Change the World"
"Behind the Mask"
"It's in the Way That You Use It"
"Pretending"
"Riding with the King"—with
    B. B. King

"Circus"
"Revolution"

Disc 2—Live
"Badge"
"Sunshine of Your Love"
"White Room"
"Wonderful Tonight"
"Worried Life Blues"
"Cocaine"
"Layla (Unplugged)"
"Nobody Knows You When You're
    Down and Out (Unplugged)"
"Walkin' Blues (Unplugged)"
"Them Changes"—with
    Steve Winwood
"Presence of the Lord"—with
    Steve Winwood
"Hoochie Coochie Man"
"Goin' Down Slow"
"Over the Rainbow"

Disc 3—Blues
"Before You Accuse Me"
"Last Fair Deal Gone Down"
"Hold On, I'm Coming"—with
    B. B. King
"Terraplane Blues"
"It Hurts Me Too"
"Little Queen of Spades"
"Third Degree"
"Motherless Child"
"Sportin' Life Blues"—with J. J. Cale
"Ramblin' On My Mind"
"Stop Breakin' Down Blues"
"Everybody Oughta Make a Change"
"Sweet Home Chicago"
"If I Had Possession Over
    Judgement Day"
"Hard Times Blues"
"Got You on My Mind"
"I'm Tore Down"
"Milkcow's Calf Blues"
"Key to the Highway"—with
    B. B. King

index